The Great Means Expansive Buddha Flower Adornment Sutra

Chapter Twenty-six
The Ten Grounds
Part One - The First Ground

Commentary by
Tripitaka Master Hsuan Hua

FLOWER ADORNMENT SUTRA: THE TEN GROUNDS, PART ONE

Chinese Text:

    Commentary by the Venerable Master Hsüan Hua

    Transcribed by Bhikshuni Heng Hua

    Reviewed and Edited by Bhikshuni Heng Tao

        Technical Assistance: Upasaka Chou Kuo Li,
        Upasikas Yun Yu and Lisa Choi

Translated from the Chinese by the Buddhist Text
Translation Society of the Sino-American Buddhist
Association:

    Primary Translation by Bhikshuni Heng Hsien

    Reviewed by Bhikshuni Heng Ch'ih, Bhikshuni
      Heng Tao, and Upasaka Hsing Tsun Lee

    Edited by Bhikshuni Heng Ch'ih.

    Certified by the Venerable Master Hsüan Hua
      and Bhikshuni Heng Tao

Chinese Calligraphy, cover: Venerable Master Hua

English Calligraphy, cover and interior
    and interior: Jerri-jo Idarius

Cover Design: Upasika Kuo Ling (Linda) Pecaites

Photograph of Master Hua: Upasaka Kuo Ying
    (William) Brevoort

        Technical Assistance: Upasikas Kuo Shan
          (Susan) Anderson and Kuo Li (Patricia)
          Hensley, Kathy Dinwiddie and Ina Koch

First Printing Spring, 1980, for the Occasion of
    the Birthday of Shakyamuni Buddha

for information address:

    The Sino-American Buddhist Association
    City of Ten Thousand Buddhas
    Talmage, California, U. S. A. 95481
    Telephone (707) 642-0939

大方廣佛華嚴經華嚴海會佛菩薩

過新年

今逢一九八〇年

衲請各位上法船

同遊華嚴毘盧海

再登妙高極樂山

宣化上人寫於萬佛城

無言堂

THE VENERABLE TRIPITAKA MASTER HUA

When his filial service was completed, the Master
went into seclusion in Amitabha Cave in the Manchurian
Mountains. There he delved deeply into Ch'an meditation
and practiced rigorous asceticism, eating only pine nuts
and drinking spring water. The area abounded with wild
beasts, but they never disturbed the Master. In fact,
wolves and bears were tamed, and tigers were subdued by
his compassion and fearlessness. Wild birds gathered
to hear the Dharma.

After his stay in the mountains, the Master returned to reside at Three Conditions Monastery where he
helped the Venerable Master Ch'ang Chih and Elder Master
Ch'ang Jen establish monasteries and spread the Dharma.

His skill was such that he wore only three layers
of cotton clothing even during the severe winters, and
could walk barefoot in the snow without being affected
by the cold. He compassionately responded to people's
needs and reinforced their faith by healing the sick,
taking ghosts across, and subduing demons. Thousands
of beings took refuge with the Master during those early
years, and he relieved countless sufferings.

During that time, the Master visited many local
Buddhist monasteries, attended meditation and recitation
sessions, walked miles and miles to listen to lectures
on the Sutras, and also explained the Sutras himself.
He also visited various non-Buddhist religious establish-
ments and obtained a thorough grounding in the range of
their specific beliefs.

In 1946, the Master began a pilgrimage which took
him first to P'u T'o Mountain, where he received the
complete precepts in 1947. Then, in 1948, after three
thousand miles of travel, the Master arrived at Nan-hua
Monastery and bowed before the Venerable Master Hsü Yün,
who was then 109 years old. The Elder Master Yün, the
Forty-fourth Patriarch from Shakyamuni Buddha, recognized
the Master immediately as a vessel worthy of the Dharma
and capable of its propagation. He sealed and certified
the Master's spiritual skill and transmitted to him the
wonderful mind-to-mind seal of all Buddhas. Thus the
Master became the Forty-fifth Patriarch from Shakyamuni
Buddha, the Nineteenth Patriarch in China from Bodhi-
dharma, and the Ninth Patriarch of the Wei Yang Sect.

The Noble Yün saw me and said, "Thus it is."
I saw the Noble Yün and verified, "Thus it is."
The Noble Yün and I both Thus,
Universally vow that all beings will also be Thus.

— by Tripitaka Master Hua

vi

TABLE OF CONTENTS

VERSE FOR THE NEW YEAR

NOW WE HAVE REACHED THE YEAR NINETEEN EIGHTY,

AND ALL ARE INVITED TO BOARD THE DHARMA BOAT,

AND TOGETHER ROAM THE FLOWER ADORNMENT
VAIROCANA SEA,

THEN ASCEND THE WONDROUS, LOFTY MOUNT
OF ULTIMATE BLISS!

--TRIPITAKA MASTER HUA

ABOUT THE VENERABLE MASTER HUA

"...WITH GREAT COMPASSION RESCUE ALL."

"If you want to be a person, the very first thing you should know is that compared to the sea, your parents' kindness is deeper; compared to the sky your parents' kindness is higher...If you plan to repay them, you must first learn to have virtue and to teach living beings to cultivate the Way. It is said, 'If one child obtains the Way, nine generations will leap over birth and death.'"

—from *Record of Water and Mirror Reflections*
by the Venerable Master Hua

At the turn of the century, the Master's birth itself was an extraordinary beginning. In a dream, his mother saw Amitabha Buddha emitting a brilliant light that pervaded the entire world and she awoke to give birth to the Master while a rare fragrance lingered in the room.

At eleven years of age, the Master witnessed death for the first time. He returned home to ask what it was and received two answers: it is the unavoidable end to ordinary human life; it is possible to transcend it by cultivating the Way and putting a stop to the revolving wheel of rebirth.

Upon hearing this, the Master immediately wanted to leave home, cultivate the Way, end birth and death, and then teach other living beings to do the same. But his mother asked him to remain with his parents in their old age. He honored her wishes and was so dedicated in his care for his parents that he soon became known far and wide as "Filial Son" Pai.

Nor did he cease his filiality at his parents' deaths. From the day his mother was buried on, he sat in meditation by her grave for three years. The winter wind and rain, snow and ice, and the summer's bright, hot sun were not kept out by the little hut he sat in. During that time he ate only what food was offered him; if none was offered, he did not eat. And he never lay down to sleep. He meditated unmoving for days on end, and read the Sutras until his eyes bled. Once, during his filial vigil, he left the graveside to receive the Shramanera precepts and become a novice monk.

Dharma Realm Buddhist University was founded in
1976 as well, with its campus at the City of Ten Thousand Buddhas. Countering the present-day trend of Buddhist scholars to advocate "objectivity" and condemn
"belief," to the point that their students who are
Buddhists feel forced to hide that fact from their pro-
fessors, the Master has written a song (composed in
English).

> Yes, yes, yes, indeed,
> The ways of the wise are what we study.
> Yes, yes, yes, indeed,
> The ways of the wise are what we study.
>
> The ways of thieving mouse-people aren't for us.
> We don't hide our Buddhism in the closet.
>
> We want to have wisdom that's really pure,
> We want to have wisdom that's really pure,
> We want to have wisdom that's really, really, pure.
>
> When I grow up, I'll save all the people in the world
> So that all of us can go to enlightenment.
> If that sounds like a good idea to you
> Let's all get together and fulfill our vows,
> And reach the highest summit now.

Already in America over a thousand people have
taken refuge with the Triple Jewel and bowed to the
Master as their teacher. The Master's vow about his
disciples is that as long as a single one of them has
not become a Buddha, he will not become a Buddha. He
will wait. Meanwhile the Dharma wheel continues to turn
and opportunities to teach and transform living beings
are never missed. In 1971 the Master began lectures on
National Master Ch'ing Liang's *Preface* and *Prologue* to
the *Flower Adornment Sutra*, and in 1972 the explanation of
the Sutra proper began. The daily lectures gradually
unfold the inconceivable and ineffable splendor of the
state of perfect fusion and interpenetration described
in the Sutra.

White Universe

—by Tripitaka Master Hua

> Ice in the sky, snow on the ground,
> Numberless tiny bugs die in the cold or sleep in hibernation.
> In the midst of stillness you should contemplate,
>   and within movement you should investigate.
> When you wrestle with dragons and subdue tigers,
>   in continual playful sport,

Ghosts will cry and spirits wail; surrounding
   transformations are strange.
True and actual meanings are cut off from words.
Not thought about or talked about;
   you ought to advance with haste.
With the great and small destroyed, with no inside or out,
Every mote of dust is an infinite Dharma Realm,
Complete, whole, and perfectly fused,
   interpenetrating without obstruction.
With two clenched fists break to pieces
   the covering of empty space.
In one mouthful swallow the source of seas of Buddhalands.
With great compassion rescue all, sparing no blood or sweat,
   and never pause to rest!

→•←

biography compiled by
Bhikshuni Heng Ch'ih

After a brief time with the Venerable Elder Master Yün, Master Hua went on south to Hong Kong where he again took up meditation in Kuan Yin Cave. After a year he rose to the occasion of the influx of Sangha members from the north and began establishing temples and monasteries, sponsoring the carving of sacred images, printing Sutras, conducting meditation and recitation sessions and lecturing on the Dharma. His Great Compassion Dharmas of healing continued to relieve the suffering of many, and thousands more people took refuge with the Triple Jewel and bowed to the Master as their teacher. He instructed them in the universality of the Pure Land Dharma door, and assured them of its efficacy if they single-mindedly recited. ○

> Pick it up! Put it down! Who is mindful
>   of the Buddha? Ha, ha, ha!
> Put it down! Pick it up! Who is the
>   Buddha mindful of? Hee, hee, hee!
> It's not you, it's not me:
> Between you and me there are too many,
>   that's all.
> It's just you, it's just me:
> When Sumeru topples, who can there be?

> —by Tripitaka Master Hua

In 1962, the Master came to America and once again took up meditation, this time "in the grave." In the Ch'an School it is said, "If you want to end birth and death, you first must become a 'living dead person.'" This is the task the Master undertook. Several years later, a group of young Americans, eager for the Dharma, asked him to come out and lecture the *Shurangama Sutra*. The Master consented.

> Each of you now meets
>   a monk in the grave.
> Above there is no sun and moon,
>   below there is no lamp.
> Affliction and enlightenment:
>   ice is water.
> Birth and death, nirvana
>   are empty dharmas.
> Let go of self-seeking
>   be apart from the false.
> When the mad mind ceases,
>   enlightenment pervades all.
> Enlightened, attain brightness,
>   the treasury of the self-nature.

vii

*Basically the retribution body
is the Dharma Body.*

—by Tripitaka Master Hua

The Shurangama Lecture and Study Session lasted for 96
days, and from then on the Dharma wheel has turned con-
tinually as the Master delivered complete commentaries
on the *Heart Sutra*, *The Diamond Sutra*, *The Sixth Patriarch's
Sutra*, *the Amitabha Sutra*, *The Sutra of the Past Vows of Earth
Store Bodhisattva*, *The Great Compassion Heart Dharani Sutra*, *The
Dharma Flower Sutra*, *The Sutra in Forty-two Sections*, *the
Shramanera Vinaya*, and others.

In 1971 Gold Mountain Monastery was established as
a place of practice of the orthodox Dharma. The Master
has made a vow that wherever he goes, the proper Dharma
will prevail and the Dharma Ending Age will not manifest. *The Gold Mountain Doctrine* expresses the force of
this vow:

*Freezing, we do not scheme.
Starving, we do not beg.
Dying of poverty, we ask for nothing.
We accord with conditions, but do not change.
We do not change, and yet accord with conditions.
These are our three great principles.*

*We renounce our lives to do the Buddha's work.
We shape our lives to create the ability
To make revolution in the Sangha order.
In our actions we understand the principles,
So that our principles are revealed in our actions.
We carry out the pulse of the Patriarch's mind-to-mind seal.*

—by Tripitaka Master Hua

In 1973, the Master established the International
Institute for the Translation of Buddhist Texts with
the aim of translating the entire Tripitaka, the Buddhist Canon, into the languages of the Western world. To
date some twenty sutras and Buddhist texts have been
published by the Buddhist Text Translation Society.

The City of Ten Thousand Buddhas was established
in 1976. Located at Wonderful Enlightenment Mountain,
the center spreads over 237 acres and contains more
than sixty major buildings. Tathagata Monastery, Great
Compassion House, Great Joyous Giving House, and the
Hall of Ten Thousand Buddhas are all part of the monas-
tice complex.

Empress came to understand the meaning.
(*Sung Kao Seng Chuan*, Vol. 45, pp. 663-667,
translated by Bodde.)

2. The Philosophy of Hua Yen:

In Hua Yen we have seen the melting pot in
which a new broth of transcendental philosophy was
concocted out of the ingredients of Indian Maha-
yana Buddhism and Chinese Taoism and Confucianism.
Like other schools of Buddhism, the philosophy of
Hua Yen centers around the theory of causation by
mere ideation (萬 法 一 心). So it is said in the
Avatamsaka Sutra:

> If there are people who wish to know
> all the Buddhas in three periods of time
> and ten directions of space, they should
> first of all realize that the nature of
> the Dharma Realm is the creation of the
> mind.

The mind mentioned above is often referred to as
the realm of absolute principle 一 眞 法 界. It is
the fountainhead of everything phenomenal and nou-
menal. It is omnipresent and omnipotent, pervading the universe in three periods of time and ten
directions of space. It is the moving spirit behind the operation of the universe and the trans-
migration of life. It finds itself manifested in
myriad things and myriad things are no more than
its pale reflection. It is in everything and
everything is in it. In a broad sense, it is syn-
onymous with the Tao of *Lao Tzu* and *Chuang Tzu* and
the Masculine Prime Mover (乾 元) of the *Book
of Changes* as represented below:

> The Great Tao flows everywhere, both to
> the left and to the right. The ten thou-
> sand things depend upon it; it holds no-
> thing back. It nourishes the ten thousand
> things, and yet it is not their lord. It
> has no aim; it is very small. The ten
> thousand things return to it, yet it is
> not their lord. It is very great. It
> does not show greatness. And is, there-
> fore, truly great. (*Tao Teh Ching*, pg. 34)

xiii

Tung Kuo-tzu asked Chuang Tzu, "Where is the Tao you mentioned?"

"Everywhere," he answered.

"Please specify it," asked Tung Kuo-tzu.

"It resides in ants," he answered

"What comes below them?"

"It resides in weeds," answered Chuang Tzu.

"Something still lower?"

"It resides in tiles."

"Oh, still lower?"

"In excrement."

Then Tung Kuo-tzu had nothing to say.

"...There is nothing that escapes the Tao," said Chuang Tzu. "All-inclusive, Omnipresent, and Oneness are three words adequate to qualify the nature of the Tao," he added. (*Chuang Tzu*, Chapter 22.)

> Great, indeed, is the sublimity of the masculine prime mover to which everything under the universe owes its origin and which permeates all heaven. (*Book of Changes*, Vol. 1, pg. 1.)

However, the Realm of Absolute Principle represented in Hua Yen is something more than the master mind behind the operation of the universe and the development of myriad things. It is rather a field of activity in which the myriad things (萬 法) identify themselves with the one mind (一 心) as their universality, and the one mind manifests itself in the myriad things as its projections. In the Realm of Absolute Principle all opposites, diversities, contraries, and relativities are completely interfused and identified. So Lao Tzu said:

> When unity is achieved through indentification of all particularities with the absolute, the heavens will become clearer, the earth stabler, the gods more divine. The valleys will become fuller, and all things will grow into better shapes. (*Tao Teh Ching*, Chapter 39)

In a relative sense, everything in the universe is conditioned by time and space. So we say

by Professor H.T. Lee
Chinese Language Department
Dharma Realm Buddhist
University

1. Historical Background:

The *Avatamsaka Sutra* (*Hua Yen Ching* 華嚴經 · was said to have been preached by the Buddha soon after his enlightenment under the Bodhi tree. The esoteric·principle represented in this Sutra was so profound and abstruse as to baffle the comprehension of many Arhats and Bodhisattvas attending the lecture. For this reason, the Buddha could not help preaching the four Agamas (·四阿含·) and other Hinayana doctrines which are easier to learn than the *Avatamsaka Sutra*.

Prior to the establishment of the Avatamsaka School, there flourished in China a school of Buddhism named after the *Dasa-bhumi Sutra* (Ti Lun School 地論宗). The school was later divided into two sects--the Northern Path (北道派) and the Southern Path (南道派)--due to divergence of opinion on the interpretation of·the Sutra. At the outset, the Northern Path had an edge over the Southern Path as the founder of the former named Tao Chung (道寵) exercised a great influence on the people of Lo Yang (洛陽 and other major Chinese cities. He claimed to have over ten thousand disciples throughout China. At one time, he was honored as one of the Six Great Virtuous Men of the Ch'en Dynasty (557-587 A.D.), and, later, he ranked among the Ten Great Virtuous Men of the Sui Dynasty (589-618 A.D.). However, after his passing, the school witnessed a rapid decline in popularity and influence until it escaped public notice.

The Southern Path was in the heyday of popularity under the leadership of Hui Kuang 慧光 468- 537 A.D.). He was well versed in Sanskrit and *Dasabhumi* scriptures and, therefore, he stood high in public estimation. He had ten bright disciples, among whom Fa-shang (法上 495-580 A.D.) was the most prominent.

The Ti Lun School was eventually fused with the Avatamsaka School when Tu Shun (杜·順 557-640 A.D.), the nominal founder of the latter school,

came into prominence as one of the greatest Buddhist Masters of the Tang Dynasty (618-907 A.D.).
Tu Shun, whose priestly name is Fa Shun (法順),
received the royal patronage of Emperor Tang. Having heard of his profound erudition in Buddhism,
Emperor Tai Tsung (唐太宗 600-649 A.D.) invited him
to his royal court for an audience and conferred
upon him the title of "The Venerable Imperial Heart
(帝心尊者)." After his passing, his able disciple, named Chih Yen (智儼 602-668 A.D.), suc-
ceeded as the Second Patriarch of the School. He
wrote many commentaries on the *Avatamsaka Sutra*, such
as the *Hua Yen Ching Yi Hai Pai Men* (- 華嚴經義海百門
the *Hua Yen Huan Yuan Kuan* (華嚴還原觀----r, etc.

The Hua Yen School did not reach the height
of popularity and influence until Fa Tsang (法藏
643-712 A.D.), the Third Patriarch, assumed full
responsibility for the systematization of its gospel. Aside from his academic efforts he also took
pains to propagate the gospel of Hua Yen wherever
possible. It went on record that while lecturing
on the Realm of Absolute Principle (一眞法界 ,
the Chinese philosophy of organism) for Empress Wu
Tse-tien (則天武后), he pointed at a golden lion
guarding the door of the inner palace as an example
to illustrate his point. Thence-forth the lecture
(in written form) bore the title of "The Essay on
the Gold Lion." Quoted in part is the biography of
Fa Tsang included in the *Sung Kao Seng Chuan* (宋高僧
傳-):

> Tsang expounded the new version of the
> *Avatamsaka Sutra* for Tse-tien, but when he
> came to the theories of the ten mysteries
> of Indra's net, the samadhi of the ocean
> symbol, the harmonizing of the six quali-
> ties, and the realm of universal perception,
> the chapters of which all constitute gen-
> eral or special principles in the *Avatamsaka*,
> the Empress became puzzled and undecided.
> Then Tsang pointed to the golden lion guard-
> ing the palace hall by way of illustration.
> In this way he presented his theories so
> that they were explained quickly and easily.
> In the resulting work written by him,
> called the "Essay on the Gold Lion," he
> enumerated ten principles, with their gen-
> eral or special qualities. Thereupon the

PREFACE TO THE TEN GROUNDS

by Bhikshu Heng Sure,
bowing every third step
to the City of Ten
Thousand Buddhas

THE STILL EXTINCTION WHICH THE BUDDHAS PRACTICE,
CANNOT BE DESCRIBED IN WORDS.
THE PRACTICE OF THE GROUNDS IS ALSO THUS:
DIFFICULT TO EXPRESS, DIFFICULT TO ACCEPT.

AS THE TRACES OF A BIRD IN SPACE,
ARE DIFFICULT TO EXPRESS, DIFFICULT TO DISCERN,
SO, TOO, ARE THE GROUNDS' MEANINGS,
INCOMPREHENSIBLE TO MIND AND THOUGHT.

Avatamsaka Sutra
Ten Grounds

How hard it is to express my thoughts on the
Flower Adornment Sutra. I believe the only way to
really experience the Sutra is to use it: to wear,
and eat and sleep its principles. Then it's real.
There is magic in the book. Its words are not ordinary words. They act on the mind in an inconceivable way. They make deep changes for the good.
The only way to know it's true is to try it out.
Just like food: no matter how well the menu des-
cribes it, if you don't eat, you'll still be hungry.

The important thing to say is that the Sutra
explains methods for becoming good people to the
ultimate. It gives the rules for purifying the
body, mouth, and mind. It tells of Buddhas and
Bodhisattvas who cultivated the Dharma-methods and
changed from common people to enlightened beings.
Their glory is so brilliant and their behavior so
lofty, I can't talk about it.

The best thing to do is point to the Sutra and
urge everyone to open it, read it, bow to it,
praise and make offerings to it, repent before it,
practice its truths. Then the door to the treas-
ure house of wisdom magically opens. The dazzling
light shines out, the darkness retreats.

This is an indication that each object in the world
is not merely itself but involves every other object. Like the flows and ebbs of a rolling sea,
the rise of the one is contingent upon the fall of
the other, or vice versa. The network represents
the universality, and the pearls stand for the particularities. The universality is the substance
of the particularities, and the particularities
are the projections of the universality. Hence,
unity is seen in diversities, and order is established in disorder (見色明空，雜中立純). Likewise,
the Realm of Absolute Principle also finds manifestation in the Four-fold Universe (四法界) of
Six Characteristics (六相) shrouded in the Ten
Mysteries (十玄).
    This is the magnificent edifice of Hua Yen,
conjured up by the cosmic mind through the intricate chain reactions of causations.

INTRODUCTION TO THE TEN GROUNDS

by Bhikshu Heng Ch'au,
bowing every third step
to the City of Ten
Thousand Buddhas.

AS ONE THIRSTY THINKS OF ICY WATER,
AS ONE HUNGRY DREAMS ABOUT GOOD FOOD,
AS ONE SICK REFLECTS ON WHOLESOME MEDICINE,
AS A BEE IS GREEDY FOR GOOD HONEY,
SO, TOO, DO WE, IN JUST THAT WAY
WISH TO HEAR THESE DHARMAS OF SWEET DEW.

Avatamsaka Sutra
"Ten Grounds" Chapter
(The Ground of Happiness)

Vajra Treasury Bodhisattva, based on the Buddhas spiritual power, entered the Bodhisattva's
Great Wisdom Light Samadhi and spoke the Ten Grounds.
Everyone assembled was ready and anxious to "hear
these Dharmas of sweet dew." But Vajra Treasury
Bodhisattva hesitated and remained silent. Why?
He felt the Ten Grounds were too profound to grasp,
too difficult to accept, even for Bodhisattvas.
The Grounds are the most supreme source of all Buddhas. "They leave thought and transcend the ground
of the mind." One has to be unselfish and have
deep faith to listen to this most profound wisdom.
Otherwise, those who hear will be confused and
doubt. So it says,

IF ONE HOLDS THE MIND LIKE VAJRA,
WITH DEEP FAITH IN THE BUDDHA'S FOREMOST WISDOM,
KNOWING THAT THE MIND-GROUND LACKS A SELF,
ONE CAN HEAR THESE DHARMAS MOST SUPREME.

LIKE PICTURES THAT ARE PAINTED IN THE AIR,
LIKE TRACES OF THE WIND IN EMPTY SPACE,
THE WISDOM OF THE MUNI IS THAT WAY,
ITS DISTINCTIONS VERY HARD FOR ONE TO SEE.

Avatamsaka Sutra
"Ten Grounds" Chapter
(The Ground of Happiness)

On a rainy day in Southern California, a fire-
man and school teacher from a nearby town crowd
together with the two bowing monks in the back of
their old '56 station wagon. They came to make an
offering of food and hot tea and to listen to the
Avatamsaka Sutra. The monks read the Sutra every day
after lunch. Heng Sure reads in Chinese and translates. Heng Ch'au writes it into English.
    "Hey, that's *good*!" says the school teacher.
    "Yeah, *really* good!" exclaims the fireman.
"Could you read it again? I want to copy it down."
    The monk reads the passage again.
    "Boy, I could chew on those words for years."
reflects the teacher.
    Near Mono Bay, California, three or four
couples and their families drive out every weekend
to listen to the King of Kings of Sutras, the *Avatamsaka*. On a highway pullout or under a grove of
trees alongside the road they sit together on
blankets as the monks do their daily reading. "I've
never heard anything like that before," says one.
"I mean, it's so true!"
    The world is hungry for the real thing. So
many people we met were fascinated and drawn to
the *Flower Adornment Sutra*. They shared two things:
one, the Sutra's words naturally made sense and
filled a space in their hearts and minds that had
been vacant for too long; two, they were captiva-
ted by the translation of totally "greek looking"
Chinese characters into English they could understand. Time and again, people came back for this
experience.
    Science and material abundance have left many
of us disenchanted and unfulfilled. All along our
eight hundred mile trek we found people of the
minds who longed for true principle and the real
thing. They shared a sense of futility and emptiness with seeking peace and happiness in externals
and material wealth. We all wanted to come to
grips with the big issue of birth and death and to
find ultimate peace and happiness, and so the first
of the Ten Grounds, the Ground of Happiness, seems
particularly relevant and basic.
    Real happiness is within, not found outside.
The source of the deep happiness of Bodhisattvas
of the First Ground comes from diligently cultivating morality, concentration, and wisdom and put-
xviii

ting an end to greed, hatred, and stupidity. Moreover, they are happy because they have put down the
big hang-up of the self. They have no fear or worries any more, because they have no ego.

> "IT IS BECAUSE THESE BODHISATTVAS
> ARE FREE FROM THE THOUGHT OF SELF. THEY
> DO NOT CHERISH THEIR OWN BODIES, HOW MUCH
> THE LESS WEALTH AND POSSESSIONS. THEY
> HAVE LEFT THE VIEW OF SELF FAR BEHIND, AND
> HAVE NO THOUGHT OF SELF.

> Avatamsaka Sutra
> "Ten Grounds" Chapter
> (The Ground of Happiness)

   For myself, the Avatamsaka Sutra didn't come
"alive" until months into the pilgrimage. Why?
It was the case that I was confused, not that the
Sutra was confusing. My mind was just too turbid
and my view of self too big to see and "hear these
Dharmas most supreme." Only after about half a
year of bowing in repentance and reform, no T.V.
or newpapers or letters, no talking, and eating
pure vegetarian food and drink, did the Sutra begin
to open up and reveal its wonder. My selfish pride
is just like being deaf and blind.
   The Western scientific and intellectual tradi-
tion has come to an inevitable brink and standstill
Our lives and spiritual growth seem to have, too.
We now face the emptiness of things (dharmas) and
the truth of no-self like one standing on a bridge
that stops abruptly half way across the water. We
don't know where to go, what to follow. In the
West, the self is the very heart and foundation of
our world view and identity. The prospect that it
is an illusion and unreal sends a shiver through
us as did the discovery that the earth moves and
is not the center of the universe for people in the
late Middle Ages. Buddhism appears at an auspi-
cious and ripe moment to complete the bridge and
take us all to the other shore. The truth of no
self is not the "end" that we fear, but, really
the beginning of true wisdom and real happiness.
So it's said,

   If you can't put down what's
   false, you can't pick up what's true.

xix

             If you can't put down death,
             you can't pick up life.

     Even the children we met on our journey were
drawn to this Sutra. It was as if they recognized
it intuitively--past words and thoughts--just
straight from their hearts. On Christmas, 1977,
23 had made camp on the sandy bank of a levee outside the small village of Oceana, California. Four
boys watched us from an old wooden railroad tres-
tle. They slowly approached and soon a lively con-
versation was going about life and Buddhism. The
boys stood in the mud and rain watching and listening as we studied the *Avatamsaka Sutra* by a flickering
oil lamp inside our car. The words of the Sutra
are special, and they took it all in. "Like bees
that are mindful of their honey, like thirsty people thinking of sweet dew."
     Later they returned with a money offering they
pooled from their savings and half a box of oat-
meal and a card signed, "from Jackie, Sonny, Bobbie,
and John." But, mostly they returned because they
were fascinated with the *Avatamsaka* and wanted to
hear Heng Sure do that "magic thing" and turn the
foreign looking Chinese characters into words and
thoughts they knew. They were in awe. "I ain't
never run across anything like this before in my
whole life!" said one.
     "Hey it's for real, man!" said another. "Just
like that, he can read them and know what they say
and tell us all. Neat, far out!"
     Finally, John the skeptic of the group blurted
out,
     "You aren't prayin' to God, and you don't want
to go to heaven... Seems pretty useless and empty."
     Before we could answer, Sonny looked squarely
at his friend and quietly said, "It's all in the
mind, John. It's all in how you look at it, you
know? You can do *anything* if you set your mind to
it."
     It's said in Buddhism,

             Peoples' minds are the Buddha,
          the Buddha is just people's mind-

The wonderful principles of the *Avatamsaka Sutra* exist
in the minds of people. Everyone has this wisdom

and everyone can speak the Sutra. We forget and
cover over our natural, bright understanding. But,
it doesn't ever leave us. It's just waiting to be
remembered and thawed out. The Sutras flow from
the minds of all living beings.

The happiness of the Bodhisattvas on the First
Ground is already inside of us. It exists inherent-
ly within our self-nature. One only needs to cultivate the Way to experience this ultimate bliss.
Anyone can do it. It's like John said, "You can
do anything if you set your mind to it." This little boy was expressing the core principle of the
Avatamsaka Sutra. He knew it naturally, without ever
having read it. The Sutra was inside of him.

> IF ONE WISHES TO KNOW,
> ALL BUDDHAS OF THE THREE PERIODS OF TIME,
> CONTEMPLATE THE NATURE OF THE DHARMAREALM,
> EVERYTHING IS MADE FROM THE MIND ALONE.

> *Avatamsaka Sutra*
> *Chapter Twenty*

Namo to *The Great Expansive Buddha Flower Adornment Sutra,*
and the oceanwide Flower Adornment Assembly of Buddhas and Bodhisattvas.

> February 2, 1980
> City of Ten Thousand
> Buddhas

Note: *Dharma Master Heng Ch'au and*
Dharma Master Heng Sure, whose
Preface follows, completed a
2½ year pilgramage bowing every
third step from Gold Wheel Temple
in Los Angeles, California, to the
City of Ten Thousand Buddhas in
Northern California. They are now
continuing to bow every third step
within the City of Ten Thousand
Buddhas with the hope of bringing
peace and allieviating disasters
in the world by ridding their own
natures of greed, hatred and
stupidity and transferring merit.

that this city is as big as Rome, and that man is
as old as your grandpa. However, viewed from the
standpoint of the infinite space, there is nothing
bigger and smaller in the world. Measured by the
yardstick of endless eternity, there is nobody
short-lived or long-lived. When the relative is
identified with the absolute, there is no distinc-
tion between things big and small, short-lived or
long-lived, because all differentiations are interfused and eliminated. So, Chuang Tzu said:

> When nothing in the world is bigger than
> the tip of an autumn hair, Mt. Tai will be
> small. When nobody enjoys a longer exis-
> tence than the child that dies in infancy,
> our Methuselah, Peng Tsu, will have died
> prematurely. Since Sky, Earth, and I all
> came into existence at the same time, all
> creation and I are one. And, if all is
> one, can there be any talk about existence,
> or talk about nonexistence? (*Chuang Tzu*,
> Chapter 2, "All Created Equal.")

In Hua Yen, the universe is represented as an
organic whole of intricate structure and dynamic
character. It is a field of activity in which
everything is interfused with and connected to
everything else in perfect harmony within the intricate framework of cosmic patterns. The intricate interpenetration and harmonious cooperation
of all things and events are dictated by their internal nature and have nothing to do with a per-
ior authority external to them. The concepti n of
"One in Many and Many in One" represented in the
Avatamsaka Sutra is better illustrated by the Indra's
Net (帝網千珠):

> In the Heaven of Indra, there is a net-
> work of pearls so intricately arranged that
> when the network is on the move, each pearl
> in every single loop keeps on rolling, re-
> flecting all other pearls in its different
> facets, thus producing a grand view of mul-
> titudinous images of beautiful colors. The
> same is true of other pearls within the
> meshwork of the net.

> *FROM COMPASSION, KINDNESS, AND THE*
> *POWER OF VOWS APPEAR AND ENTER THE PRAC-*
> *TICES OF THE GROUNDS. GRADUALLY REACH*
> *PERFECTION OF THE MIND. WISDOM'S PRAC-*
> *TICES ARE NOT REFLECTION'S REALM.*

We look into the magic mirror and measure our behavior against the perfect wisdom and virtue of the Worthy Sages of the Avatamsaka Assembly, and we know shame. We try to change. Change is painful, but it "hurts good." The Sutra guides our efforts with kindness and compassion. It says,

"Anyone can be a Bodhisattva. Peace of mind and deep joy can be yours. All you need to do is offer up your conduct according to these teachings. Watch your thoughts; purify them. Change your behavior towards the good. Control your words. Follow these rules. They really work."

As we bow and contemplate the Sutra, we get the feeling that Buddhadharma is the "deepest contours" of the natural mind. In this way it is the teaching of all beings, for it transcends age, race, sex, nationality, species, space, and time. It's just always been true. Particularly the Five Precepts, the Ten Goods, the Six Perfections, and the Ten Thousand Conducts, and the Ten Kings of Vows of Universal Worthy. These are the fundamental patterns for proper living. They are the basic shape, the original mold of perfect humanity. It's said,

> When you are a person to perfection,
> The Buddha's way accomplishes itself.

The Sutra is not foreign, not obscure or irrelevant to the problems of the world today. It is the original road-map for the journey into the mind and its states.

The more we apply Sutra-Dharma to our behavior, the more our bad habits and faults appear. It's clear that in one's own heart there is enough light to "illuminate the mind and see the nature." But, our thoughts and attachments obstruct the light and cover it over. By letting go of the false, the true appears without effort. I cause all my own troubles. My greed, anger, and stupidity are huge. These poisons arise from ignorance.

Cultivating Way-virtue according to the Sutra's
wisdom melts the darkness of ignorance bit by bit,
day by day. The less we seek selfish benefit, the
less we worry. The more we let go and just watch
things work out according to the Tao, the more
everything's okay. The more we give up trying to
figure out the world, the more things make sense.
The more we cultivate, the happier we get.

     Outside Point Sur Lighthouse, a big sedan
slides to a stop on a dusty turn-off. A man gets
out and walks to the side of the monks who are bow
ing to the ground. He is heavy-set, middle-aged,
and a flashy dresser. His face is full of emotion

     "My name is Riley. You're Buddhists? Buddha,
Buddha, Wow! Listen! I was in prison for five
years, and a little book of Buddhist parables kept
me going the whole time. They really talked to me
deep inside, you know. You're American monks?
Caucasians?"

     Heng Ch'au answers, "Buddhism doesn't have a
certain country or people..."

     Riley breaks in, "...or color or race. It's
in the heart, in the mind, right?"

     "Right."

     "So here I am, speeding on my way to L.A., and
I saw you bowing and listen, I've seen Christians,
Krishnas, Muslims, Jews, and some nobody's ever
heard of (tears start to come to his eyes). But,
nothing has ever moved me like this. What I read
in that Buddhist book was true. And here you are,
practicing it for real. I can't tell you what
this means to everyone, and it's everywhere!"

     Riley left happy and crying and shaking, full
of something he couldn't find words for. His eyes
were like crystal platters.

     The first of the Bodhisattva's wisdom grounds
is here in bilingual version. It's like the sun
breaking through clouds.

>   SUCH STATES AS THESE ARE DIFFICULT TO PERCEIVE.
>   THEY CAN BE KNOWN BUT CANNOT BE EXPRESSED.
>   THROUGH THE BUDDHAS' POWER, THEY ARE PROCLAIMED.
>   YOU SHOULD RECEIVE THEM WILL ALL REVERENCE.

                              February 3, 1980
                              City of Ten Thousand
                              Buddhas

     xxiv

The First Ground

SUTRA:

THE TEN GROUNDS, CHAPTER TWENTY-SIX, PART ONE

COMMENTARY:

The *Flower Adornment Sutra* has eighty-one rolls
and thirty-nine chapters, of which this is *CHAPTER
TWENTY-SIX, THE TEN GROUNDS.* Why are these ten
called "grounds?" All things that exist are born
from the ground, grow because of the ground, come
to maturity by means of the ground, and obtain liberation due to the ground.

Within the ground are found a variety of
treasuries like gold mines, diamond mines, silver
mines, copper, iron, and various other kinds of
mines which people excavate. The Ten Grounds contain the mines of Buddhas, the mines of Bodhisattvas, the mines of Sound Hearers and those Enlightened to Conditions, the mines of gods and people,
and the mines of animals, hungry ghosts, and hellbeings. In all the ten dharma realms there are
mines. If we knew how to excavate them, then we
could obtain a variety of treasures.

The Dharma doors of the Ten Grounds contain
all Dharma doors; there is an interconnection between them. If we want to cultivate the Bodhisattva path, it will come about through cultivation of
the Grounds. If we want to develop the Bodhisattva
path, we will do it through development of the
Dharma doors of the Ten Grounds. If we want to
bring cultivation of the Bodhisattva path to maturity, we will do it through maturation of the

Ten Grounds. If we want to obtain liberation by
means of the Bodhisattva path, we even more must
rely on the Dharma doors of the Ten Grounds in our
cultivation in order to gain that liberation.
     The Dharma doors of the Ten Grounds, then,
make up the twenty-sixth chapter in the *Flower Adornment Sutra*, and this is PART ONE of the chapter.

SUTRA:

     AT THAT TIME, THE WORLD-HONORED ONE WAS IN
THE ROYAL PALACE IN THE HEAVEN OF THE COMFORT FROM
OTHERS' TRANSFORMATIONS, IN THE HALL OF TREASURIES
OF MANI JEWELS, TOGETHER WITH A GATHERING OF GREAT
BODHISATTVAS. ALL THESE BODHISATTVAS, WHO WERE
IRREVERSIBLE FROM ANUTTARASAMYAKSAMBODHI, HAD AS-
SEMBLED FROM THE WORLDS OF THE OTHER DIRECTIONS.
THEY DWELT IN THE STATES OF WISDOM IN WHICH ALL
BODHISATTVAS DWELL, HAD ENTERED THE PLACE OF WIS-
DOM WHICH ALL THUS COME ONES ENTER, AND DILIGENTLY
PRACTICED WITHOUT REST. THEY WERE WELL ABLE TO
MANIFEST ALL KINDS OF SPIRITUAL PENETRATIONS, AND
ALL THAT THEY DID TO TEACH, TRANSFORM, TAME, AND
SUBDUE LIVING BEINGS WAS DONE AT THE RIGHT TIME.
IN ORDER TO ACCOMPLISH ALL BODHISATTVAS' GREAT
VOWS, IN ALL WORLDS, IN ALL KALPAS, IN ALL LANDS,
THEY DILIGENTLY CULTIVATED ALL PRACTICES, WITHOUT
SLACKING EVEN MOMENTARILY. THEY WERE REPLETE WITH
A BODHISATTVA'S BLESSINGS AND WISDOM, THE AIDS TO
THE WAY, BY WHICH THEY UNIVERSALLY BENEFITTED LIV-
ING BEINGS WITHOUT SHIRKING. THEY HAD ARRIVED AT
THE ULTIMATE SHORE OF A BODHISATTVA'S WISDOM AND
EXPEDIENTS.

COMMENTARY:

     After Vajra Banner Bodhisattva had finished
speaking the Ten Transferences Chapter, and before
he'd begun to explain the Ten Grounds Chapter,
AT THAT TIME, THE WORLD-HONORED ONE, Shakyamuni
Buddha, WAS IN THE ROYAL PALACE IN THE HEAVEN OF
THE COMFORT FROM OTHERS' TRANSFORMATIONS. In this
heaven, others' bliss is easily transformed into
one's own. The Buddha was IN THE HALL OF TREASUR-
IES OF MANI JEWELS, TOGETHER WITH A GATHERING OF

GREAT BODHISATTVAS, a limitless number of them, who
were Bodhisattvas of long-standing, with the Way-
Virtue, wisdom, and cultivation requisite for them
to be IRREVERSIBLE FROM ANUTTARASAMYAKSAMBODHI.
These Bodhisattvas did not retreat from the Unsurpassed, Right and Equal, Proper Enlightenment in
either thought, conduct, or position. They had attained these Three Kinds of Irreversibility.

The Unsurpassed, Right and Equal, Proper Enlightenment is the culmination of Three Levels of
Enlightenment. Those of the Two Vehicles--the
Sound Hearers and Those Enlightened to Conditions
--obtain Proper Enlightenment. They are enlightened themselves, but they have not obtained Right
and Equal Enlightenment, and so they cannot enlighten others. The Bodhisattvas' enlightenment
is described as Right and Equal because they enlighten themselves, enlighten others, and cultivate
Dharma-doors equal to the Buddhas' Dharma doors.
"Surpassed Lords" is the title given to Bodhisattvas because the Buddhas are above them. Their
enlightenment is not unsurpassed.

Each level of enlightenment is delineated.
People cannot be something just because they claim
to be. They must be recognized as such by others
for it to count. The Buddhas can enlighten themselves and others and have perfected their enlightenment and practice. So they attain Unsurpassed,
Right and Equal, Proper Enlightenment, that is,
Anuttarasamyaksambodhi. The great Bodhisattvas
spoken of here, although they are not yet totally
unsurpassed, still are irreversible, and in the
future they are certain to become Buddhas.

THEY HAD ALL ASSEMBLED FROM THE WORLDS OF THE
OTHER DIRECTIONS. Not all of those great Bodhisattvas come from the Saha world; they came from
worlds as many as fine motes of dust. THEY DWELT
IN THE STATES OF WISDOM IN WHICH ALL BODHISATTVAS
DWELL. THEY HAD ENTERED THE PLACE OF WISDOM WHICH
ALL BODHISATTVAS DWELL. THEY HAD ENTERED THE PLACE
OF WISDOM WHICH ALL THUS COME ONES ENTER. Not only
did they have the wisdom of Bodhisattvas, they
also had the wisdom of a Buddha, though not quite
so profound. AND they DILIGENTLY PRACTICED WITH-
OUT REST. They were courageously vigorous and
diligently cultivated the Bodhisattva Path without
resting. THEY WERE WELL ABLE TO MANIFEST ALL KINDS

OF SPIRITUAL PENETRATIONS. They all had various
kinds of wisdom and manifested all kinds of spiritual penetrations, *AND ALL THAT THEY DID TO TEACH,
TRANSFORM, TAME, AND SUBDUE LIVING BEINGS WAS DONE
AT THE RIGHT TIME.* The vocation of a Bodhisattva
is to teach and transform living beings, tame and
subdue living beings, and cause all living beings
quickly to accomplish Buddhahood, all at the right
time. Sometimes if one speaks inappropriately,
and teaches living beings before their roots have
ripened or the time is right by blasting Dhārma at
them, they cannot receive it. They get scared,
have doubts, and they never want to listen to the
Buddhadharma again. Bodhisattvas teach and transform living beings at the most appropriate moment.
It is just like planting seeds: if planted at the
wrong time, they will not come up, and the planting will have been done in vain. If one plants
the seeds at the exact time they should be planted,
they will grow. Right at the time the seeds of
Bodhi should be planted, Bodhisattvas break open
the mind-ground of living beings, teach them to
bring forth the thought for Bodhi, and plant the
seeds which gradually grow, ripen, and yield a har-
vest of liberation. That is the meaning of "at
the right time."
     *IN ORDER TO ACCOMPLISH ALL BODHISATTVAS' GREAT
VOWS, IN ALL WORLDS, IN ALL KALPAS, IN ALL LANDS,*
within the kshetra lands of all Buddhas, *THEY DILI-
GENTLY CULTIVATED ALL PRACTICES.* They were hero-
ically vigorous and diligently cultivated all the
doors of conduct that all Bodhisattvas cultivate,
WITHOUT SLACKING EVEN MOMENTARILY. Not even for
an instant were they lazy, but they were ever vigorous. *THEY WERE REPLETE WITH A BODHISATTVA'S
BLESSINGS AND WISDOM, THE AIDS TO THE WAY, BY
WHICH THEY UNIVERSALLY BENEFITTED LIVING BEINGS
WITHOUT SHIRKING.* They not only cultivated for
themselves, but for all living beings as well.
They never stopped, never got tired, and were never
lazy. They would never say, "I've had it! I'm
going to quit cultivating the Bodhisattva Way and
stop benefitting living beings." They weren't
like that. They always wanted to benefit living
beings. *THEY HAD ARRIVED AT THE ULTIMATE SHORE
OF A BODHISATTVA'S WISDOM AND EXPEDIENTS.* They

had reached the ultimate shore of wisdom and skill-
in-means of all Bodhisattvas--the highest position
--and had obtained the purity of Nirvana that con-
sists in permanence, bliss, true self, and purity.

SUTRA:

*THEY MANIFESTED ENTRY INTO BIRTH AND DEATH AS
IDENTICAL WITH NIRVANA, YET THEY DID NOT RENOUNCE
THE CULTIVATION OF BODHISATTVA PRACTICES. THEY
WERE SKILLED AT ENTERING ALL BODHISATTVAS' DHYANAS,
LIBERATIONS, SAMADHIS, SAMAPATTIS, SPIRITUAL PENE-
TRATIONS, AND CLEAR KNOWLEDGES. IN ALL THEY DID
THEY OBTAINED COMFORT. THEY ACQUIRED ALL BODHI-
SATTVAS' COMFORTABLE SPIRITUAL POWERS, AND IN AN
INSTANT, WITHOUT MOVEMENT OR EXERTION, THEY COULD
GO TO THE ASSEMBLIES OF ALL THUS COME ONES' BODHI-
MANDAS, ACT AS LEADERS OF THE ASSEMBLY, AND REQUEST
THE BUDDHA TO SPEAK DHARMA. THEY PROTECTED AND
UPHELD THE BUDDHAS' PROPER DHARMA WHEEL. THEY USED
A VAST, GREAT MIND TO MAKE OFFERINGS TO AND SERVE
ALL BUDDHAS. THEY ALWAYS DILIGENTLY PRACTICED THE
DEEDS WHICH ALL BODHISATTVAS PRACTICE. THEIR BOD-
IES UNIVERSALLY APPEARED IN ALL WORLDS. THEIR
VOICES REACHED THROUGHOUT THE DHARMA REALMS OF THE
TEN DIRECTIONS. THEIR MINDS' WISDOM WAS UNOBSTRUC-
TED. THEY UNIVERSALLY SAW THE MERIT AND VIRTUE OF
ALL BODHISATTVAS OF THE THREE PERIODS OF TIME. THEY
HAD ALREADY CULTIVATED AND OBTAINED PERFECTION. IN
INEFFABLY MANY KALPAS THEY COULD NOT COMPLETELY BE
DESCRIBED.*

COMMENTARY:

*THEY MANIFESTED ENTRY INTO BIRTH AND DEATH AS
IDENTICAL WITH NIRVANA.* Bodhisattvas who cultivate the Bodhisattva Way have freedom over birth
and death and, for them, samsara is just Nirvana,
and afflictions are just Bodhi. Everything about
them is a manifestation. They manifest all sorts
of births and manifest various kinds of deaths.
They appear as various kinds of living beings.
From gods, humans, and asuras, to the animals,
hungry ghosts, and hell-beings, within every des-
tiny, Bodhisattvas appear to go through birth and

death. They are born in various ways and influence those around them to bring forth the thought for Bodhi. They die in various ways in order to cause living beings to understand the pain of samsara. Therefore, they manifest entry into birth and death as identical with Nirvana: how one is born, how one dies, and how birth and death become Nirvana. *YET THEY DID NOT RENOUNCE THE CULTIVATION OF BODHISATTVA PRACTICES.* Although Bodhisattvas manifest all those births and deaths and sufferings in order to teach and transform living beings, and then cultivate ascetic practices and enter Nirvana, still, they return to continue cultivating the Bodhisattva Way among living beings. Wherever they are, they do not renounce that cultivation. They cultivate the Bodhisattva path to help living beings and cause them to resolve themselves upon Bodhi.

THEY WERE SKILLED AT ENTERING ALL BODHISATTVAS' DHYANAS, LIBERATIONS, SAMADHIS. They were good at realizing the dhyana-samadhis, the liberations, and the proper concentration and proper receptiveness that Bodhisattvas cultivate, and *SAMAPATTIS, SPIRITUAL PENETRATIONS AND CLEAR KNOWLEDGES.* "Samapatti" is a Sanskrit word which translates as "arrival at equanimity," which refers to the state reached when one is free of torpor and agitation. They also had attained the wonderful functioning of various kinds of spiritual penetrations: the Three Clarities and the Six Penetrations. The Three Clarities are:

1. The clarity of the heavenly eye.
2. The clarity of the heavenly ear.
3. The clarity concerning former lives.

Another rendering of this list is:

1. The clarity of the heavenly eye.
2. The clarity concerning former lives.
3. The clarity of the extinction of outflows.

The Six Penetrations are:

1. The penetration of the heavenly eye.
2. The penetration of the heavenly ear.
3. The penetration of others' thoughts.

4. The penetration of former lives.
5. The penetration of the extinction of
   outflows.
6. The penetration of spiritual fulfillments.

IN ALL THEY DID THEY OBTAINED COMFORT. In all of
their activities, they were independent and sovereign.

THEY ACQUIRED ALL BODHISATTVAS' COMFORTABLE
SPIRITUAL POWERS. They could manifest birth and
death, Nirvana, and the cultivation of the Bodhisattva Way in all places. At all times they were
at ease with the power of wonderful functioning
of their spiritual penetrations, just as all Bodhisattvas are; AND IN AN INSTANT, WITHOUT MOVE-
MENT OR EXERTION, THEY COULD GO TO THE ASSEMBLIES
OF ALL THUS COME ONES' BODHIMANDAS. You see the
Bodhisattva as just walking along, but he can go
anywhere in the ten directions within the space
of a single instant, with no need to move or act.
You see him eating, but his spiritual powers have
already taken him in the assemblies of the Bodhimandas of all Thus Come Ones. You see the Bodhisattva as asleep, but he has already transformed
bodies and gone to other Buddhalands. You see the
Bodhisattva as doing something, or as doing nothing, but he can be transforming bodies and going
to limitless and boundlessly many other worlds to
teach and transform living beings. He has that
kind of wonderful ability. So the Bodhisattvas
at all times and in all places go to see all Buddhas of the ten directions, draw near and pay their
respects, and make offerings to them. Don't think
they're just asleep. If it's just an ordinary person who's asleep, of course it's not very inter-
esting. They may be having nightmares about wanting to jump off the Golden Gate Bridge or the Em-
pire State Building. In the dream they may even
fall from the sky-scraper and die, but when they
wake up, they are still in their beds. They may
dream of being the 555th person to jump from the
Golden Gate Bridge only to find themselves on the
couch upon awakening. That is an ordinary person's
dream-state.

The state of a Bodhisattva also resembles
dreaming, but the Bodhisattva goes off to rescue

living beings and to teach and transform them.
Wherever he sees beings experiencing disaster, he
manifests a body and goes to save them. Bodhisattvas also *ACT AS LEADERS OF THE ASSEMBLY* and *REQUEST
THE BUDDHA TO SPEAK DHARMA.* Someone must request
the Dharma or the Buddha does not speak it. Someone circumambulates three times, bows, kneels, and
requests that the Buddha speak the Dharma and turn
the Dharma wheel.

    *THEY PROTECTED AND UPHELD THE BUDDHAS' PROPER
DHARMA WHEEL.* Bodhisattvas go everywhere to protect and support the assemblies of the Bodhimandas
of all Buddhas, just as here where we daily turn
the Proper Dharma wheel, yet no one realizes it and
this country's disciples treat it as a very ordinary event when, in fact, it is an earth-shaking,
heaven-startling matter. *THEY USED A VAST, GREAT
MIND TO MAKE OFFERINGS TO AND SERVE ALL BUDDHAS.
THEY ALWAYS DILIGENTLY PRACTICED THE DEEDS WHICH
ALL BODHISATTVAS PRACTICE. THEIR BODIES UNIVER-
SALLY APPEARED IN ALL WORLDS.* Bodies of theirs
went everywhere in all worlds of the ten directions.

    *THEIR VOICES REACHED THROUGHOUT THE DHARMA
REALMS OF THE TEN DIRECTIONS.* In all the deeds
the Bodhisattvas cultivated, their bodies manifested in all worlds, and the sound of their voices
also manifested in the Dharma Realms of the ten
directions. *THEIR MINDS' WISDOM WAS UNOBSTRUCTED.*
Their minds and their wisdom were perfectly fused
without obstruction. *THEY UNIVERSALLY SAW THE
MERIT AND VIRTUE OF ALL BODHISATTVAS OF THE THREE
PERIODS OF TIME.* They could see all the merit and
virtue of all Bodhisattvas of the past, present,
and future. *THEY HAD ALREADY CULTIVATED AND OB-
TAINED PERFECTION.* They had cultivated to perfection the merit and virtue of all Bodhisattvas. *IN
INEFFABLY MANY KALPAS THEY COULD NOT COMPLETELY BE
DESCRIBED.* In kalpas so long, one still could not
portray them.

SUTRA:

    *THEIR NAMES WERE: VAJRA TREASURY BODHISATTVA,
JEWELED TREASURY BODHISATTVA, LOTUS TREASURY BODHI-
SATTVA, VIRTUE TREASURY BODHISATTVA, TREASURY OF*

LOTUS VIRTUES BODHISATTVA, SUN TREASURY BODHISAT-
TVA, TREASURY OF SURYA BODHISATTVA, TREASURY OF
UNDEFILED MOONS BODHISATTVA, TREASURY OF ADORNMENTS
UNIVERSALLY MANIFESTING IN ALL COUNTRIES BODHISAT-
TVA, TREASURY OF VAIROCANA WISDOM BODHISATTVA,
TREASURY OF WONDERFUL VIRTUES BODHISATTVA, TREASURY
OF CHANDANA VIRTUES BODHISATTVA, TREASURY OF FLOWER
VIRTUES BODHISATTVA, TREASURY OF KUSUMA VIRTUES
BODHISATTVA, TREASURY OF UTPALA VIRTUES BODHISAT-
TVA, TREASURY OF HEAVENLY VIRTUES BODHISATTVA,
TREASURY OF BLESSINGS AND VIRTUES BODHISATTVA,
TREASURY OF UNOBSTRUCTED PURE WISDOM'S VIRTUE BO-
DHISATTVA, TREASURY OF MERIT AND VIRTUES BODHISAT-
TVA, TREASURY OF NARAYANA VIRTUES BODHISATTVA,
TREASURY OF NON-DEFILEMENT BODHISATTVA, TREASURY
OF FREEDOM FROM FILTH BODHISATTVA, TREASURY OF VER-
SATILE ELOQUENCE ADORNMENTS BODHISATTVA, TREASURY
OF GREAT BRIGHT-LIGHT NETS BODHISATTVA, TREASURY
OF PURE, AWESOME VIRTUES' LIGHT KING BODHISATTVA,
TREASURY OF GOLD ADORNMENTS AND THE LIGHT OF GREAT
MERIT AND VIRTUES KING BODHISATTVA, TREASURY OF
ADORNMENTS OF ALL MARKS' PURE VIRTUES BODHISATTVA,
TREASURY OF VAJRA BLAZING VIRTUES AND ADORNING
MARKS BODHISATTVA, TREASURY OF BLAZING LIGHT BODHI-
SATTVA, TREASURY OF LIGHT ILLUMINATION CONSTELLA-
TION KING BODHISATTVA, TREASURY OF EMPTY SPACE AND
UNOBSTRUCTED WISDOM BODHISATTVA, TREASURY OF UN-
OBSTRUCTED WONDROUS SOUNDS BODHISATTVA, TREASURY
OF DHARANI MERIT AND VIRTUES TO MAINTAIN THE VOWS
OF LIVING BEINGS BODHISATTVA, TREASURY OF SEA
ADORNMENTS BODHISATTVA, TREASURY OF SUMERU VIRTUES
BODHISATTVA, TREASURY OF PURITY OF MERIT AND VIR-
TUES BODHISATTVA, THE THUS COME ONE'S TREASURY
BODHISATTVA, TREASURY OF THE BUDDHAS' VIRTUES BO-
DHISATTVA, MOON OF LIBERATION BODHISATTVA, AND ALL
OTHER NUMBERLESS, LIMITLESS, BOUNDLESS, INCOMPAR-
ABLE, UNCOUNTABLE, INDESCRIBABLE, INCONCEIVABLE,
ILLIMITABLE AND INEFFABLE MULTITUDES OF BODHISAT-
TVAS, MAHASATTVAS, WITH VAJRA TREASURY BODHISATTVA
AS THEIR LEADER.

COMMENTARY:

THEIR NAMES WERE as follows. There was one
Bodhisattva called VAJRA TREASURY BODHISATTVA.
Another Bodhisattva was called JEWELED TREASURY

BODHISATTVA.   There was another Bodhisattva called
LOTUS TREASURY BODHISATTVA.   There was another
Bodhisattva called VIRTUE TREASURY BODHISATTVA.
There was another Bodhisattva called TREASURY OF
LOTUS VIRTUES BODHISATTVA.   Another Bodhisattva
was called SUN TREASURY BODHISATTVA.   There was
another Bodhisattva called TREASURY OF SURYA BODHI-
SATTVA, that is to say, "Store of Suns" Bodhisat-
tva.   THERE WAS ANOTHER BODHISATTVA CALLED TREASURY
OF UNDEFILED MOONS BODHISATTVA.   Another Bodhisat-
tva was called TREASURY OF ADORNMENTS UNIVERSALLY
MANIFESTING IN ALL COUNTRIES BODHISATTVA.   That
Bodhisattva, a store of adornments, manifested in
all worlds.   There was another Bodhisattva called
TREASURY OF VAIROCANA WISDOM BODHISATTVA.   Another
Bodhisattva was called TREASURY OF WONDERFUL VIR-
TUES BODHISATTVA.   There was another Bodhisattva
called TREASURY OF CHANDANA VIRTUES BODHISATTVA.
Another Bodhisattva was called TREASURY OF KUSUMA
VIRTUES BODHISATTVA.   "Kusuma" means "large flow-
ers."   Another Bodhisattva was named TREASURY OF
UTPALA VIRTUES BODHISATTVA.   "Utpala" means "Azure
Flowers."   Another Bodhisattva was called TREASURY
OF HEAVENLY VIRTUES BODHISATTVA.   There was another
Bodhisattva named TREASURY OF BLESSINGS AND VIR-
TUES BODHISATTVA.   Another Bodhisattva was named
TREASURY OF UNOBSTRUCTED PURE WISDOM'S VIRTUES BO-
DHISATTVA.   Another Bodhisattva went by the name
of TREASURY OF MERIT AND VIRTUES BODHISATTVA.   Yet
another Bodhisattva was called TREASURY OF NARAYANA
VIRTUES BODHISATTVA.   One was named TREASURY OF
NON-DEFILEMENT BODHISATTVA.   Another Bodhisattva
was called TREASURY OF FREEDOM FROM FILTH BODHI-
SATTVA.   There was yet another Bodhisattva who was
known as TREASURY OF VERSATILE ELOQUENCE AND ADORN-
MENTS BODHISATTVA.   TREASURY OF GREAT BRIGHT-LIGHT
NETS BODHISATTVA was one Bodhisattva's name, while
another Bodhisattva's name was TREASURY OF PURE,
AWESOME VIRTUES' LIGHT KING BODHISATTVA.   Further-
more, there was a Bodhisattva called TREASURY OF
GOLD ADORNMENTS AND THE LIGHT OF GREAT MERIT AND
VIRTUES KING BODHISATTVA.   Present was also TREAS-
URY OF ADORNMENTS OF ALL MARKS' PURE VIRTUES BO-
DHISATTVA, as well as a Bodhisattva called TREAS-
URY OF VAJRA BLAZING VIRTUES AND ADORNING MARKS
BODHISATTVA.   TREASURY OF BLAZING LIGHT BODHISAT-
TVA was there, along with TREASURY OF LIGHT ILLUMI-

NATION CONSTELLATION KING BODHISATTVA, TREASURY OF
EMPTY SPACE AND UNOBSTRUCTED WISDOM BODHISATTVA,
and TREASURY OF UNOBSTRUCTED WONDROUS SOUNDS BODHI-
SATTVA. There was, further, a Bodhisattva who had
the name TREASURY OF DHARANI MERIT AND VIRTUES TO
MAINTAIN THE VOWS OF LIVING BEINGS BODHISATTVA.
TREASURY OF SEA ADORNMENTS BODHISATTVA was in the
assembly, and so, too, was a Bodhisattva called
TREASURY OF SUMERU VIRTUES BODHISATTVA. There was
another named TREASURY OF PURITY OF MERIT AND VIR-
TUES BODHISATTVA. Another was called THE THUS COME
ONE'S TREASURY BODHISATTVA. Yet another Bodhisat-
tva went by the appelation TREASURY OF THE BUDDHAS'
VIRTUES BODHISATTVA. Another Bodhisattva was named
MOON OF LIBERATION BODHISATTVA. That Bodhisattva
AND ALL THE OTHER NUMBERLESS, LIMITLESS, BOUNDLESS,
INCOMPARABLE, UNCOUNTABLE, INDESCRIBABLE, INCON-
CEIVABLE, ILLIMITABLE, AND INEFFABLE MULTITUDES OF
BODHISATTVAS, MAHASATTVAS. They were so many that
you could not measure them, ascertain their bounds,
compare them to anything, count them up, define
them, or conceptualize them if you tried. The
Great Bodhisattvas were there with VAJRA TREASURY
BODHISATTVA AS THEIR LEADER.

SUTRA:

     AT THAT TIME VAJRA TREASURY BODHISATTVA RE-
CEIVED THE BUDDHAS' SPIRITUAL POWER AND ENTERED
"THE BODHISATTVAS' GREAT WISDOM LIGHT SAMADHI."
AFTER HE ENTERED THAT SAMADHI, IN EACH OF THE TEN
DIRECTIONS WERE WORLDS BEYOND THE NUMBER OF FINE
MOTES OF DUST IN TEN MILLION BUDDHALANDS, EACH OF
WHICH CONTAINED BUDDHAS TO THE NUMBER OF FINE MOTES
OF DUST IN TEN MILLION BUDDHALANDS, ALL BEARING
THE SAME NAME, "VAJRA TREASURY."

COMMENTARY:

     AT THAT TIME VAJRA TREASURY BODHISATTVA RE-
CEIVED THE BUDDHAS' SPIRITUAL POWER AND ENTERED
"THE BODHISATTVAS' GREAT WISDOM LIGHT SAMADHI."
Because he was receiving the awesome spiritual
power of Shakyamuni Buddha and of all the Buddhas
of the ten directions, he entered the proper con-

centration and proper reception that great Bodhisattvas enter. *AFTER HE ENTERED THAT SAMADHI*, then
something wonderful occurred. *IN EACH OF THE TEN
DIRECTIONS WERE WORLDS BEYOND THE NUMBER OF FINE
MOTES OF DUST IN TEN MILLION BUDDHALANDS, EACH OF
WHICH CONTAINED BUDDHAS TO THE NUMBER OF FINE MOTES
OF DUST IN TEN MILLION BUDDHALANDS.* Each of the
worlds to the number of fine motes of dust in ten
million Buddhalands had in it Buddhas to the number of fine motes of dust in ten million Buddhalands, *ALL BEARING THE SAME NAME, "VAJRA TREASURY."*
They were all called Vajra Treasury Buddha, Vajra
Treasury Thus Come One.

SUTRA:

*ALL THOSE BUDDHAS APPEARED BEFORE HIM AND
SAID, "GOOD INDEED, GOOD INDEED, VAJRA TREASURY,
THAT YOU ARE ABLE TO ENTER THIS BODHISATTVAS' GREAT
WISDOM LIGHT SAMADHI. GOOD MAN, THIS IS DUE TO
THE COMBINED AID OF BUDDHAS THROUGHOUT THE TEN
DIRECTIONS TO THE NUMBER OF FINE MOTES OF DUST IN
TEN MILLION BUDDHALANDS. IT IS ALSO DUE TO THE
POWER OF THE BASIC VOWS AND THE AWESOME SPIRITUAL
MIGHT OF VAIROCANA, THUS COME ONE, ARHAT, OF RIGHT
AND EQUAL ENLIGHTENMENT. AND IT IS DUE TO THE
POWER OF YOUR SUPREME WISDOM. THEY WISH TO CAUSE
YOU TO HAVE THE LIGHT TO SPEAK ALL INCONCEIVABLE
BUDDHADHARMAS FOR ALL BODHISATTVAS, THAT IS, TO
BRING ABOUT ENTRY INTO THE GROUND OF WISDOM; THE
GATHERING IN OF GOOD ROOTS; THE SKILLFUL SELECTION
OF BUDDHADHARMAS;...*

COMMENTARY:

ALL THOSE BUDDHAS APPEARED BEFORE HIM, they
manifested before Vajra Treasury Bodhisattva in
samadhi, *AND SAID, "GOOD INDEED, GOOD INDEED, VAJ-
RA TREASURY, THAT YOU ARE ABLE TO ENTER THIS BO-
DHISATTVAS' GREAT WISDOM LIGHT SAMADHI."* They
praised him, saying, "You are really good, you are
really fine, Vajra Treasury, that you can gain
access into this right concentration and right reception of the great Bodhisattvas' light of wisdom."

    "GOOD MAN, THIS IS DUE TO THE COMBINED AID OF
BUDDHAS THROUGHOUT THE TEN DIRECTIONS TO THE NUM-
BER·OF FINE MOTES OF DUST IN TEN MILLION BUDDHA-
LANDS. They are all helping you enter this sama-
dhi," they explained. "IT IS ALSO DUE TO THE POWER
OF THE BASIC VOWS AND THE AWESOME SPIRITUAL MIGHT
OF VAIROCANA THUS COME ONE, ARHAT, OF RIGHT AND
EQUAL ENLIGHTENMENT. It is due to the Unsurpassed
One of Right and Equal Enlightenment, whose light
pervades all places. The power of that Buddha's
basic vows and his awesome spiritual might aid you
to enter this proper concentration. AND IT IS DUE
TO THE POWER OF YOUR SUPREME WISDOM. The power of
supreme wisdom that you obtained from cultivating
Bodhisattva practices enables you to enter this
right samadhi."
    "THEY WISH TO CAUSE YOU TO HAVE THE LIGHT TO
SPEAK ALL INCONCEIVABLE BUDDHADHARMAS FOR ALL BO-
DHISATTVAS. Another reason you are able to enter
this Great Wisdom Light Samadhi is because the
Buddhas of the ten directions want you to have the
light of wisdom to speak all the inconceivable
Dharmas expressed by all Buddhas for the sake of
all Bodhisattvas. THAT IS, TO BRING ABOUT ENTRY
INTO THE GROUND OF WISDOM. Then you will be able
to cause all beings to enter the ground of wisdom.
It is to bring about THE GATHERING IN OF GOOD·
ROOTS. It is so you can collect together all the
good roots of living beings amassed in cultivation
that you are enabled to enter this samadhi. It is
to effect THE SKILLFUL SELECTION OF BUDDHADHARMAS.
In order to make use of the Selective Dharma Eye
so as to understand all Dharmas spoken by all Buddhas, you are able to enter this Great Wisdom Light
Samadhi."

SUTRA:

"...VAST KNOWLEDGE OF ALL DHARMAS; SKILLFUL ABILITY
TO SPEAK DHARMA; PURIFICATION OF UNDISCRIMINATING
WISDOM; NON-DEFILEMENT OF ALL WORLDLY DHARMAS;
PURIFICATION OF WORLD-TRANSCENDING GOOD ROOTS; OB-
TAINING INCONCEIVABLE STORES OF WISDOM; OBTAINING
ALL WISDOM AND ENTRY TO STATES OF WISDOM.
    "THEY ALSO WISH TO BRING ABOUT OBTAINING OF
BODHISATTVAS' TEN GROUNDS FROM BEGINNING TO END:

AN ACCURATE SPEAKING OF THE DISTINCTIVE CHARACTER-
ISTICS OF THE BODHISATTVAS' TEN GROUNDS:...

COMMENTARY:

"VAST KNOWLEDGE OF ALL DHARMAS" means being
able to,

>   Deeply enter the Sutra store,
>   And have wisdom like the sea.

The Buddhadharma is like the great sea. It is
necessary to have vast, great wisdom in order to
know all dharmas. But, just knowing is not enough
one must also have "SKILLFUL ABILITY TO SPEAK DHAR-
MA." You must be good at employing clever, expedient methods to speak all dharmas, and have the
"PURIFICATION OF UNDISCRIMINATING WISDOM." You
require the Four Wisdoms:

1. The wisdom that accomplishes what is done
2. The wisdom of wonderful contemplation.
3. The wisdom of sameness.
4. The great, perfect mirror wisdom.

Then, right within non-discrimination you will be
able to understand all pure, wonderful dharmas.
"NON-DEFILEMENT OF ALL WORLDLY DHARMAS." Defiled
worldly dharmas need only be turned around to become undefiled, world-transcending dharmas. It is
also to bring about the "PURIFICATION OF WORLD-
TRANSCENDING GOOD ROOTS." Obtaining all world-
transcending dharmas, you can cultivate world-
transcending good roots, and attain to purity, as
well as "OBTAINING INCONCEIVABLE STATES OF WISDOM"
and "OBTAINING ALL WISDOM AND ENTRY TO STATES OF
WISDOM." Upon obtaining all-wisdom, one is able
to enter the states of wisdom.
     "THEY ALSO WISH TO BRING ABOUT OBTAINING OF
THE BODHISATTVAS' TEN GROUNDS FROM BEGINNING TO
END." This is to bring about understanding of and
certification to the progressive states of the
grounds of a Bodhisattva from the First to the
Tenth. Those of the First Ground do not understand the state of those of the Second Ground, and
those of the Tenth Ground do not understand the

state of those of Equal Enlightenment. So in cultivation, each person has his or her own skill and
his or her own states, which differ from those of
others; and the Ten Grounds have a progression
from beginning to end, from the First Ground to
the Tenth Ground. "AN ACCURATE SPEAKING OF THE
DISTINCTIVE CHARACTERISTICS OF THE BODHISATTVAS'
TEN GROUNDS" means accurately explaining different
characteristics of the Bodhisattvas' Ten Grounds.
People who cultivate the Way should recognize
states. The Buddhas wish the Bodhisattvas to
thoroughly understand the states of the Ten Grounds
and to accurately explain the different characteristics of the Ten Grounds.

SUTRA:

"...FOLLOWING AND BEING MINDFUL OF ALL BUDDHAS'
DHARMAS; CULTIVATING, STUDYING, AND DISCRIMINATING
NON-OUTFLOWING DHARMAS; CLEVERLY ADORNING THROUGH
THE LIGHT OF GREAT WISDOM OF SKILLFUL SELECTION
AND CONTEMPLATION; SKILLFULLY ENTERING THE DOOR OF
DECISIVE WISDOM; ACCORDING TO DWELLING PLACES MANI-
FESTING IN SEQUENCE AND SPEAKING WITHOUT FEAR; OB-
TAINING THE LIGHT OF UNOBSTRUCTED ELOQUENCE; DWELL-
ING ON THE GROUND OF GREAT ELOQUENCE AND HAVING
SKILLFUL DECISIVENESS; BEING SO MINDFUL OF THE BO-
DHISATTVAS THAT ONE NEVER FORGETS THEM; MATURING
ALL THE REALMS OF LIVING BEINGS; BEING ABLE PER-
VASIVELY TO GO TO ALL PLACES AND BE SURE TO BE EN-
LIGHTENED.

COMMENTARY:

"FOLLOWING AND BEING MINDFUL OF ALL BUDDHAS'
DHARMAS/" Following means singlemindedly adapting to, according with, and being mindful of all
the Dharmas spoken by the Buddhas. "CULTIVATING,
STUDYING, AND DISCRIMINATING NON-OUTFLOWING DHAR-
MAS/" One should clearly understand what has outflows and what has no outflows, as well as to what
extent there are outflowing dharmas present within
non-outflowing dharmas, and to what extent there
are non-outflowing dharmas present within outflowing dharmas. That means on the one hand cultivat-

ing and on the other hand studying and discriminating what are dharmas with outflows and what are dharmas without outflows. *"CLEVERLY ADORNING THROUGH THE LIGHT OF GREAT WISDOM OF SKILLFUL SELECTION AND CONTEMPLATION/"* One who is good at employing the Selective Dharma Eye can contemplate all the dharmas of great wisdom. When one has great wisdom, then one can have great wisdom light, and then one is able cleverly and expediently to adorn all Buddhalands. *"SKILLFULLY ENTERING THE DOOR OF DECISIVE WISDOM/"* One is also able to be very exact and clear about discriminating, to enter the door of all-wisdom, and to have no doubts.

"ACCORDING TO DWELLING PLACES MANIFESTING IN SEQUENCE AND SPEAKING WITHOUT FEAR/" In accord with where Bodhisattvas are dwelling, in a clear and orderly fashion they speak the precise meaning of the Dharmas and have no fear. *"OBTAINING THE LIGHT OF UNOBSTRUCTED ELOQUENCE/"* The light of wisdom reveals itself in unimpeded eloquence. *"DWELLING ON THE GROUND OF GREAT ELOQUENCE AND HAVING SKILLFUL DECISIVENESS/"* One has great eloquence and one applies it to all Dharmas. *"BEING SO MINDFUL OF THE BODHISATTVAS THAT ONE NEVER FORGETS THEM/"* They always remember all Bodhisattvas. *"MATURING ALL THE REALMS OF LIVING BEINGS/"* One is also able to bring all living beings to maturity, that is:

1. To cause those who have not yet planted good roots to plant them;
2. To cause already planted good roots to grow;
3. To cause good roots that have already grown to come to maturity;
4. To cause those whose roots have already matured to obtain liberation.

"BEING ABLE PERVASIVELY TO GO TO ALL PLACES AND BE SURE TO BE ENLIGHTENED." They visit all assemblies in the Bodhimandas of all Buddhas of the three periods of time and, upon arriving there, are certain to become enlightened and to obtain great wisdom, great eloquence, long life, and happiness. They are certified as being enlightened to the real mark of all dharmas.

SUTRA:

. "GOOD MAN, YOU SHOULD ELOQUENTLY DISCUSS THESE
DISTINCTIONS OF DHARMA DOORS AND GOOD AND CLEVER
METHODS, WHICH IS TO SAY, RECEIVING THE BUDDHAS'
SPIRITUAL POWER, TO BE AIDED BY THE THUS COME ONES'
LIGHT OF WISDOM; TO PURIFY ONE'S OWN GOOD ROOTS;
TO UNIVERSALLY PURIFY THE DHARMA REALMS; TO COM-
PLETELY GATHER IN LIVING BEINGS; TO DEEPLY ENTER
THE DHARMA BODY AND THE WISDOM BODY; TO RECEIVE ALL
BUDDHAS' ANOINTMENT OF ONE'S CROWN; TO OBTAIN THE
TALLEST, LARGEST BODY IN ALL WORLDS; TO TRANSCEND
ALL WORLDLY WAYS; TO PURIFY WORLD-TRANSCENDING GOOD
ROOTS; TO PERFECT THE WISDOM OF ALL-WISDOM."

COMMENTARY:

When Vajra Treasury Bodhisattva entered the
Great Wisdom Light Samadhi, all the Buddhas of the
ten directions praised him and said to him, "GOOD
MAN, YOU SHOULD ELOQUENTLY DISCUSS THESE DISTINC-
TIONS OF DHARMA DOORS AND GOOD AND CLEVER METHODS."
They told him, "You should use your unobstructed
eloquence to explain the various aspects of the
Great Wisdom Light Samadhi, and of expedient skill-
ful methods, WHICH IS TO SAY, RECEIVING THE BUD-
DHAS' SPIRITUAL POWER/ You are based in great
spiritual power of all Buddhas of the ten direc-
tions, as well as that of Vairocana Buddha and
Shakyamuni Buddha. TO BE AIDED BY THE THUS COME
ONES' LIGHT OF WISDOM, the light of the Buddhas
will come to your assistance. TO PURIFY ONE'S OWN
GOOD ROOTS of Bodhi; TO UNIVERSALLY PURIFY THE
DHARMA REALMS with your light of wisdom. TO COM-
PLETELY GATHER IN LIVING BEINGS/ Your wisdom will
gather in and receive all living beings, as well
as TO DEEPLY ENTER THE DHARMA BODY AND THE WISDOM
BODY. TO RECEIVE ALL BUDDHAS' ANOINTMENT OF ONE'S
CROWN/ All the Buddhas of the ten directions and
the three periods of time will come and give you a
prediction and rub your crown to aid you. TO OB-
TAIN THE TALLEST, LARGEST BODY IN ALL WORLDS/ You
will gain the worlds' greatest wisdom and the tallest Dharma Body. TO TRANSCEND ALL WORLDLY WAYS/
You will be able to excel in all mundane Dharma
doors and paths. TO PURIFY WORLD-TRANSCENDING GOOD

ROOTS of Bodhi, and TO PERFECT THE WISDOM OF ALL-
WISDOM. You will perfect the ground of all-wisdom
and then enable all living beings to obtain the
wisdom among wisdoms."

SUTRA:

    AT THAT TIME THE BUDDHAS OF THE TEN DIRECTIONS
BESTOWED UPON VAJRA TREASURY BODHISATTVA A PEER-
LESS BODY; BESTOWED UNOBSTRUCTED ELOQUENCE OF DE-
LIGHT IN SPEECH; BESTOWED SKILLFULLY DISCRIMINAT-
ING PURE WISDOM; BESTOWED THE POWER OF GOOD MEMORY
AND NON-FORGETFULNESS; BESTOWED SKILLFULLY DECISIVE
WISDOM OF UNDERSTANDING; BESTOWED THE WISDOM TO
REACH ALL PLACES AND BECOME ENLIGHTENED; BESTOWED
THE POWER OF EASE IN ACCOMPLISHING THE WAY; BE-
STOWED THE THUS COME ONES' FEARLESSNESSES; BESTOWED
THOSE OF ALL WISDOMS' WISDOM OF ELOQUENCE TO CON-
TEMPLATE AND DISCRIMINATE ALL DHARMA DOORS; BE-
STOWED ALL THUS COME ONES' PERFECTED, SUPERIOR,
WONDERFUL ADORNMENTS OF BODY, SPEECH, AND MIND.
AND WHY? BECAUSE, UPON OBTAINING THIS SAMADHI, THE
DHARMA IS THAT WAY; BECAUSE OF THE ARISAL FROM
PAST VOWS; BECAUSE OF PROFOUND THOUGHT BEING WELL-
PURIFIED; BECAUSE OF THE WHEEL OF WISDOM BEING
WELL-PURIFIED; BECAUSE OF AIDS TO THE WAY BEING
WELL-ACCUMULATED; BECAUSE OF WHAT ONE DOES BEING
WELL-CULTIVATED; BECAUSE OF MINDFULNESS OF ONE AS
A LIMITLESS DHARMA VESSEL; BECAUSE OF KNOWLEDGE
THAT ONE HAS PURE FAITH AND UNDERSTANDING; BECAUSE
OF FLAWLESS MAINTAINING AND UPHOLDING BEING OB-
TAINED; BECAUSE OF SKILLFUL APPLICATION OF THE
SEAL OF WISDOM OF THE DHARMA REALM.

COMMENTARY:

    AT THAT TIME THE BUDDHAS OF THE TEN DIREC-
TIONS BESTOWED UPON VAJRA TREASURY BODHISATTVA A
PEERLESS BODY. They aided Vajra Treasury Bodhisattva in obtaining a body whose radiance could
not be obscured, and BESTOWED UNOBSTRUCTED ELO-
QUENCE OF DELIGHT IN SPEECH, out of great compassion giving him the perfectly fused and unobstructed eloquence. They BESTOWED SKILLFULLY DISCRIMI-

NATING PURE WISDOM and BESTOWED THE POWER OF GOOD
MEMORY AND NON-FORGETFULNESS upon Vajra Treasury
Bodhisattva. They BESTOWED SKILLFULLY DECISIVE :
WISDOM OF UNDERSTANDING. They BESTOWED THE WISDOM
TO REACH ALL PLACES AND BECOME ENLIGHTENED. They
also gave Vajra Treasury Bodhisattva their aid and
BESTOWED THE POWER OF EASE IN ACCOMPLISHING THE
WAY, the power of free and easy success on the
Path; and they BESTOWED THE THUS COME ONES' FEAR-
LESSNESSES, and BESTOWED THOSE OF ALL WISDOM'S WIS-
DOM OF ELOQUENCE TO CONTEMPLATE AND DISCRIMINATE
ALL DHARMA DOORS; and they BESTOWED ALL THUS COME
ONES', Buddhas', PERFECTED, SUPERIOR WONDERFUL
ADORNMENTS OF BODY, SPEECH, AND MIND, the perfec-
tion of limitless adornments. AND WHY? Why was
that? BECAUSE, UPON OBTAINING THIS SAMADHI, when
one attains to the Great Wisdom Light Samadhi, THE
DHARMA IS THAT WAY. A necessary correlary of this
dharma is that it has to be that way. It is also
BECAUSE OF THE ARISAL FROM PAST VOWS, that is, this
kind of dharma comes into being through the vows
of the Buddhas and Bodhisattvas of the ten directions. It is also BECAUSE OF PROFOUND THOUGHT
BEING WELL-PURIFIED, because Vajra Treasury Bodhisattva was good at purifying deep thought; and BE-
CAUSE OF THE WHEEL OF WISDOM BEING WELL-PURIFIED,
and BECAUSE OF AIDS TO THE WAY BEING WELL-ACCUMU-
LATED. Furthermore, it is BECAUSE OF WHAT ONE DOES
BEING WELL-CULTIVATED, bringing those Dharma doors
that one should to accomplishment. It is BECAUSE
OF MINDFULNESS OF ONE AS A LIMITLESS DHARMA VESSEL.
The Buddhas of the ten directions are aware that
Vajra Treasury Bodhisattva can act as a vessel for
limitlessly many Dharmas. BECAUSE OF KNOWLEDGE
THAT ONE HAS PURE FAITH AND UNDERSTANDING. They
know that he is someone who has accomplished faith
and understanding. It is also BECAUSE OF FLAWLESS
MAINTAINING AND UPHOLDING BEING OBTAINED, and BE-
CAUSE OF SKILLFUL APPLICATION OF THE SEAL OF WISDOM
OF THE DHARMA REALM, from being skilled at employ-
ing the Jeweled Seal of the Dharma Realm to seal
and certify all Dharmas.

SUTRA:

AT THAT TIME, ALL THE BUDDHAS OF THE TEN DI-
RECTIONS EXTENDED THEIR RIGHT HANDS AND RUBBED

VAJRA TREASURY BODHISATTVA ON THE CROWN. AFTER
THEY HAD RUBBED HIS CROWN, VAJRA TREASURY BODHI-
SATTVA AROSE FROM SAMADHI AND TOLD ALL THE ASSEM-
BLY OF BODHISATTVAS, "DISCIPLES OF THE BUDDHA, ALL
BODHISATTVAS' VOWS ARE WELL-DECIDED. THEY ARE UN-
ADULTERATED, IMPERCEPTIBLE, VAST AND GREAT LIKE THE
DHARMA REALM, ULTIMATELY LIKE EMPTY SPACE, EXHAUST-
ING THE BOUNDARIES OF THE FUTURE. THESE BODHISAT-
TVAS PERVADE ALL BUDDHALANDS AND RESCUE AND PRO-
TECT ALL LIVING BEINGS. THEY ARE PROTECTED BY ALL
BUDDHAS. THEY ENTER THE GROUNDS OF WISDOM OF ALL
BUDDHAS OF THE PAST, THE FUTURE, AND THE PRESENT.
    "DISCIPLES OF THE BUDDHA, WHAT ARE THE GROUNDS
OF WISDOM OF THE BODHISATTVAS, MAHASATTVAS? DIS-
CIPLES OF THE BUDDHA, THE GROUNDS OF WISDOM OF THE
BODHISATTVAS, MAHASATTVAS, ARE OF TEN KINDS, WHICH
ALL BUDDHAS OF THE PAST, THE FUTURE, AND THE PRE-
SENT HAVE SPOKEN, WILL SPEAK AND ARE SPEAKING. I
ALSO SPEAK THEM THUS.

COMMENTARY:

    AT THAT TIME, after the Buddhas of the ten
directions had praised Vajra Treasury Bodhisattva,
ALL THE BUDDHAS OF THE TEN DIRECTIONS, the Buddhas
from above, below, east, west, south, and north--
the six directions--with the addition of the four
intermediate points, making ten directions, ALL
EXTENDED THEIR RIGHT HANDS. Each Buddha extended
his right hand and RUBBED VAJRA TREASURY BODHISATTVA
ON THE CROWN. AFTER THEY HAD RUBBED HIS CROWN,
VAJRA TREASURY BODHISATTVA AROSE FROM SAMADHI AND
TOLD ALL THE ASSEMBLY OF BODHISATTVAS, "DISCIPLES
OF THE BUDDHA, ALL BODHISATTVAS' VOWS ARE WELL-
DECIDED." He told them that all the great vows
made by all Bodhisattvas are decisive. "THEY ARE
UNADULTERATED," they have no admixture, and are
"IMPERCEPTIBLE." The vows made by Bodhisattvas
cannot be seen, and yet they are "VAST AND GREAT
LIKE THE DHARMA REALM, ULTIMATELY LIKE EMPTY SPACE."
At their ultimate point they are like emptiness:
you cannot find their limits. "EXHAUSTING THE
BOUNDARIES OF THE FUTURE they PERVADE ALL THE BUD-
DHALANDS." The Bodhisattvas go to the countries
of all Buddhas "AND RESCUE AND PROTECT ALL LIVING
BEINGS." They have the ability to save all beings.

"THEY ARE PROTECTED BY ALL BUDDHAS" of the three periods of time. "THEY ENTER THE GROUNDS OF WIS- DOM OF ALL BUDDHAS OF THE PAST, FUTURE, AND PRE- SENT." The Bodhisattvas are certified as having entered the grounds of wisdom of all Buddhas of the three periods of time.

"DISCIPLES OF THE BUDDHA, WHAT ARE THE GROUNDS OF WISDOM OF THE BODHISATTVAS, MAHASATTVAS" who cultivate and accumulate various kinds of good roots, and the grounds of wisdom of all Bodhisat- tvas and Buddhas? What are they? "DISCIPLES OF THE BUDDHA, THE GROUNDS OF WISDOM OF THE BODHISAT- TVAS, MAHASATTVAS, ARE OF TEN KINDS." The great Bodhisattvas who cultivate the conduct of Bodhi- sattvas have ten grounds of wisdom. If spoken in even further detail, there are limitless and bound- lessly many kinds, "WHICH ALL BUDDHAS OF THE PAST, THE FUTURE, AND THE PRESENT HAVE SPOKEN, WILL SPEAK, AND ARE SPEAKING." The Buddhas of the past, the future, and the present have spoken, will in the future speak, and right now are speaking them, "I ALSO SPEAK THEM THUS. I, too, just like the Buddhas of the past, the future, and the present, will speak the ten kinds of grounds of wisdom of the Bodhisattvas."

SUTRA:

"WHAT ARE THE TEN? ONE, THE GROUND OF HAPPI- NESS; TWO, THE GROUND OF LEAVING FILTH; THREE, THE GROUND OF EMITTING LIGHT; FOUR, THE GROUND OF BLAZ- ING WISDOM; FIVE, THE GROUND OF INVINCIBILITY; SIX, THE GROUND OF MANIFESTATION; SEVEN, THE GROUND OF TRAVELLING FAR; EIGHT, THE GROUND OF IMMOVABILITY; NINE, THE GROUND OF GOOD WISDOM; TEN, THE GROUND OF THE DHARMA CLOUD.

"DISCIPLES OF THE BUDDHA, THESE TEN GROUNDS HAVE BEEN EXPLAINED, WILL BE EXPLAINED, AND ARE BE- ING EXPLAINED BY ALL BUDDHAS OF THE THREE PERIODS OF TIME. DISCIPLES OF THE BUDDHA, I HAVE NOT SEEN ANY THUS COME ONES IN ANY BUDDHALANDS WHO DO NOT SPEAK THESE TEN GROUNDS. AND WHY? THEY ARE THE BODHISATTVAS' MAHASATTVAS' MOST SUPERIOR PATH TO BODHI. THEY ARE ALSO DOORS OF PURE DHARMA LIGHT, NAMELY, THE DETAILED EXPLANATION OF ALL BODHISAT- TVAS' GROUNDS. DISCIPLES OF THE BUDDHA, THIS PLACE

IS INCONCEIVABLE, NAMELY THE WISDOM ACCORDINGLY
CERTIFIED TO BY BODHISATTVAS."
    AT THAT TIME, AFTER VAJRA TREASURY BODHISAT-
TVA HAD FINISHED SPEAKING THE NAMES OF THE TEN
GROUNDS, HE REMAINED SILENT AND DID NOT FURTHER
DISTINGUISH THEM.   THEREUPON, ALL THE ASSEMBLY OF
BODHISATTVAS, UPON HEARING THE NAMES OF THE BODHI-
SATTVAS' TEN GROUNDS, BUT NOT HEARING THEIR EXPLAN-
ATION, ALL LOOKED UP IN THIRST AND HAD THIS THOUGHT,
"WHAT IS THE CAUSE, AND WHAT IS THE REASON, THAT
VAJRA TREASURY BODHISATTVA ONLY SPEAKS THE NAMES
OF THE BODHISATTVAS' TEN GROUNDS YET DOES NOT EX-
PLAIN THEM?"   MOON OF LIBERATION BODHISATTVA, KNOW-
ING WHAT WAS BEING THOUGHT BY ALL THOSE IN THE
GREAT ASSEMBLY, USED VERSES TO QUESTION VAJRA TREAS-
URY BODHISATTVA, SAYING:
    "WHY IS IT THAT THE PURE ENLIGHTENED ONE,
    REPLETE WITH MINDFULNESS, WISDOM, AND VIRTUE,
    SPEAKS OF THE SUPERIOR, WONDROUS GOUNDS, YET
    WITH POWER TO DO SO STILL DOES NOT EXPLAIN
    THEM?"

COMMENTARY:

    "WHAT ARE THE TEN?" What are the ten grounds
called? Their names are as follows: "ONE, THE
GROUND OF HAPPINESS." Upon arriving at this ground
one is very happy. "TWO, THE GROUND OF LEAVING
FILTH." At the Second Ground, all filth of false
thinking is cut off,' that is, all view delusions,
thought delusions, and delusions like dust and
sand. "THREE, THE GROUND OF EMITTING LIGHT." At
the Third Ground, one eliminates all the dust-
fatigue of false thinking, and the light of one's
own original wisdom manifests. "FOUR, THE GROUND
OF BLAZING WISDOM." At the Fourth Ground, not only
does one emit light, but one even blazes with the
flaming light of wisdom. "FIVE, THE GROUND OF IN-
VINCIBILITY." It is hard to cultivate to this position. It is not at all easy to attain to this
ground. "SIX, THE GROUND OF MANIFESTATION." At
this Ground, all wisdom manifests. "SEVEN, THE
GROUND OF TRAVELLING FAR." At the Seventh Ground,
one can fly and do transformations. "EIGHT, THE
GROUND OF IMMOVABILITY." At the Eighth Ground,
without moving from the Bodhimanda, one travels

pervasively throughout the ten directions. *"NINE, THE GROUND OF GOOD WISDOM."* Upon arriving at this Ground, one has the best of wisdoms. *"TEN, THE GROUND OF THE DHARMA CLOUD."* The Dharma cloud universally shades all living beings.

"DISCIPLES OF THE BUDDHA"--Vajra Treasury again calls out, "All of you disciples of the Buddha, *THESE TEN GROUNDS HAVE BEEN EXPLAINED, WILL BE EXPLAINED, AND ARE BEING EXPLAINED BY ALL BUDDHAS OF THE THREE PERIODS OF TIME."* The names of the Bodhisattvas' Ten Grounds had already been spoken by all future Buddhas, and are now being spoken by the Buddhas of the present. *"DISCIPLES OF THE BUDDHA, I HAVE NOT SEEN ANY THUS COME ONES IN ANY BUDDHALANDS WHO DO NOT SPEAK THESE TEN GROUNDS."* He said, "I have never seen any Buddha in all the Buddhalands who fails to speak the doctrines of the Ten Grounds. *"AND WHY? THEY ARE THE BODHISATTVAS' MAHASATTVAS' MOST SUPERIOR PATH TO BODHI."* The great Bodhisattvas among Bodhisattvas use these Dharma doors as the superior path for cultivating Bodhi. *"THEY ARE ALSO DOORS OF PURE DHARMA LIGHT."* The Ten Grounds are also entrances into the light of pure Dharma wisdom, *"NAMELY, THE WISDOM ACCORDINGLY CERTIFIED TO BY BODHISATTVAS."* All Bodhisattvas accordingly cultivate and certify to this wisdom.

AT THAT TIME, AFTER VAJRA TREASURY BODHISATTVA HAD FINISHED SPEAKING THE NAMES OF THE TEN GROUNDS, HE REMAINED SILENT AND DID NOT FURTHER DISTINGUISH THEM. He did not open his mouth. He said nothing, withdrew to one side, and did not explain the meaning of the Ten Grounds any further. *THEREUPON, THE ASSEMBLY OF BODHISATTVAS,* all the great Bodhisattvas who had come there from the ten directions, *UPON HEARING THE NAMES OF THE BODHISATTVAS' TEN GROUNDS, BUT NOT HEARING THEIR EXPLANATION,* when they did not hear Vajra Treasury Bodhisattva give any deeper explanation of their principles, *ALL LOOKED UP IN THIRST.* Turning up their heads, they waited for Vajra Treasury Bodhisattva to explain, *AND HAD THIS THOUGHT, "WHAT IS THE CAUSE, AND WHAT IS THE REASON THAT VAJRA TREASURY BODHISATTVA ONLY SPEAKS THE NAMES OF THE BODHISATTVAS' TEN GROUNDS YET DOES NOT EXPLAIN THEM?* Why did he only tell us the names of the Ten Grounds of a Bodhisattva, with no commentary or explanation?" *MOON OF LIB-*

ERATION BODHISATTVA, KNOWING WHAT WAS BEING THOUGHT
BY ALL THOSE IN THE GREAT ASSEMBLY, USED VERSES TO
QUESTION VAJRA TREASURY BODHISATTVA, SAYING: "WHY
IS IT THAT THE PURE ENLIGHTENED ONE/ you, Bodhisattva, REPLETE WITH MINDFULNESS, WISDOM, AND VIRTUE/
who have perfected pure mindfulness, the light of
wisdom, and all meritorious qualities, SPEAKS OF
THE SUPERIOR, WONDROUS GROUNDS/ you give the names
of the Ten Grounds--YET WITH POWER TO DO SO STILL
DOES NOT EXPLAIN THEM?/ Why is it that even though
you have the power to explain them in detail, you
do not do so for all of us?".

SUTRA:

> "YOU HAVE DECISIVENESS AND JUDGMENT,
> ARE COURAGEOUS AND ARE NOT WEAK-WILLED;
> WHY DO YOU ONLY NAME THE GROUNDS,
> WITHOUT GOING ON THEN TO DISCUSS THEM?
>
> "THE WONDERFUL DOCTRINES OF THE GROUNDS,
> ALL THOSE ASSEMBLED WISH TO HEAR;
> THEIR MINDS SHOW NO TRACE OF COWARDICE.
> THEY WISH YOU TO SPEAK THEM IN DETAIL.
>
> "THE MULTITUDES ASSEMBLED ARE ALL PURE,
> DEVOID OF LAXNESS, STERN THEY ARE AND CLEAR,
> ABLE TO BE SOLID AND UNMOVING,
> WITH MERIT, VIRTUE, WISDOM, ALL ENDOWED.
>
> "MUTUALLY THEY LOOK TO YOU IN REVERENCE,
> ALL OF THEM INTENT WITH UPWARD GAZE,
> LIKE BEES THAT ARE MINDFUL OF THEIR HONEY,
> LIKE THIRSTY PEOPLE THINKING OF SWEET DEW."

COMMENTARY:

Moon of Liberation Bodhisattva went on to say
to Vajra Treasury Bodhisattva, "YOU HAVE DECISIVE-
NESS AND JUDGMENT/ You have the decisive wisdom to
understand right and wrong, ARE COURAGEOUS AND ARE
NOT WEAK-WILLED/You cultivate the Bodhisattva Way
with courageous vigor, and are not afraid of anything, so WHY DO YOU ONLY NAME THE GROUNDS?/ Why
did you just speak the names of the Ten Bodhisattva

Grounds *WITHOUT GOING ON THEN TO DISCUSS THEM?/* You
did not expound them for everyone.

   "THE WONDERFUL DOCTRINES OF THE GROUNDS/--each
of the Grounds is sure to have very inconceivable
and subtle doctrines--*ALL THOSE ASSEMBLED WISH TO
HEAR.* Right now all of the multitudes in the Dharma Assembly wish to hear those doctrines. *THEIR
MINDS SHOW NO TRACE OF COWARDICE/* The hearts of all
the Bodhisattvas have no fear whatsoever. *THEY
WISH YOU TO SPEAK THEM IN DETAIL/* If you would just
speak this Dharma, they would all like to hear it.
   *"THE MULTITUDES ASSEMBLED ARE ALL PURE/ DE-
VOID OF LAXNESS, STERN AND CLEAR/* The Bodhisattvas
in this Bodhimanda are all courageously vigorous,
stern, strict, and pure. With their great resolve
for Bodhi, they are *ABLE TO BE SOLID AND UNMOVING/*
and are *WITH MERIT, VIRTUE, WISDOM ALL ENDOWED/*
   "MUTUALLY THEY LOOK TO YOU IN REVERENCE/ Their
eyes are all upon you as they wait with much respect for you, oh Bodhisattva, to speak to them.
ALL OF THEM INTENT WITH UPWARD GAZE/ All the great
Bodhisattvas are looking towards you single-minded,
thirsty for the explanation, *LIKE BEES THAT ARE
MINDFUL OF THEIR HONEY/ LIKE THIRSTY PEOPLE THINK-
ING OF SWEET DEW/* They are waiting just that sin-
cerely in single-minded, eager anticipation."

SUTRA:

   *AT THAT TIME, THE GREATLY WISE AND FEARLESS
BODHISATTVA, VAJRA TREASURY, HAVING HEARD WHAT WAS
SAID, AND WISHING TO MAKE THE ASSEMBLED MULTITUDES
HAPPY, FOR ALL DISCIPLES OF THE BUDDHA USED VERSES
AND SAID:*

COMMENTARY:

   AT THAT TIME, THE GREATLY WISE/ If you have
great wisdom, then, no matter what happens, you
have no problems. People who lack wisdom, however,
have problems no matter what happens. *AND FEAR-
LESS/* You should not be afraid of people, but you
also must not go around bullying people. Fearing
and bullying people amount to the same thing. To
be fearless does not mean to beat up on people or

to argue with them. It is just that, as a result
of your own great wisdom, there is nothing that you
fear. *BODHISATTVA VAJRA TREASURY/* Who was it who
was greatly wise and fearless? It was Vajra Treasury Bodhisattva who, *HAVING HEARD WHAT WAS SAID*
by Moon of Liberation Bodhisattva in his verses,
*AND WISHING TO MAKE THE ASSEMBLED MULTITUDES HAPPY,
FOR ALL DISCIPLES OF THE BUDDHA/* for all the great
Bodhisattvas, *USED VERSES AND SAID:*

SUTRA:

> *"THE DEEDS OF BODHISATTVAS' GROUNDS OF
>   PRACTICE,*
> *ARE SOURCES MOST SUPREME OF BUDDHAS ALL:*
> *CLEAR DISCUSSION OF THEM IN DETAIL*
> *IS FOREMOST, RARE, AND HARD TO COME UPON.*

> *"THEIR SUBTLETIES ARE DIFFICULT TO SEE,*
> *APART FROM THOUGHT, THEY GO BEYOND THE*
>   *MIND;*
> *THE STATES AND REALMS OF BUDDHAS THAT*
>   *APPEAR,*
> *CAUSE THOSE WHO HEAR TO BE CONFUSED AND*
>   *DOUBT.*

COMMENTARY:

   *"THE DEEDS OF BODHISATTVAS' GROUNDS OF PRAC-
TICE"/* Bodhisattva Vajra Treasury said, "During a
Bodhisattva's cultivation on the causal ground,
he experiences the events on the Ten Bodhisattva
Grounds, which *ARE SOURCES MOST SUPREME OF BUDDHAS
ALL /* There is nothing higher than they are, and
they are the basic Dharma-doors for accomplishing
Buddhahood. *CLEAR DISCUSSION OF THEM IN DETAIL
IS FOREMOST, RARE, AND HARD TO COME UPON/* They
are rarely explained.
   "THEIR SUBTLETIES ARE DIFFICULT TO SEE
practices of Bodhisattvas have fine points which
are not easy to understand. *APART FROM THOUGHT,
THEY GO BEYOND THE MIND/* These kinds of Dharma-
doors are such that the path of language is cut
off, and the place of the mind's workings is ex-
tinguished. They go beyond all reflection and

deliberation. THE STATES AND REALMS OF BUDDHAS
THAT APPEAR/--all that manifest are the Buddhas'
states--CAUSE THOSE WHO HEAR TO BE CONFUSED AND TO
DOUBT/ It is very hard for those who hear of these
Dharma-doors to understand them, and it is very
easy for them to give rise to doubts and confusion.

SUTRA:

> "IF ONE HOLDS THE MIND LIKE VAJRA,
> WITH DEEP FAITH IN THE BUDDHAS' FOREMOST
>   WISDOM,
> KNOWING THAT THE MIND-GROUND LACKS A SELF,
> ONE CAN HEAR THESE DHARMAS MOST SUPREME.
>
> "LIKE PICTURES THAT ARE PAINTED IN THE AIR,
> LIKE TRACES OF THE WIND IN EMPTY SPACE,
> THE WISDOM OF THE MUNI IS THAT WAY,
> ITS DISTINCTIONS VERY HARD FOR ONE TO SEE.
>
> "I AM MINDFUL THAT THE WISDOM OF THE BUDDHAS,
> IS SUPERIOR BEYOND CONCEPTION;
> THERE'S NO ONE IN THE WORLD WHO CAN
>   RECEIVE IT.
> SILENT, THEN, AM I AND DO NOT SPEAK."

COMMENTARY:

"IF ONE HOLDS THE MIND LIKE VAJRA/ Living beings give rise to doubts and confusion, because they
do not have the wisdom to understand these most
superior Dharma-doors. If they can hold onto their
minds with vajra-like solidity, WITH DEEP FAITH IN
THE BUDDHAS' FOREMOST WISDOM/ KNOWING THAT THE MIND-
GROUND LACKS A SELF/ ONE CAN HEAR THESE DHARMAS
MOST SUPREME. Knowing that the entrances into the
mind-ground are necessarily devoid of self, they
will be able to hear these most supreme Dharmas."
"LIKE PICTURES THAT ARE PAINTED IN THE AIR/
One should not become attached upon hearing of
these magnificent Dharmas. They are all like paint-
ings in space, with no shape or characteristics,
and LIKE TRACES OF THE WIND IN EMPTY SPACE/ which
also lack shape or characteristics. THE WISDOM OF
THE MUNI IS THAT WAY/ Shakyamuni Buddha's wisdom

is also like that, *ITS DISTINCTIONS VERY HARD FOR ONE TO SEE/* No matter how hard you try, they are not easily understood or seen.

"*I AM MINDFUL THAT THE WISDOM OF THE BUDDHAS/ IS SUPERIOR BEYOND CONCEPTION/* It is excellent and not easy to conceive of. *THERE'S NO ONE IN THE WORLD WHO CAN RECEIVE IT/* No one in the world can understand this Dharma or accept these principles. *SILENT, THEN, AM I AND DO NOT SPEAK.* Therefore, I remain silent and do not explain them for anyone."

SUTRA:

AT THAT TIME, WHEN MOON OF LIBERATION BODHISATTVA HEARD THIS SAID, HE ADDRESSED VAJRA TREASURY BODHISATTVA, SAYING, "DISCIPLE OF THE BUDDHA, THE MULTITUDES ARE ALREADY GATHERED HERE. THEY ALL HAVE WELL PURIFIED THE DEPTHS OF THEIR MINDS AND HAVE WELL CLEANSED THEIR THOUGHTS. THEY HAVE WELL CULTIVATED MANY PRACTICES. THEY HAVE WELL ACCUMULATED THE AIDS TO THE PATH. THEY HAVE BEEN WELL ABLE TO DRAW NEAR HUNDREDS OF THOUSANDS OF MILLIONS OF BUDDHAS. THEY HAVE ACCOMPLISHED LIMITLESS GOOD ROOTS OF MERIT AND VIRTUE. THEY HAVE CAST OFF ALL STUPIDITY AND DOUBT. THEY HAVE NO DEFILEMENTS. THEY HAVE DEEP FAITH AND UNDERSTANDING. WITHIN THE BUDDHADHARMAS THEY DO NOT FOLLOW OTHER TEACHINGS. ALL IS WELL, DISCIPLE OF THE BUDDHA; YOU SHOULD RECEIVE THE BUDDHAS' SPIRITUAL POWER AND SPEAK. ALL THESE BODHISATTVAS WILL BE ABLE TO BE CERTIFIED AS KNOWING ALL THESE PROFOUND PLACES."

AT THAT TIME, MOON OF LIBERATION BODHISATTVA, WISHING TO RESTATE HIS MEANING, SPOKE VERSES, SAYING:

COMMENTARY:

AT THAT TIME, WHEN MOON OF LIBERATION BODHISATTVA finished listening to Vajra Treasury Bodhisattva, and having HEARD THIS SAID. HE ADDRESSED VAJRA TREASURY BODHISATTVA, SAYING, "DISCIPLE OF THE BUDDHA, THE MULTITUDES ARE ALREADY GATHERED HERE THEY ALL HAVE WELL PURIFIED THE DEPTHS OF THEIR

MINDS of faith, *AND HAVE WELL CLEANSED THEIR
THOUGHTS. THEY HAVE WELL CULTIVATED ALL PRACTICES.
THEY HAVE WELL ACCUMULATED THE AIDS OF THE PATH.
THEY HAVE BEEN WELL ABLE TO DRAW NEAR HUNDREDS OF
THOUSANDS OF MILLIONS OF BUDDHAS. THEY HAVE AC-
COMPLISHED LIMITLESS GOOD ROOTS OF MERIT AND VIR-
TUE. THEY HAVE CAST OFF ALL STUPIDITY AND DOUBT.*
All of them have already done away with ignorance
and confusion. *THEY HAVE NO DEFILEMENTS,* no filth.
THEY HAVE DEEP FAITH AND UNDERSTANDING. They be-
lieve in and understand the Buddhadharmas, and
*WITHIN THE BUDDHADHARMAS, THEY DO NOT FOLLOW OTHER
TEACHINGS.* They always study and practice Buddha-
dharma and do not follow other teaching methods
of side doors and outside ways.

"*ALL IS WELL, DISCIPLE OF THE BUDDHA,*" he said.
"You are really good, Vajra Treasury Bodhisattva,
great disciple of the Buddha, *YOU SHOULD RECEIVE
THE BUDDHAS' SPIRITUAL POWER AND SPEAK.* You
should receive the Buddhas' great, awesome spiritual might and, for this great assembly, speak the
Buddhadharma. *ALL THESE BODHISATTVAS,* in this assembly, *WILL BE ABLE TO BE CERTIFIED AS KNOWING
ALL THESE PROFOUND PLACES.* They will certify to
the profound Dharma-doors of the Ten Grounds. They
are all capable of realizing and understanding
them."

*AT THAT TIME, MOON OF LIBERATION BODHISATTVA,
WISHING TO RESTATE HIS MEANING, SPOKE VERSES SAY-
ING:* He used verses to reiterate what he had just
said.

SUTRA:

"*WE WISH YOU TO SPEAK OF THE MOST TRANQUIL,
BODHISATTVAS' PRACTICES UNSURPASSED,
DISCRIMINATING EACH AND EVERY GROUND,
WISDOM PURE, AND ACCOMPLISHMENT OF PROPER
        ENLIGHTENMENT.*

"*THIS ASSEMBLY IS FREE FROM ALL DEFILEMENTS,
THEIR DETERMINATION AND UNDERSTANDING ARE
        BRIGHT AND PURE.
THEY HAVE SERVED LIMITLESS BUDDHAS:
THEY CAN KNOW THE MEANING OF THESE GROUNDS.*"

AT THAT TIME, VAJRA TREASURY BODHISATTVA SAID,
"DISCIPLES OF THE BUDDHA, ALTHOUGH THE ASSEMBLY
GATHERED HERE ALL HAVE WELL PURIFIED THEIR THOUGHTS,
HAVE CAST OFF STUPIDITY AND DOUBT, AND IN THE
DEEPLY PROFOUND DHARMA THEY DO NOT FOLLOW OTHERS'
TEACHINGS, THERE ARE STILL OTHER LIVING BEINGS
WITH DEFICIENT WISDOM, WHO, UPON HEARING THESE
PROFOUND AND DIFFICULT-TO-CONCEIVE-OF MATTERS WOULD
GIVE RISE TO MORE DOUBTS, AND, IN THE LONG NIGHT
THEY WOULD SUFFER MUCH DISTRESS. I TAKE PITY UPON
THEM AND, THEREFORE, REMAIN SILENT."
    AT THAT TIME, VAJRA TREASURY BODHISATTVA, WISH-
ING TO RESTATE HIS MEANING, SPOKE VERSES, SAYING:

COMMENTARY:

"WE WISH YOU TO SPEAK OF THE MOST TRANQUIL"/
Moon of Liberation Bodhisattva said, "I wish that
you, great Bodhisattva, would speak these most
peaceful Dharmas, BODHISATTVAS' PRACTICES UNSUR-
PASSED/ The most superior Dharma-doors of cultiva-
tion, DISCRIMINATING EACH AND EVERY GROUND, and
analyze and explain the principles of the Ten
Grounds, WISDOM PURE AND ACCOMPLISHMENT OF PROPER
ENLIGHTENMENT/ causing all living beings to obtain
pure wisdom, and in the future to become Buddhas.
THIS ASSEMBLY IS FREE FROM ALL DEFILEMENTS"/ He
said, "THEIR DETERMINATION AND UNDERSTANDING ARE
BRIGHT AND PURE/ Their resolution and their com-
prehension are both very, very pure. THEY HAVE
SERVED LIMITLESS BUDDHAS/ THEY CAN KNOW THE MEAN-
ING OF THESE GROUNDS."

AT THAT TIME, right after that, VAJRA TREASURY
BODHISATTVA SAID, "DISCIPLE OF THE BUDDHA, ALTHOUGH
THE ASSEMBLY GATHERED HERE HAVE WELL PURIFIED THEIR
THOUGHTS, HAVE CAST OFF STUPIDITY AND DOUBT, AND
IN THE DEEPLY PROFOUND DHARMA THEY DO NOT FOLLOW
OTHERS' TEACHINGS, they are not turned by the ex-
ternalist teachings of side doors and outside ways,
THERE ARE STILL OTHER LIVING BEINGS WITH DEFICIENT
WISDOM. Although this assembly may understand,
there are other living beings besides them who do
not understand. They, WHO, UPON HEARING THESE PRO-
FOUND AND DIFFICULT-TO-CONCEIVE-OF MATTERS, unsur-
passed, subtle and wonderful dharmas, are ones who

WOULD GIVE RISE TO MORE DOUBTS. They would easily
produce doubts, *AND, IN THE LONG NIGHT* of ignorance
and stupidity, *THEY WOULD SUFFER MUCH DISTRESS.*
They themselves would constantly be unable to see
through it all, put it all down, and would not obtain comfort, but would undergo vexation. *I TAKE
PITY UPON THEM AND, THEREFORE, REMAIN SILENT.* Since
I pity those kinds of living beings, I am silent
and do not speak."

SUTRA:

> "*ALTHOUGH THESE MULTITUDES HAVE PURE, VAST
>   WISDOM,
> AND THEIR PROFOUND AND SHARP UNDERSTANDING
>   CAN MAKE DECISIVE CHOICES,
> THEIR MINDS UNMOVING LIKE THE KING OF
>   MOUNTAINS,
> AND CANNOT BE OVERTURNED, LIKE THE GREAT
>   SEA,*
>
> "*THERE ARE THOSE WHO HAVE NOT PRACTICED
>   LONG NOR YET UNDERSTOOD,
> THEY PRACTICE WITH CONSCIOUSNESS, NOT
>   WITH WISDOM.
> HEARING THIS THEY WILL DOUBT AND FALL
>   INTO BAD PATHS.
> I TAKE PITY ON THEM AND, THEREFORE,
>   DO NOT SPEAK.*"

COMMENTARY:

"*ALTHOUGH THESE MULTITUDES HAVE PURE, VAST
WISDOM*"/ Vajra Treasury Bodhisattva says, "Although most of the multitudes in this Dharma Assembly are pure and undefiled and have great wisdom, *AND THEIR PROFOUND AND SHARP UNDERSTANDING
CAN MAKE DECISIVE CHOICES*/ They also have the
capacity which is durable, bright, and sharp due
to their profound Prajna wisdom, *THEIR MINDS UN-
MOVING LIKE THE KING OF MOUNTAINS*/ Each one of the
great Bodhisattvas has a mind which does not move,
like Mount Sumeru, *CANNOT BE OVERTURNED, LIKE THE
GREAT SEA*/ They cannot be turned over, in the
same way that no one is able to overturn the ocean.

"However, *THERE ARE THOSE WHO HAVE NOT PRAC-
TICED LONG NOR YET UNDERSTOOD/* Within the Great
Assembly there are also those who first gave rise
to the thought for Bodhi perhaps ten or twenty
years ago, which is a very short time. They have
not yet attained to the understanding which comes
from wisdom. *THEY PRACTICE WITH CONSCIOUSNESS,
NOT WITH WISDOM.* They go along with their discriminating consciousness in what they do and do not
use wisdom." To use wisdom is to recognize all
states. If one employs consciousness, one merely
discriminates states and does not recognize them.
*"HEARING THIS THEY WILL DOUBT AND FALL INTO BAD
PATHS/* As soon as they hear about the Dharma-doors
of the Ten Grounds, they will have doubts and will
either fall into the hells, the hungry ghosts, or
the animals--the three evil destinies. *I TAKE PITY
ON THEM AND, THEREFORE, DO NOT SPEAK/* Since I pity
the living beings who are like that, therefore I
don't speak, for if I did speak, they would doubt
and disbelieve, and that would be their downfall,
because you cannot slander the Dharma-doors of the
Ten Grounds without falling into the three evil
destinies."

SUTRA:

AT THAT TIME, MOON OF LIBERATION BODHISATTVA
AGAIN ADDRESSED VAJRA TREASURY BODHISATTVA, SAYING,
"DISCIPLE OF THE BUDDHA, I HOPE YOU WILL RECEIVE THE
BUDDHAS' SPIRITUAL POWER AND EXPLAIN IN DETAIL
THESE INCONCEIVABLE DHARMAS. THESE PEOPLE SHOULD
OBTAIN THE THUS COME ONES' PROTECTION AND MINDFUL-
NESS AND GIVE RISE TO FAITH AND RECEPTIVITY. AND
WHY? WHEN ONE EXPLAINS THE TEN GROUNDS, THE DHAR-
MA OF ALL BODHISATTVAS IS THAT WAY: THAT THEY OB-
TAIN THE BUDDHAS' PROTECTION AND MINDFULNESS. BE-
CAUSE THEY OBTAIN THE BUDDHAS' PROTECTION AND MIND-
FULNESS, THEY CAN BE COURAGEOUS ABOUT THESE GROUNDS
OF WISDOM. AND WHY? THESE ARE THE BODHISATTVAS'
MOST INITIAL PRACTICES FOR ACCOMPLISHING ALL BUD-
DHAS' DHARMAS.
"JUST AS WRITTEN WORDS WHICH SAY NUMEROUS
THINGS ARE BASED UPON AN ALPHABET IN THAT THE AL-
PHABET IS FUNDAMENTAL TO THEM AND NONE OF THEM

DEPARTS FROM IT IN THE SLIGHTEST, SO TOO, DISCIPLE
OF THE BUDDHA, ALL BUDDHAS' DHARMAS ARE BASED UPON
THE TEN GROUNDS IN THAT THE TEN GROUNDS ARE FUNDA-
MENTAL TO THEM. THROUGH SUCCESSFUL CULTIVATION OF
THEM, ONE OBTAINS ALL WISDOM. THEREFORE, DISCIPLE
OF THE BUDDHA, I WISH YOU WOULD EXPLAIN THEM. THESE
PEOPLE WILL CERTAINLY BE PROTECTED BY THE THUS COME
ONES AND CAUSED TO BELIEVE AND RECEIVE THESE DHAR-
MAS."
        AT THAT TIME, MOON OF LIBERATION BODHISATTVA,
WISHING TO RESTATE HIS MEANING. SPOKE VERSES, SAY-
ING:

COMMENTARY:

        AT THAT TIME, MOON OF LIBERATION BODHISATTVA
AGAIN ADDRESSED VAJRA TREASURY BODHISATTVA, SAYING,
"DISCIPLE OF THE BUDDHA, I HOPE YOU WILL RECEIVE
THE BUDDHAS' SPIRITUAL POWER. Great Bodhisattva,
I wish that you would receive the power of spiri-
tual penetrations of the Buddhas of the ten direc-
tions and of Shakyamuni Buddha, AND EXPLAIN IN DE-
TAIL THESE INCONCEIVABLE DHARMAS. Analyze and des-
cribe these Dharma-doors for us. THESE PEOPLE
SHOULD OBTAIN THE THUS COME ONES' PROTECTION AND
MINDFULNESS. The people who are here in this Dhar-
ma Assembly should be protected and remembered by
all Buddhas, AND GIVE RISE TO FAITH AND RECEPTIV-
ITY. They will have faith. AND WHY? WHEN ONE
EXPLAINS THE TEN GROUNDS, THE DHARMA IS THAT WAY:
THAT THEY OBTAIN THE BUDDHAS' PROTECTION AND MIND-
FULNESS. When all Bodhisattvas hear the Dharma,
it should be that way for them. All Buddhas should
protect and remember them. BECAUSE THEY OBTAIN
THE BUDDHAS' PROTECTION AND MINDFULNESS, THEY CAN
BE COURAGEOUS ABOUT THESE GROUNDS OF WISDOM. They
can give rise to great courage. AND WHY? THESE
ARE THE BODHISATTVAS' MOST INITIAL PRACTICES. These
are Dharma-doors which Bodhisattvas cultivate at
the very beginning FOR ACCOMPLISHING ALL BUDDHAS'
DHARMAS. The Dharmas spoken by all Buddhas are
produced within the Ten Grounds and accomplished
through them.
        "JUST AS WRITTEN WORDS WHICH SAY NUMEROUS
THINGS ARE BASED UPON AN ALPHABET, they all need
a basic alphabet, IN THAT THE ALPHABET IS FUNDA-

MENTAL TO THEM AND NONE OF THEM DEPARTS FROM IT IN
THE SLIGHTEST. In the final analysis, not even a
minute portion of them is not of the alphabet. SO,
TOO, DISCIPLE OF THE BUDDHA, ALL BUDDHAS' DHARMAS
ARE BASED UPON THE TEN GROUNDS IN THAT THE TEN
GROUNDS ARE FUNDAMENTAL TO THEM. The Dharmas spo-
ken by all Buddhas all take the Ten Grounds as
their basis. BY SUCCESSFUL CULTIVATION OF THEM,
ONE OBTAINS ALL WISDOM. If you cultivate the Ten
Grounds to the ultimate point, and accomplish the
wisdom of the Ten Grounds, you give rise to all
wisdoms. THEREFORE, DISCIPLE OF THE BUDDHA, I
WISH YOU WOULD EXPLAIN THEM. Due to that, Great
Disciple of the Buddha, we all want you to explain
them for us. THESE PEOPLE WILL CERTAINLY BE PRO-
TECTED BY THE THUS COME ONES. The people who hear
these Dharmas will definitely be protected and remembered by the Buddhas, and CAUSED TO BELIEVE AND
RECEIVE THESE DHARMAS, they will offer up their
conduct according to them."
    AT THAT TIME, MOON OF LIBERATION BODHISATTVA,
WISHING TO RESTATE HIS MEANING, SPOKE VERSES, SAY-
ING: He repeated in verse form what he had said
before.

SUTRA:

    "GOOD INDEED, DISCIPLE OF THE BUDDHA, I
        WISH YOU WOULD PROCLAIM
    ALL THE GROUNDS OF PRACTICE TO APPROACH
        AND ENTER BODHI;
    OF ALL THE COMFORTABLE HONORED ONES
        THROUGHOUT THE TEN DIRECTIONS,
    NONE IS NOT PROTECTIVE OF AND MINDFUL OF
        THE BASIC ROOTS OF WISDOM.

    "SECURED IN THEM, THAT WISDOM IS ALSO
        FUNDAMENTAL;
    ALL THE BUDDHAS' DHARMAS ARE PRODUCED
        FROM THEM;
    JUST AS WRITTEN WORDS ARE COMPRISED BY
        ALPHABETS,
    SO, TOO, THE BUDDHAS' DHARMAS ARE BASED
        UPON THESE GROUNDS."

COMMENTARY:

"GOOD, INDEED, DISCIPLE OF THE BUDDHA." Moon
of Liberation Bodhisattva said, "How good you are!
You are the Buddhas' great disciple. I WISH YOU
WOULD PROCLAIM/ Take pity on all living beings
and speak the Dharma-doors of the Ten Grounds.
ALL THE GROUNDS OF PRACTICE TO APPROACH AND ENTER
BODHI. Teach us how to tend toward, enter, go
along, and cultivate the Bodhisattvas' path of
Enlightenment. OF ALL THE COMFORTABLE HONORED
ONES THROUGHOUT THE TEN DIRECTIONS"/ Comfortable
Honored Ones are the Buddhas. "NONE IS NOT PRO-
TECTIVE OF AND MINDFUL OF THE BASIC ROOTS OF WIS-
DOM/ They always wish to aid and uphold, protect
and remember people who hear the Dharma doors of
the Ten Grounds and who cultivate the Dharma-doors
of the Ten Grounds, because the Ten Grounds are
the basic root of wisdom.
      "SECURED IN THEM, THAT WISDOM IS ALSO FUNDA-
MENTAL. The wisdom derived from cultivating the
Ten Grounds is fundamental to them. ALL THE BUD-
DHAS' DHARMAS ARE PRODUCED FROM THEM. Why are
the Ten Grounds called 'Grounds?' It is because
they are the foundation for all Dharmas spoken by
the Buddhas. JUST AS WRITTEN WORDS ARE COMPRISED
BY ALPHABETS"/ Just as when one writes words or
characters, they are all based either upon an alphabet or syllabary, like "A, B, C"; or upon radi-
cals, as, for example, for Chinese characters the
three drops of water (氵), the simple standing
person radical (亻), or the double standing person
radical (彳), etc. "Alphabet" stands for all of
those, which are the basis of written words. "SO,
TOO, THE BUDDHAS' DHARMAS ARE BASED UPON THESE
GROUNDS, because the Buddhas' Dharmas are all produced from the Ten Grounds, in the same way as
all written words are based upon the alphabet."

SUTRA:

      AT THAT TIME, ALL THE ASSEMBLY OF GREAT BO-
DHISATTVAS, SIMULTANEOUSLY AND WITH A SINGLE
SOUND, SPOKE VERSES TO VAJRA TREASURY BODHISATTVA,
SAYING:

"YOU OF SUPERIOR, WONDROUS WISDOM
      UNDEFILED,
OF BOUNDLESS, DISCRIMINATING ELOQUENCE,
PLEASE PROCLAIM PROFOUND AND WONDERFUL
      WORDS,
INTERACTIVE WITH THE FOREMOST MEANING.

COMMENTARY:

AT THAT TIME, ALL THE ASSEMBLY OF GREAT BO-
DHISATTVAS/ After Moon of Liberation Bodhisattva
had finished speaking his verses, all the Great
Bodhisattvas of the ten directions, limitless like
fine motes of dust, SIMULTANEOUSLY AND WITH A SIN-
GLE SOUND, said the same thing at the same time.
They SPOKE VERSES to Vajra Treasury Bodhisattva,
SAYING: "YOU OF SUPERIOR, WONDROUS WISDOM UNDE-
FILED"/ They said, "Vajra Treasury Bodhisattva,
great disciple of the Buddhas that you are, you
have already certified to the attainment of the
most superior, subtle and wonderful wisdom that
is pure and free from defilement. You OF BOUND-
LESS, DISCRIMINATING ELOQUENCE, which enables you
to speak in great detail and with a great deal of
principle, PLEASE PROCLAIM PROFOUND AND WONDERFUL
WORDS/ We hope you will explain the unsurpassed,
deeply profound, subtle and wonderful principles
of the Ten Grounds, INTERACTIVE WITH THE FOREMOST
MEANING/ The Dharma doors of the Ten Grounds are
interactive with the Primary Truth."

SUTRA:

"YOU WHO MINDFULLY MAINTAIN PURE PRACTICES,
AND ARE REPLETE WITH VIRTUES FROM TEN
      POWERS,
WITH ELOQUENCE TO DISCRIMINATE THE
      MEANINGS,
PLEASE EXPLAIN THE MOST SUPERIOR GROUNDS.

"WITH SAMADHI AND PRECEPTS JOINED TO FORM
      UPRIGHT THOUGHT,
FREE FROM ARROGANCE AS WELL AS DEVIANT
      VIEWS,
THIS ASSEMBLY HAS NO DOUBTS IN MIND,
AND ONLY WANTS TO HEAR THEM WELL EXPLAINED.

"AS ONE THIRSTY THINKS OF ICY WATER,
AS ONE HUNGRY DREAMS ABOUT GOOD FOOD,
AS ONE SICK REFLECTS ON WHOLESOME MEDICINE,
AS A BEE IS GREEDY FOR GOOD HONEY,

"SO, TOO, DO WE IN JUST THAT WAY,
WISH TO HEAR THESE DHARMAS OF SWEET DEW.

"GOOD, INDEED, ONE OF WISDOM VAST AND GREAT,
PLEASE TELL US HOW TO ENTER THE TEN GROUNDS,
ACCOMPLISHING TEN POWERS WITHOUT OBSTRUCTION,
AND THE WELL-GONE ONES' PRACTICES, ONE AND
      ALL."

COMMENTARY:

     "YOU WHO MINDFULLY MAINTAIN PURE PRACTICES/
All of these people are mindful of and cultivate
all pure practices, AND ARE REPLETE WITH VIRTUE
FROM TEN POWERS"/ They all cultivate the Buddhas
ten kinds of powers and amass all kinds of merit
and virtue. "WITH ELOQUENCE TO DISCRIMINATE THE
MEANINGS/ PLEASE EXPLAIN THE MOST SUPERIOR GROUNDS/
We request the great Bodhisattva to speak the su-
preme Dharma-doors of the Ten Grounds. WITH SAMA-
DHI AND PRECEPTS JOINED TO FORM UPRIGHT THOUGHT/
All of those listening cultivate samadhi and hold
precepts, and they all have proper knowledge and
proper views. FREE FROM ARROGANCE AS WELL AS DE-
VIANT VIEWS/ They have no overbearing pride or
arrogance, nor any considerations of deviant views.
THIS ASSEMBLY HAS NO DOUBTS IN MIND/ Those in the
Great Assembly now have no doubts about the Dharma-
doors of the Ten Grounds, AND ONLY WANT TO HEAR
THEM WELL EXPLAINED"/ They all wish the Bodhisattva would speak the Dharma-doors of the Ten Grounds.
     "AS ONE THIRSTY THINKS OF ICY WATER/ Like
someone hot and thirsty wanting to eat some ice
cream, or perhaps drink a milk-shake, or some
other cold, refreshing drink. AS ONE HUNGRY DREAMS
ABOUT GOOD FOOD"/ They are also like famished people dreaming of finding some bread to eat, or something to cure their hunger pangs. They think of
good things to eat, the finest food. "AS ONE SICK
REFLECTS ON WHOLESOME MEDICINE"/ They are like
sick people who think about the best medicines to

cure their illnesses. AS A BEE IS GREEDY FOR GOOD
HONEY/ They are also like honey bees which are
greedy for the pollen to become honey and be ready
for them to eat." But, as it turns out, when the
honey is ready, people come and steal it from them.
      "SO, TOO, DO WE IN JUST THAT WAY/ All the Bo-
dhisattvas WISH TO HEAR THESE DHARMAS OF SWEET DEW.
We wish to hear those Dharmas which quench thirst,
satisfy hunger, cure sickness, and satisfy all one
might be greedy for.
      "GOOD, INDEED, ONE OF WISDOM VAST AND GREAT"/
They said, "Good, indeed, you of vast, great wisdom,
Vajra Treasury Bodhisattva, PLEASE TELL US HOW TO
ENTER THE TEN GROUNDS/ We would like you to speak
the Dharma-doors of the Ten Grounds, ACCOMPLISHING
TEN POWERS WITHOUT OBSTRUCTION/ You have already
accomplished the position of the Ten Powers without
obstruction, AND THE WELL-GONE ONES' PRACTICES ONE
AND ALL/ along with pretty much all of the prac-
tices of the Well-Gone Ones, the Buddhas. Great
Bodhisattva, please very compassionately speak the
Dharmas of the Ten Grounds for all of us."

SUTRA:

        AT THAT TIME, THE WORLD-HONORED ONE, FROM BE-
TWEEN HIS EYEBROWS, EMITTED A PURE LIGHT, NAMED
"BLAZING LIGHT OF BODHISATTVAS' POWERS," WITH HUN-
DREDS OF THOUSANDS OF ASAMKHYEYAS OF LIGHTS AS ITS
RETINUE, WHICH UNIVERSALLY ILLUMINED ALL THE
WORLDS THROUGHOUT THE TEN DIRECTIONS, PERVADING AB-
SOLUTELY EVERYWHERE. THE SUFFERINGS OF THE THREE
EVIL PATHS ALL CEASED TO BE. IT ALSO ILLUMINATED
THE ASSEMBLIES OF ALL THUS COME ONES, MANIFESTING
ALL BUDDHAS' INCONCEIVABLE POWERS. IT ALSO ILLU-
MINATED THE PERSONS OF ALL BODHISATTVAS SPEAKING
DHARMA WITH THE AID OF ALL BUDDHAS THROUGHOUT ALL
WORLDS IN THE TEN DIRECTIONS. WHEN FINISHED DOING
THAT, IT FORMED A GREAT PLATFORM OF NETS OF CLOUDS
OF LIGHT HIGH IN EMPTY SPACE AND REMAINED THERE.
AT THAT TIME, ALL THE BUDDHAS OF THE TEN DIRECTIONS
ALSO IN THAT WAY, FROM BETWEEN THEIR EYEBROWS EMIT-
TED PURE LIGHTS. THOSE LIGHTS' NAMES, RETINUES,
AND ACTIONS WERE ALL THE SAME AS THAT ONE'S. MORE-
OVER, THEY ILLUMINED THE BUDDHAS AND GREAT ASSEM-
BLIES OF THIS SAHA WORLD AND THE PERSON OF VAJRA

TREASURY BODHISATTVA UPON HIS LION'S THRONE, AND HIGH IN
EMPTY SPACE, THEY FORMED A LARGE PLATFORM OF NETS
OF CLOUDS OF LIGHTS. AT THAT TIME, WITHIN THE
PLATFORM OF LIGHT, THROUGH THE BUDDHAS' AWESOME
SPIRITUAL MIGHT, WERE SPOKEN VERSES, SAYING:

COMMENTARY:

AT THAT TIME, right then, THE WORLD-HONORED
ONE, Shakyamuni Buddha, FROM BETWEEN HIS EYEBROWS,
EMITTED A PURE LIGHT, NAMED "BLAZING LIGHT OF BODHI-
SATTVAS' POWERS," WITH HUNDREDS OF THOUSANDS OF
ASAMKHYEYAS OF LIGHTS AS ITS RETINUE. "Asamkhyeyas"
means "limitless numbers of" WHICH UNIVERSALLY IL-
LUMINED ALL THE WORLDS THROUGHOUT THE TEN DIREC-
TIONS, all the Buddhas worlds in the ten directions,
PERVADING ABSOLUTELY EVERYWHERE. Nowhere was there
a place upon which they did not shine. THE SUFFER-
INGS OF THE THREE EVIL PATHS ALL CEASED TO BE. The
sufferings of the hell- beings, hungry ghosts, and
animals all stopped. IT ALSO ILLUMINED THE ASSEM-
BLIES OF ALL THUS COME ONES, lighting up the assem-
blies in the Bodhimandas of all Buddhas, MANIFEST-
ING ALL BUDDHAS' INCONCEIVABLE POWERS. They used
the light to reveal the inconceivable powers of the
Buddhas. IT ALSO ILLUMINED THE PERSONS OF ALL BO-
DHISATTVAS SPEAKING DHARMA WITH THE AID OF ALL BUD-
DHAS THROUGHOUT ALL WORLDS IN THE TEN DIRECTIONS.
It shone upon all Bodhisattvas speaking with the
aid of all Buddhas of the ten directions. WHEN
FINISHED DOING THAT, when that ceremony had been
completed, IT FORMED A GREAT PLATFORM OF NETS OF
CLOUDS OF LIGHTS HIGH IN EMPTY SPACE. In the sky
above it took form as a great platform of nets of
light, AND REMAINED THERE. It settled there in
mid-air. AT THAT TIME, ALL THE BUDDHAS OF THE TEN
DIRECTIONS ALSO IN THAT WAY, also FROM BETWEEN
THEIR EYEBROWS, EMITTED PURE LIGHTS called "Blazing Lights of Bodhisattvas' Powers." THOSE LIGHTS'
NAMES, RETINUES, AND ACTIONS WERE ALL THE SAME AS
THAT ONE'S. The names of those lights, their retinues, and what they did, were all the same as
those of Shakyamuni Buddha's.
MOREOVER, THEY ILLUMINED THE BUDDHAS AND GREAT
ASSEMBLIES OF THIS SAHA WORLD. In the countries
of the other directions they emitted light, and

they also illuminated Shakyamuni Buddha and the
great multitudes of this Dharma Assembly in this
Saha world, *AND THE PERSON OF VAJRA TREASURY BO-
DHISATTVA UPON HIS LION'S THRONE,* along with the
Lion's seat upon which Vajra Treasury Bodhisattva
was sitting; *AND HIGH IN EMPTY SPACE,* in mid-air,
*THEY FORMED A LARGE PLATFORM OF NETS OF CLOUDS OF
LIGHTS. AT THAT TIME, WITHIN THE PLATFORM OF
LIGHTS,* with the nets of clouds of light, *THROUGH
THE BUDDHAS' AWESOME SPIRITUAL MIGHT,* due to the
awesome spiritual power of the Buddhas of the ten
directions, and to the awesome spiritual might of
Shakyamuni Buddha, *WERE SPOKEN VERSES, SAYING:*

SUTRA:

> "THE BUDDHA, WITH NO EQUAL,
> JUST LIKE EMPTY SPACE,
> OF TEN POWERS LIMITLESS,
> OF MERIT AND VIRTUE SUPREME;
> AMONG PEOPLE MOST VICTORIOUS,
> SUPERIOR IN THE WORLD:
> THAT SHAKYA LION'S DHARMAS
> ARE WHAT GIVES THEM AID.

> "DISCIPLE OF THE BUDDHA,
> RECEIVE ALL BUDDHAS' STRENGTH,
> SET FORTH THIS KING OF DHARMAS'
> TREASURY MOST SUPREME:
> ALL GROUNDS' EXTENSIVE WISDOM,
> PRACTICES WONDROUS AND SUPREME,
> THROUGH BUDDHAS' AWESOME SPIRIT,
> DISCRIMINATE AND SPEAK.

> "THOSE WHO HAVE THE AID
> OF ALL THE WELL-GONE ONES,
> SHOULD OBTAIN THESE DHARMA JEWELS
> ENTERING THEIR MINDS;
> THAT ALL GROUNDS UNDEFILED,
> IN ORDER BE COMPLETED,
> ONE MUST POSSESS AS WELL
> THUS COME ONES' TEN-FOLD POWER.

> "THOUGH ONE MAY DWELL IN BLAZES
> OF KALPAS LIKE THE SEA,
> IF ABLE TO ACCEPT THEM,

ONE DOUBTLESS HEARS THESE DHARMAS:
BUT THOSE WHO HARBOR DOUBTS,
AND WHO HAVE NO FAITH,
WILL NEVER COME TO HEAR
THE MEANINGS SUCH AS THESE.

"PLEASE DO EXPLAIN THE GROUNDS,
THE WAY TO SUPREME WISDOM,
ENTER, DWELL WITHIN, UNFOLD
SUCCESSIVE CULTIVATION;
FROM STATES OF CULTIVATION
ARISES DHARMA WISDOM,
TO BENEFIT AND AID
EACH AND EVERY LIVING BEING."

AT THAT TIME, VAJRA TREASURY BODHISATTVA CON-
TEMPLATED IN THE TEN DIRECTIONS, AND, IN ORDER TO
CAUSE THOSE IN THE GREAT ASSEMBLY TO INCREASE
THEIR PURE FAITH, SPOKE VERSES, SAYING:

"THE WAYS OF THE THUS COME ONES,
    GREAT IMMORTALS,
ARE SUBTLE, WONDERFUL, AND HARD
    TO COMPREHEND;
NOT THOUGHT, THEY ARE APART FROM
    EVERY THOUGHT:
THOSE SEEKING THEM IN SEEING
    CAN'T ATTAIN THEM.

COMMENTARY:

"THE BUDDHA, WITH NO EQUAL, JUST LIKE EMPTY
SPACE/ The Buddha is incomparable and like empty
space, in that there is also nothing comparable
to empty space. OF TEN POWERS LIMITLESS, OF MERIT
AND VIRTUE SUPREME/ The Buddha has ten kinds of
powers, and limitless merit and virtue. AMONG
PEOPLE MOST VICTORIOUS, SUPERIOR IN THE WORLD/
Among people, the Buddha is foremost, and the
highest in the world, too. THAT SHAKYA LION'S
DHARMAS ARE WHAT GIVE THEM AID. The Dharmas of
the Lion of the Shakya Clan, the Buddha, are what
aid those people who wish to speak the Dharma and
explain it.
"DISCIPLE OF THE BUDDHA, RECEIVE ALL BUDDHAS'-
STRENGTH/ You, Vajra Treasury Bodhisattva, should

receive the power of Shakyamuni Buddha and the
power of all the Buddhas of the ten directions, and
*SET FORTH THIS KING OF DHARMAS' TREASURY MOST SU-
PREME/* Come and explain for everyone these most
supreme Dharma-doors, the endowment of the King of
Jewels. *ALL GROUNDS' EXTENSIVE WISDOM, PRACTICES
WONDROUS AND SUPREME/* The Ten Grounds have vast,
great wisdoms, and most superior, wonderful practices. *THROUGH BUDDHAS' AWESOME SPIRIT, DISCRIMI-
NATE AND SPEAK/* The Buddhas will come to aid you,
enabling you to discriminate and explain.
      *"THOSE WHO HAVE THE AID OF ALL THE WELL-GONE
ONES,* the Buddhas' might, *SHOULD OBTAIN THESE DHAR-
MA JEWELS ENTERING THEIR MINDS* and be able to speak
according to intent. *THAT ALL GROUNDS UNDEFILED
IN ORDER BE COMPLETED/* The Ten Grounds are all
free from defilement. To be able to speak them
perfectly, and in order, *ONE MUST POSSESS AS WELL
THUS COME ONES' TEN-FOLD POWER/* By relying on the
ten kinds of powers of a Buddha, one can then
speak them perfectly.
      *"THOUGH ONE MAY DWELL IN BLAZES OF KALPAS LIKE
THE SEA/* Even though one dwells in kalpa-fires,
periods of coming into being, dwelling, going bad,
and disappearing on the part of kalpas, great kalpas, as many in quantity as there is water in the
sea, *IF ABLE TO ACCEPT THEM, ONE DOUBTLESS HEARS
THESE DHARMAS/* One can hear these kinds of Dharmas for that long a time; one definitely will be
able to hear them. *BUT THOSE WHO HARBOR DOUBTS AND
WHO HAVE NO FAITH/* Maybe there are doubters, dis-
believers. They *WILL NEVER COME TO HEAR THE MEAN-
INGS SUCH AS THESE/* They will never have the opportunity to hear these kinds of Dharmas.
      *"PLEASE DO EXPLAIN THE GROUNDS, THE WAY TO
SUPREME WISDOM/* Great Bodhisattva, you should now
speak for everyone the Bodhisattvas' Ten Grounds,
the path of most supreme wisdom. *ENTER, DWELL
WITHIN, UNFOLD SUCCESSIVE CULTIVATION/* Enter into
these Dharmas, and then open them up and set them
forth, investigating and explaining them in orderly
sequence for living beings, enabling living beings
to cultivate. *FROM STATES OF CULTIVATION ARISES
DHARMA WISDOM/* It is from cultivating and experiencing these various kinds of Dharmas that wisdom is attained and Dharma arises *TO BENEFIT AND
AID EACH AND EVERY LIVING BEING/* I hope that you,

Bodhisattva, will speak for everyone's benefit, for
the sake of all the living beings in this Dharma
Assembly."

AT THAT TIME, thereupon, VAJRA TREASURY BODHI-
SATTVA CONTEMPLATED IN THE TEN DIRECTIONS. He con-
templated the causes and conditions of living be-
ings throughout the ten directions, AND, IN ORDER
TO CAUSE THOSE IN THE GREAT ASSEMBLY TO INCREASE
THEIR PURE FAITH, the faith and understanding of
everyone present, SPOKE VERSES, SAYING: "THE WAYS
OF THE THUS COME ONES, GREAT IMMORTALS"/ He said,
"The Buddhas are like Great Immortals. Their ways
ARE SUBTLE, WONDERFUL, AND HARD TO COMPREHEND/ NOT
THOUGHT, THEY ARE APART FROM EVERY THOUGHT/ When
you have no-thought, you should still go on to become free of all thoughts. THOSE SEEKING THEM IN
SEEING CANNOT ATTAIN THEM/ If you want to see the
Buddha and the Dharma by looking at forms and seeking in sounds, that is not possible. Those who do
so cannot see the Buddha, nor can they understand
the Dharma-doors of the Ten Grounds."

SUTRA:

> "THEY ARE NOT PRODUCED,
> AND THEY ARE NOT DESTROYED;
> PURE OF NATURE ARE THEY,
> AND THEY ARE ALWAYS STILL.
> OF PEOPLE UNDEFILED,
> INTELLIGENT, AND WISE,
> THEY ARE THE PLACE OF PRACTICE,
> OF THEIR WISDOM.

> "THEIR OWN NATURE BASICALLY
> IS EMPTY AND IT'S STILL;
> NON-DUAL IT IS, BUT
> IT IS ALSO UNENDING;
> WHEN LIBERATED AND SET FREE
> FROM ALL THE DESTINIES,
> ONE DWELLS WITHIN
> THE IDENTITY THAT IS NIRVANA.

COMMENTARY:

"The Dharma-doors of the Ten Grounds are just our original Buddha-nature and they are our original wisdom, as well as being the treasury of light of everyone's own original nature. As to these Dharma-doors, *THEY ARE NOT PRODUCED, AND THEY ARE NOT DESTROYED/* They are not defiled nor immaculate, not increased and not decreased. *PURE OF NATURE ARE THEY, AND THEY ARE ALWAYS STILL/* These Dharma-doors of the Ten Grounds are always pure; thus, they are always still and unmoving. *OF PEOPLE UNDEFILED, INTELLIGENT, AND WISE/* All of you great disciples of the Buddha, since you are free from filth, you have obtained true and actual intelligence and wisdom. For each bit of defilement that's removed, a bit of purity appears. You decrease defilement by the same proportion as you increase purity, because defilement and purity are opposites. If you have defilements, that increases your stupidity. If you are pure, that increases your wisdom. If you are stupid, then day by day you fall, whereas with wisdom, day by day you rise upwards. As it is said:

> The superior person ascends;
> The inferior person descends.

That is the same principle. In cultivation one purifies the defiled mind. What is defilement? Among all worldly dharmas, the heaviest is sexual desire. That is what is most defiled and most impure, but most people can't get out of this bind. They get caught up like a silkworm spinning a cocoon, which is binding itself up without even realizing it. Sages turn defilement into purity. Ordinary people turn purity into defilement. Whenever people abandon defiled dharmas and return to original purity, they are intelligent Sages with wisdom. *THEY ARE THE PLACE OF PRACTICE OF THEIR WISDOM/* The Dharma-doors of the Ten Grounds are what is cultivated by Bodhisattvas, by intelligent persons who have wisdom.
    "*THEIR OWN NATURE BASICALLY IS EMPTY AND IT'S STILL"/* The self-nature of us all is basically pure and without anything at all; but we ourselves day by day turn our backs on enlightenment and

unite with the dust and take suffering for bliss.
Therefore, to the self-nature, which basically is
pure and still, there are added a great many afflictions. *"NON-DUAL IT IS, BUT IT IS ALSO UNEND-
ING"/* The self-nature hasn't even one, to say nothing of two. It has no shape or characteristics,
no self, others, living beings, or ones with life-
spans, "but it is also unending." Although it has
no mark, it is not that it doesn't exist. Empty
space has no mark, but you cannot deny that there
is empty space. *"WHEN LIBERATED AND SET FREE FROM
ALL THE DESTINIES"/* Liberated through the wisdom
of the Ten Grounds, one attains to freedom regarding the four evil destinies--those of asuras,
hell-beings, hungry ghosts, and animals--and *"ONE
DWELLS WITHIN IDENTITY THAT'S NIRVANA"/* If you
are able to understand the Dharma-doors of the Ten
Grounds, then you can understand that birth and
death are the same as Nirvana, that samsara is
identical with Nirvana, and that afflictions are
just Bodhi. If you do not understand the Dharma-
doors of the Ten Grounds, then, for you, birth
and death are still birth and death, and Nirvana
is still Nirvana, without any connection whatsoever.

SUTRA:

> *"THEY ARE NOT BEGINNING, NOR MIDDLE,
>   NOR END;
> THEY ARE NOT EXPRESSIBLE IN WORDS;
> THEY TRANSCEND THE THREE PERIODS
>   OF TIME;
> THEIR CHARACTERISTICS ARE LIKE
>   EMPTY SPACE.*
>
> *"THE STILL EXTINCTION WHICH THE
>   BUDDHAS PRACTICE,
> CANNOT BE DESCRIBED IN WORDS.
> THE PRACTICE OF THE GROUNDS IS
>   ALSO THUS:
> DIFFICULT TO EXPRESS, DIFFICULT
>   TO ACCEPT.*
>
> *"THE BUDDHAS' STATES THAT ARISE
>   FROM WISDOM*

> ARE NOT THOUGHT AND LEAVE THE PATH
> OF THE MIND.
> THEY ARE NOT THE DOORS OF SKANDHAS,
> REALMS, OR PLACES:
> THE WISE KNOW INTELLECT DOES NOT
> REACH THEM.

COMMENTARY:

"THEY ARE NOT BEGINNING, NOR MIDDLE, NOR END/
The wisdom of these grounds has no beginning, middle, or end. To say 'The Dharma the Buddha spoke
was good in the beginning, good in the middle, and
good in the end," does not apply here. Nor do the
grounds belong to the View of Truth, the View of
Emptiness, or the View of the Middle. THEY ARE
NOT EXPRESSIBLE IN WORDS/ The Ten Grounds can
only be known and cannot be described by words,
which is why I do not wish to speak about them.
THEY TRANSCEND THE THREE PERIODS OF TIME/ These
Dharma-doors go beyond all dharmas of the past,
the present, and the future, and THEIR CHARACTER-
ISTICS ARE LIKE EMPTY SPACE.
"THE STILL EXTINCTION WHICH THE BUDDHAS PRAC-
TICE/ These Dharma-doors are characterized by
still extinction. They:

> Cannot be seen by looking,
> Cannot be heard by listening,
> Cannot be perceived by smell.

They are what the Buddhas cultivate, most subtle
and wonderful, and CANNOT BE DESCRIBED IN WORDS.
If you wish me to explain the Ten Grounds, there
is no way that I can use words to explain them.
THE PRACTICE OF THE GROUNDS IS ALSO THUS/ The
Dharma-doors of cultivation of the Ten Grounds
are just the same as in the previous analogy, DIF-
FICULT TO EXPRESS, DIFFICULT TO ACCEPT/' It is not
easy to describe them. As it is said:

> The path of language is cut off,
> The place of the mind's workings
> is extinguished.

"*THE BUDDHAS' STATES THAT ARISE FROM WISDOM/*
All the Buddhas' states are produced from wisdom.
They *ARE NOT THOUGHT AND LEAVE THE PATH OF THE
MIND/* This again is:

> The path of language is cut off.
> The place of the mind's workings
>   is extinguished.
> Right in thought, one is apart
>   from thought:
> One thinks, and yet one has
>   no thoughts.

Hence, they are not thought and leave the path of
the mind. They are apart from all thoughts of the
mind. *THEY ARE NOT THE DOORS OF SKANDHAS, REALMS,
OR PLACES/* They are also not the Five Skandhas:
form, feeling, thinking, activities, and consciousness. Nor are they the Eighteen Realms, not the
Six Sense Faculties--eyes, ears, nose, tongue,
body, and mind; not the Six Objects of Perception
--forms, sounds, smells, tastes, objects of touch,
and dharmas; and, not the Six Consciousnesses--eye-
consciousness, ear-consciousness, nose-conscious-
ness, tongue-consciousness, body-consciousness,
and mind-consciousness. They are not the Twelve
Places--eyes, ears, nose, tongue, body, mind plus
forms, sounds, smells, tastes, objects of touch,
and dharmas. *THE WISE KNOW INTELLECT DOES NOT
REACH THEM/* If you use wisdom, then you can understand them. If you use your thinking mind, your
intellect, there is no way to understand them."

SUTRA:

> "*AS THE TRACES OF A BIRD IN EMPTY SPACE,
> ARE DIFFICULT TO EXPRESS, DIFFICULT
>   TO DISCERN,
> SO, TOO, ARE THE TEN GROUNDS' MEANINGS
> INCOMPREHENSIBLE TO MIND AND THOUGHT.*

> "*THEY WHO FROM COMPASSION, KINDNESS,
>   AND THE POWER OF VOWS,
> APPEAR AND ENTER THE PRACTICES OF
>   THE GROUNDS;
> GRADUALLY REACH PERFECTION OF THE MIND:*

WISDOM'S PRACTICES ARE NOT
     REFLECTION'S REALM.

"SUCH STATES AS THESE ARE DIFFICULT
     TO PERCEIVE;
THEY CAN BE KNOWN BUT CANNOT
     BE EXPRESSED;
THROUGH THE BUDDHAS' POWER THEY
     ARE PROCLAIMED.
YOU SHOULD RECEIVE THEM WITH ALL
     REVERENCE.

"WISDOM SUCH AS THIS ENTERS THE
     PRACTICES;
MILLIONS OF AEON'S SPEAKING DOES
     NOT EXHAUST THEM.
I NOW MERELY SPEAK THEM IN A
     GENERAL WAY:
THE TRUE AND ACTUAL MEANINGS
     ARE UNENDING.

"WITH A SINGLE MIND, AWAIT IN
     REVERENCE,
WHILE I RECEIVE THE BUDDHAS'
     POWER AND SPEAK
THE SUPREME DHARMAS' SUBTLE,
     WONDROUS SOUNDS,
WITH ANALOGIES AND WORDS APPROPRIATE.

"EVERY BUDDHA'S LIMITLESS SPIRITUAL
     POWERS
ALL COME TO BE EMBODIED BY ME!
THESE PLACES ARE DIFFICULT TO
     EXPRESS;
I SHALL NOW SPEAK A SMALL PORTION.

COMMENTARY:

"AS THE TRACES OF A BIRD IN EMPTY SPACE/ ARE
DIFFICULT TO EXPRESS, DIFFICULT TO DISCERN/ When
a bird flies through the air, what trace is there
to speak of? What traces can be shown to repre-
sent it? SO, TOO, ARE THE TEN GROUNDS' MEANINGS/
Therefore, it is not easy to express them, not
easy for me to instruct you in them, since they
are INCOMPREHENSIBLE TO MIND AND THOUGHT/ If you

use your ordinary mind and thoughts, you will not
be able to understand the meanings such as those
contained in the Ten Grounds. THEY WHO FROM COM-
PASSION, KINDNESS, AND THE POWER OF VOWS/ When Bodhisattvas speak the Dharma-doors of the Ten
Grounds, they all receive the compassion and vow-
power of the Buddhas, and they APPEAR AND ENTER
THE PRACTICES OF THE GROUNDS/ They appear in the
world to cultivate the doors of practice of the
Ten Grounds. GRADUALLY THERE IS PERFECTION OF THE
MIND/ Step by step, the mind of wisdom is caused
to be perfected, and the Enlightenment of Bodhi is
caused to be accomplished. WISDOM'S PRACTICES ARE
NOT REFLECTION'S REALM/ These Dharma-doors are
cultivated by wisdom. They are not states that
can be understood by people's thinking.

"SUCH STATES AS THESE ARE DIFFICULT TO PER-
CEIVE/ THEY CAN BE KNOWN BUT CANNOT BE EXPRESSED/
Knowing of them is easy, but to explain them is
not at all easy. THROUGH THE BUDDHAS' POWER THEY
ARE PROCLAIMED/ If they cannot be expressed, then
how does one express them? It is because the Buddhas of the ten directions lend their strength,
enabling one to explain the Dharma-doors of the
Ten Grounds. YOU SHOULD RECEIVE THEM ALL WITH
REVERENCE/ All of you Bodhisattvas should respect-
fully listen to these Dharmas. WISDOM SUCH AS THIS
ENTERS THE PRACTICES/ These doors of practice are
entered through wisdom. MILLIONS OF AEON'S SPEAK-
ING DOES NOT EXHAUST THEM/ In hundreds of thousands of ten thousands of millions of kalpas, they
cannot be expressed to the end. I NOW MERELY SPEAK
THEM IN A GENERAL WAY/ I, Vajra Treasury Bodhisattva, will now speak of them in general, not
completely. THE TRUE AND ACTUAL MEANINGS ARE UN-
ENDING/ The true and actual meanings cannot be
expressed entirely.

"WITH A SINGLE MIND, AWAIT IN REVERENCE/ WHILE
I RECEIVE THE BUDDHAS' POWER AND SPEAK/ I receive
the great, awesome strength of the Buddhas of the
ten directions in order to speak these Dharma-
doors, THE SUPREME DHARMAS' SUBTLE, WONDROUS
SOUNDS/ WITH ANALOGIES AND WORDS APPROPRIATE/ The
supreme dharmas are so subtle, no comparison would
be suitable to them. EVERY BUDDHA'S LIMITLESS
SPIRITUAL POWERS/ aid me and enable me to speak
these Dharmas of the Ten Grounds. They ALL COME

TO BE EMBODIED BY ME/ THESE PLACES ARE DIFFICULT
TO EXPRESS/ The Dharma-doors of the Ten Grounds
cannot be expressed to the end. I SHALL NOW SPEAK
A SMALL PORTION/ Therefore, I shall not be able
to explain these places completely. I shall just
explain them a little bit."

SUTRA:

"DISCIPLES OF THE BUDDHA, SUPPOSE THERE ARE
LIVING BEINGS WHO HAVE DEEPLY PLANTED GOOD ROOTS,
WELL CULTIVATED ALL PRACTICES, WELL ACCUMULATED
THE AIDS TO THE WAY, WELL MADE OFFERINGS TO ALL
BUDDHAS, WELL COLLECTED WHITE, PURE DHARMAS, BEEN
WELL GATHERED IN BY GOOD AND WISE ADVISORS, HAVE
WELL PURIFIED DEEP THOUGHT, HAVE ESTABLISHED GREAT
RESOLUTIONS, HAVE BROUGHT FORTH VAST, GREAT UNDER-
STANDING, HAVE MANIFESTED KINDNESS AND COMPASSION,
IN ORDER TO SEEK THE WISDOM OF THE BUDDHAS, IN
ORDER TO OBTAIN THE TEN POWERS, IN ORDER TO OBTAIN
THE GREAT FEARLESSNESSES, IN ORDER TO OBTAIN THE
BUDDHAS' DHARMAS OF EQUALITY, IN ORDER TO RESCUE
ALL THOSE IN THE WORLD, IN ORDER TO PURIFY GREAT
KINDNESS AND COMPASSION, IN ORDER TO OBTAIN THE
WISDOM WITHOUT RESIDUE OF THE TEN POWERS, IN OR-
DER TO PURIFY ALL BUDDHALANDS WITHOUT OBSTRUCTION;
IN ORDER TO KNOW ALL THE THREE PERIODS OF TIME IN
A SINGLE THOUGHT, IN ORDER TO TURN THE GREAT DHAR-
MA WHEEL WITHOUT FEAR.

COMMENTARY:

"DISCIPLES OF THE BUDDHA"/ Vajra Treasury
Bodhisattva again says, "All of you disciples of
the Buddha, SUPPOSE THERE ARE LIVING BEINGS WHO
HAVE DEEPLY PLANTED GOOD ROOTS and WELL CULTIVATED
ALL PRACTICES. They are good at practicing the
Dharma-doors of the Six Perfections and the ten
thousand conducts. They have WELL ACCUMULATED
THE AIDS TO THE WAY. They have well assembled
the Dharma-doors that aid in cultivation of the
Way and have WELL MADE OFFERINGS TO ALL BUDDHAS.
They are skilled at making offerings to all Bud-
dhas of the ten directions and the three periods
of time, and HAVE WELL COLLECTED WHITE, PURE

DHARMAS. They know very well how to accumulate
pure, white Dharmas, and have BEEN WELL GATHERED
IN BY GOOD AND WISE ADVISORS. Great and wise tea-
chers are well able to tame and subdue living beings. They HAVE WELL PURIFIED DEEP THOUGHT. They
themselves are well able to have pure, deep thoughts
with no defiled or mixed-up thoughts, and they
HAVE ESTABLISHED GREAT RESOLUTIONS, and HAVE
BROUGHT FORTH VAST, GREAT UNDERSTANDING. They have
produced limitless and boundless powers of understanding and they HAVE MANIFESTED KINDNESS AND
COMPASSION. We who cultivate the Way should al-
ways be compassionate, no matter towards whom it
may be. Why is that? IN ORDER TO SEEK THE WIS-
DOM OF THE BUDDHAS, IN ORDER TO OBTAIN THE TEN
POWERS, IN ORDER TO OBTAIN THE GREAT FEARLESSNESS-
ES, IN ORDER TO OBTAIN THE BUDDHAS' DHARMAS OF
EQUALITY, IN ORDER TO RESCUE ALL THOSE IN THE
WORLD, to save all living beings in the world. IN
ORDER TO PURIFY GREAT KINDNESS AND COMPASSION/ It
is also IN ORDER TO OBTAIN THE WISDOM WITHOUT RESI
DUE OF THE TEN POWERS, to obtain the Buddhas' ten
kinds of powers without residue, and IN ORDER TO
PURIFY ALL BUDDHALANDS WITHOUT OBSTRUCTION, to
adorn and purify all Buddhas' lands and cause them
to be without obstruction. It is, furthermore,
IN ORDER TO KNOW ALL THE THREE PERIODS OF TIME IN
A SINGLE THOUGHT, to know the causes and effects
of past, present, and future times, and IN ORDER
TO TURN THE GREAT DHARMA WHEEL WITHOUT FEAR/ For
those reasons they wish to listen to the Dharma-
doors of the Ten Grounds."

SUTRA:

"DISCIPLES OF THE BUDDHA, WHEN BODHISATTVAS
BRING FORTH THOSE KINDS OF THOUGHTS, THEY PUT COM-
PASSION FOREMOST. THEIR WISDOM INCREASES. THEY
ARE DRAWN IN BY GOOD AND CLEVER EXPEDIENTS. THEY
MAINTAIN MOST SUPERIOR DEEP THOUGHTS. THEY CON-
TEMPLATE AND DISTINGUISH THE LIMITLESS POWERS OF
THE THUS COME ONES. WITH THE POWER OF COURAGE AND
THE POWER OF WISDOM THEIR UNOBSTRUCTED WISDOM MANI-
FESTS. THEY HAVE COMPLIANT AND SPONTANEOUS WIS-
DOM. THEY CAN ACCEPT ALL BUDDHAS' DHARMAS. THEY
USE WISDOM TO TEACH AND TRANSFORM. THAT IS VAST

AND GREAT AS THE DHARMA REALM, ULTIMATELY LIKE EMP-
TY SPACE, TO THE EXHAUSTION OF THE BOUNDARIES OF
THE FUTURE.

"DISCIPLES OF THE BUDDHA, WHEN BODHISATTVAS
FIRST BRING FORTH THOSE KINDS OF THOUGHTS, THEY
IMMEDIATELY TRANSCEND THE GROUND OF ORDINARY PEO-
PLE AND ENTER THE POSITION OF A BODHISATTVA. THEY
ARE BORN IN THE HOUSEHOLD OF THE THUS COME ONES.
NO ONE CAN PRONOUNCE ANY FAULTS IN THEIR LINEAGE.
THEY ABANDON THE WORLDLY DESTINIES AND ENTER THE
WAY OF WORLD-TRANSCENDENCE. THEY OBTAIN THE DHAR-
MAS OF BODHISATTVAS. THEY DWELL IN THE PLACES OF
BODHISATTVAS. THEY ENTER INTO THE SAMENESS OF THE
THREE PERIODS OF TIME. WITHIN THE THUS COME ONES'
FAMILY, THEY ARE CERTAIN TO OBTAIN UNSURPASSED
BODHI.

"WHEN BODHISATTVAS DWELL IN DHARMAS SUCH AS
THOSE, IT IS CALLED DWELLING ON THE BODHISATTVAS'
GROUND OF HAPPINESS, BECAUSE OF THE CONNECTION
WITH NON-MOVING.

COMMENTARY:

"DISCIPLES OF THE BUDDHA"/ Vajra Treasury Bodhisattva again calls out "All you disciples of
the Buddha, WHEN BODHISATTVAS BRING FORTH THOSE
KINDS OF THOUGHTS, then THEY PUT COMPASSION FORE-
MOST. Great compassion can relieve living beings
so they separate from suffering and attain bliss.
Bodhisattvas on the First Ground make the thought
of great compassion their foremost work of primary
importance. THEIR WISDOM INCREASES. If you cultivate the Dharmas of Bodhisattvas, then you will
obtain the Bodhisattvas' wisdom. The more you
cultivate the practices of Bodhisattvas, the more
your wisdom will increase. THEY ACCUMULATE GOOD
AND CLEVER EXPEDIENTS. You will also obtain the
unimpeded eloquence of clever expedient methods in
speaking Dharma. THEY MAINTAIN MOST SUPERIOR DEEP
THOUGHTS. What they maintain are the most superior, subtle, and wonderful deep thoughts. THEY
CONTEMPLATE AND DISTINGUISH THE LIMITLESS POWERS
OF THE THUS COME ONES. WITH THE POWER OF COURAGE
AND THE POWER OF WISDOM/ The wisdom of their skill
in contemplation discerns all states, and they have
the power of very bravely and vigorously going

forward in their cultivation. *THEIR UNOBSTRUCTED WISDOM MANIFESTS/* It always manifests. No matter what state comes, it will not get in the way. *THEY HAVE COMPLIANT AND SPONTANEOUS WISDOM,* natural wisdom and *THEY CAN ACCEPT ALL BUDDHAS' DHARMAS/* They are able to receive all Dharma-doors spoken by all Buddhas. *THEY USE WISDOM TO TEACH AND TRANSFORM* all living beings. *THAT IS VAST AND GREAT AS THE DHARMA REALM/* Those states are as vast and as great as the Dharma Realm. *ULTIMATELY LIKE EMPTY SPACE. TO THE EXHAUSTION OF THE BOUNDARIES OF THE FUTURE/* To the ends of the future time it is that way.

"*DISCIPLES OF THE BUDDHA, WHEN BODHISATTVAS,* great beings, *FIRST BRING FORTH THOSE KINDS OF THOUGHTS* of great compassion, *THEY IMMEDIATELY TRANSCEND THE GROUND OF ORDINARY PEOPLE AND ENTER THE POSITION OF A BODHISATTVA. THEY ARE BORN IN THE HOUSEHOLD OF THE THUS COME ONES. NO ONE CAN PRONOUNCE ANY FAULTS THEIR LINEAGE/* There is no one who can find faults in the Bodhisattvas of the Buddha's household. *THEY ABANDON THE WORLDLY DESTINIES/* They leave behind the four evil destinies, those of asuras, hell-beings, hungry ghosts, and animals, *AND ENTER THE WAY OF WORLD-TRANSCENDENCE/* They certify to the attainment of the Way which transcends the three realms. *THEY OBTAIN THE DHARMAS OF BODHISATTVAS. THEY DWELL IN PLACES OF BODHISATTVAS. THEY ENTER EQUALLY INTO THE THREE PERIODS OF TIME/* They obtain the wisdom to enter equally into the past, the present, and the future. *WITHIN THE THUS COME ONES' FAMILY,* the lineage of the Buddhas, *THEY ARE CERTAIN TO OBTAIN UNSURPASSED BODHI,* the fruit of enlightenment, and there is nothing higher than that.

"*WHEN BODHISATTVAS DWELL IN DHARMAS SUCH AS THOSE, IT IS CALLED DWELLING ON THE BODHISATTVAS' GROUND OF HAPPINESS/* What is it called when Bodhisattvas dwell in such Dharmas as those? It is the First Ground. They attain the Bodhisattvas' Ground of Happiness and become very happy. Why is that? It is *BECAUSE OF THE CONNECTION WITH NON-MOVING/* Because they already have samadhi-power, and this happiness is derived from samadhi, they are joined with non-movement."

SUTRA:

"DISCIPLES OF THE BUDDHA, WHEN BODHISATTVAS
DWELL ON THE GROUND OF HAPPINESS, THEY ACCOMPLISH
MUCH HAPPINESS, MUCH PURE FAITH, MUCH DELIGHT, MUCH
BLISS, MUCH ELATION, MUCH ENTHUSIASM, MUCH COURAGE,
MUCH FREEDOM FROM CONTENTION, MUCH ABSENCE OF
TROUBLING, MUCH ABSENCE OF ANGER.. DISCIPLES OF
THE BUDDHA, WHEN BODHISATTVAS DWELL ON THE GROUND
OF HAPPINESS, THEY GIVE RISE TO HAPPINESS BECAUSE
THEY ARE MINDFUL OF ALL BUDDHAS. THEY GIVE RISE
TO HAPPINESS BECAUSE THEY ARE MINDFUL OF ALL BUD-
DHAS' DHARMAS. THEY GIVE RISE TO HAPPINESS BECAUSE
THEY ARE MINDFUL OF ALL BODHISATTVAS. THEY GIVE
RISE TO HAPPINESS BECAUSE THEY ARE MINDFUL OF ALL
BODHISATTVAS' PRACTICES. THEY GIVE RISE TO HAPPI-
NESS BECAUSE THEY ARE MINDFUL OF THE PURITY OF ALL
PARAMITAS. THEY GIVE RISE TO HAPPINESS BECAUSE
THEY ARE MINDFUL OF THE SUPREMACY OF ALL BODHISAT-
TVAS' GROUNDS. THEY GIVE RISE TO HAPPINESS BECAUSE
THEY ARE MINDFUL OF ALL BODHISATTVAS' INDESTRUCTI-
BILITY. THEY GIVE RISE TO HAPPINESS BECAUSE THEY
ARE MINDFUL OF THE THUS COME ONES' TEACHING AND
TRANSFORMING OF LIVING BEINGS. THEY GIVE RISE TO
HAPPINESS BECAUSE THEY ARE MINDFUL OF THE ABILITY
TO BENEFIT LIVING BEINGS.

COMMENTARY:

"DISCIPLES OF THE BUDDHA," calls out Vajra
Treasury Bodhisattva again, saying, "All of you
disciples of the Buddha, WHEN BODHISATTVAS DWELL
ON THE GROUND OF HAPPINESS THEY ACCOMPLISH MUCH
HAPPINESS/ They have a great deal of happiness,
and MUCH PURE FAITH/ Their thoughts of pure faith
also increase, and they have MUCH DELIGHT/ They
produce more fondness for the Buddhadharma than
you can possibly imagine. They have MUCH BLISS/
At all times they feel very happy and serene. No
matter where they are, they are blissful and there
are no obstacles. It does not matter what situations may present themselves, they do not feel
them to be obstacles; and no matter what causes
for afflictions may arise, they never become afflicted. In all situations and circumstances,
they are content at heart. They have MUCH ELATION/

They are always elated that they can hear the Buddhadharma and practice the Bodhisattva Way. They
have MUCH ENTHUSIASM/ They are always enthusiastic, always vigorous, and never lazy. They have
MUCH COURAGE/ They are always courageously vigorous. They have MUCH FREEDOM FROM CONTENTION/ They
never fight or argue with anyone. They have MUCH
ABSENCE OF TROUBLING/ They never cause people to
become afflicted, nor do they ever deliberately
trouble others or obstruct them in their cultivation. They have MUCH ABSENCE OF ANGER/ The Bodhisattvas who have realized the First Ground, that
of Happiness, never become angry no matter how you
treat them.

"DISCIPLES OF THE BUDDHA"/ Vajra Treasury Bodhisattva calls out again saying, "All of you disciples of the Buddha, WHEN BODHISATTVAS DWELL ON
THE GROUND OF HAPPINESS, THEY GIVE RISE TO HAPPI-
NESS, BECAUSE THEY ARE MINDFUL OF ALL BUDDHAS"/
They constantly remember and think about all Buddhas, and for that reason they are happy. They
are not like us common people who, day in and day
out, are jealous and obstructive of one another
and have no thought for the Way. Because they
singlemindedly concentrate on thinking of all Buddhas, they have no time to be jealous or obstructive. "THEY GIVE RISE TO HAPPINESS, BECAUSE THEY
ARE MINDFUL OF ALL BUDDHAS' DHARMAS"/ They also
always remember all the Dharmas spoken by all Buddhas, and they practice in accord with those Dharmas; and so they are very happy. "THEY GIVE RISE
TO HAPPINESS, BECAUSE THEY ARE MINDFUL OF ALL BO-
DHISATTVAS/" Not only are they mindful of the Buddhas and their Dharmas, they are mindful of the
Sangha, too. They always recollect all the sagely
Sangha members, the great Bodhisattvas of the ten
directions and the three periods of time, and so
they are very happy. If we cultivators of the Way
could at all times be mindful of the Buddha, the
Dharma, and the Sangha, when could we have time to
be jealous or obstructive? We would never have
the time to spend looking at others' faults. We
would always be seeing our own faults, returning
the light and illumining inwards.

"THEY GIVE RISE TO HAPPINESS, BECAUSE THEY
ARE MINDFUL OF ALL BODHISATTVAS' PRACTICES"/ They
are also always thinking of the practices culti-

vated by all Great Bodhisattvas. Of all the great
Bodhisattvas, the Buddhas of the future, some cultivate the doors of the practice of giving, others of
holding precepts, others that of patience, others
that of vigor, others dhyana-samadhi, and others
wisdom. The Bodhisattvas cultivate those various
kinds of practices, the Six Paramitas and the ten
thousand practices. Therefore, when Bodhisattvas
certify to the Ground of Happiness, they also have
the opportunity to cultivate all of those Dharma-
doors, and because of that they become very happy.
    *"THEY GIVE RISE TO HAPPINESS, BECAUSE THEY
ARE MINDFUL OF THE SUPREMACY OF ALL BODHISATTVAS'
GROUNDS/* They are always thinking of the supremacy of the positions of all Bodhisattvas, and so
they become happy. *THEY GIVE RISE TO HAPPINESS,
BECAUSE THEY ARE MINDFUL OF ALL BODHISATTVAS' IN-
DESTRUCTIBILITY/* They think of the Bodhisattvas'
realization of the Three Irreversibilities--in
thought, in position, and in conduct--and how no
heavenly demons or externalist ways can destroy
them. Therefore, they become very happy. *THEY
GIVE RISE TO HAPPINESS, BECAUSE THEY ARE MINDFUL
OF THE THUS COME ONES' TEACHING AND TRANSFORMING
OF LIVING BEINGS/* They always remember and are
mindful of how the Buddhas always compassionately
take care of all living beings, causing them to
end suffering and attain bliss, and so they become
very happy. *THEY GIVE RISE TO HAPPINESS, BECAUSE
THEY ARE MINDFUL OF THE ABILITY TO BENEFIT LIVING
BEINGS/* They are mindful of being able to cause
all living beings identically to obtain benefits
of the greatest kind, causing all living beings to
hear the Dharma and be saved and end birth and
death--those doors of practice which are most beneficial to living beings. Bodhisattvas, once they
can cultivate those various kinds of activities,
can obtain the highest kinds of causes and conditions, and for that reason they become very happy."

SUTRA:

    *"THEY GIVE RISE TO HAPPINESS, BECAUSE THEY
ARE MINDFUL OF ENTRY INTO ALL THUS COME ONES' WIS-
DOM AND EXPEDIENTS.*
    *"THEY ALSO HAVE THIS THOUGHT, 'I GIVE RISE TO
HAPPINESS, BECAUSE I HAVE TURNED AWAY FROM AND LEFT*

ALL WORLDLY STATES. I GIVE RISE TO HAPPINESS, BE-
CAUSE I DRAW NEAR TO ALL BUDDHAS. I GIVE RISE TO
HAPPINESS, BECAUSE I HAVE LEFT ALL GROUNDS OF OR-
DINARY PEOPLE FAR BEHIND. I GIVE RISE TO HAPPI-
NESS, BECAUSE I DRAW NEAR THE GROUNDS OF WISDOM.
I GIVE RISE TO HAPPINESS, BECAUSE I HAVE ETERNALLY
CUT OFF ALL EVIL DESTINIES. I GIVE RISE TO HAPPI-
NESS, BECAUSE I AM A PLACE OF RELIANCE FOR ALL LIV
ING BEINGS. I GIVE RISE TO HAPPINESS, BECAUSE I
SEE ALL THUS COME ONES. I GIVE RISE TO HAPPINESS,
BECAUSE I GIVE RISE TO THE EXPERIENCES OF ALL BUD-
DHAS. I GIVE RISE TO HAPPINESS, BECAUSE I ENTER
INTO SAMENESS WITH ALL BODHISATTVAS. I GIVE RISE
TO HAPPINESS, BECAUSE I HAVE LEFT ALL ALARMING,
HAIR-RAISING, AND OTHER SUCH EXPERIENCES FAR BE-
HIND.'
   "AND WHY? ONCE THESE BODHISATTVAS ATTAIN THE
GROUND OF HAPPINESS, THEY LEAVE ALL FEARS BEHIND.
THAT IS TO SAY: FEAR OF NOT STAYING ALIVE, FEAR OF
A BAD REPUTATION, FEAR OF DEATH, FEAR OF THE EVIL
DESTINIES, FEAR OF THE AWESOME VIRTUE OF THE GREAT
ASSEMBLY. ALL SUCH FEARS ARE ETERNALLY LEFT BE-
HIND.

COMMENTARY:

   "THEY GIVE RISE TO HAPPINESS, BECAUSE THEY
ARE MINDFUL OF ENTRY INTO ALL THUS COME ONES' WIS-
DOM AND EXPEDIENTS"/ The Bodhisattvas who realize
the Ground of Happiness have thoughts, but the
thoughts are pure. We living beings also have
thoughts, but they are defiled. Our every thought
involves the five desires: wealth, sex, fame, food,
and sleep. What Bodhisattvas think of are the pure
states of the Buddhas, the Dharma, and the Sangha,
along with the Six Paramitas and the ten thousand
conducts. Because they know they have already entered into the Thus Come Ones' wisdom and obtained
all kinds of expedients, they become very happy.
   "THEY ALSO HAVE THIS THOUGHT:/ The Bodhisattvas who have certified to the position of the
Ground of Happiness also think in this way, saying,
'I GIVE RISE TO HAPPINESS, BECAUSE I HAVE TURNED
AWAY FROM AND LEFT BEHIND ALL WORLDLY STATES/

          Turning the common into the sagely,
          Turning confusion into enlightenment,

> Turning away from defilement,
> And returning to purity.-

Because I have turned all worldly states away,
therefore, I have become very happy.'"

You are not aware of it, but those of you here
in this Bodhimanda, even though you have false
thinking, are far better off than those people outside. If you go outside, what your eyes see and
what your ears hear are all unclean dharmas. But,
inside the Bodhimanda, although you have false
thoughts, nonetheless, your self-nature is still
pure. That is what is known as turning away from-
and leaving behind all worldly states; and that is
why·they become very happy.

"'*I GIVE RISE TO HAPPINESS, BECAUSE I DRAW
NEAR TO ALL BUDDHAS*'/ Bodhisattvas of the First
Ground are always able to see the Buddhas and draw
near them, and they are very happy. '*I GIVE RISE
TO HAPPINESS, BECAUSE I HAVE LEFT ALL GROUNDS OF
ORDINARY PEOPLE FAR BEHIND*'/ The common person's
thoughts and what he or she pays attention to are
not what Bodhisattvas think about or pay attention
to. Conversely, what ordinary people do not think
of and pay no attention to is precisely what Bodhisattvas wish to study and to think of. That is
how they are able to leave the position of ordinary
people far behind and turn the common into the
sagely. '*I GIVE RISE TO HAPPINESS, BECAUSE I DRAW
NEAR THE GROUNDS OF WISDOM*'/ To leave the ordinary is to leave the grounds of ignorance and stupidity far behind. To draw near good, wise advisors is to draw near the grounds of wisdom. For
that reason they become happy. '*I GIVE RISE TO
HAPPINESS, BECAUSE I HAVE ETERNALLY CUT OFF ALL
EVIL DESTINIES*'/ Bodhisattvas who certify to the
First Ground, the Ground of Happiness, cut off all
of the bad paths and never again fall into the
four evil destinies. It may happen that they make
a vow to go to the four evil destinies to teach
and transform living beings, but that is another
matter. '*I GIVE RISE TO HAPPINESS, BECAUSE I AM
A PLACE OF RELIANCE FOR ALL LIVING BEINGS*'/ All
living beings depend upon the Bodhisattvas, which
makes the Bodhisattvas very happy.

"'*I GIVE RISE TO HAPPINESS, BECAUSE I SEE ALL
THUS COME ONES*'/ They can see the Buddhas all the

time, and so they are happy. '*I GIVE RISE TO HAP-
PINESS, BECAUSE I GIVE RISE TO THE EXPERIENCES OF
ALL BUDDHAS. I GIVE RISE TO HAPPINESS, BECAUSE I
ENTER INTO SAMENESS WITH ALL BODHISATTVAS*'/ They
are in nature the same as all Bodhisattvas who cultivate the Bodhisattva Way, and so they become happy. '*I GIVE RISE TO HAPPINESS, BECAUSE I HAVE LEFT
ALL ALARMING, HAIR-RAISING, AND OTHER SUCH EXPER-
IENCES FAR BEHIND*'"/ They are able to leave far
behind all fearsome and terrifying experiences of
the sort which make the hair on one's head stand
on end or give one goose bumps. "And other such
experiences" refers to the Five Fearsome Matters,
which are explained below.

"*AND WHY? What are the reasons? ONCE THESE
BODHISATTVAS ATTAIN THE GROUND OF HAPPINESS, THEY
LEAVE ALL FEARS BEHIND*"/ They are not afraid of
anything, because they have seen through everything
and put everything down. People, however, are
afraid of this and afraid of that--afraid of everything. That is due to not having cultivated and
certified to the Ground of Happiness. Once you
certify to the Ground of Happiness, with nothing
to fear, what is there to be afraid of? If it
comes to dying, just die and be done with it. What
is there to fear? What are all the fears that they
have left behind? "*THAT IS TO SAY, FEAR OF A BAD
REPUTATION*"/ If someone gives me a bad name, what
do I do? I get really scared and wonder how I can
get my reputation back. That is the fear of people
giving you a bad name. Are you afraid of someone
saying that you are bad? If someone says that you
are a thief, are you in terror? What if they say
you rob, kill...don't keep the precepts? Do you
fear their saying that you lie and take intoxi-
cants? Those are all examples of bad reputations.
"*FEAR OF DEATH*"/ Then there is the fear of dying.
If you are about to die, you become panic stricken.
"*FEAR OF EVIL DESTINIES*"/ There is the further
fear of falling into the three evil paths. However, when Bodhisattvas certify to the Ground of
Happiness, they do not die and they are unable to
fall into the three evil destinies. Therefore,
they are unafraid.

They also have no "*FEAR OF THE AWESOME VIRTUE
OF THE GREAT ASSEMBLY*"/ The awesome virtue of the
Great Assembly refers to several hundred or several

thousand--at any rate, a lot of people--who invite
you to lecture. When you get there, you can't say
a word. That is fear of the awesome virtue of the
Great Assembly, which makes you so scared you don't
dare speak. Furthermore, you may be wondering if
what you are about to say will be right or not.
You keep thinking, figuring to speak when you get
it clearer; but the more you think, the worse it
gets. "ALL SUCH FEARS ARE ETERNALLY LEFT BEHIND."
There are no such fears as those just described.
All of them are completely left behind, forever.
Therefore, your being afraid of this and being
afraid of that is due to not cultivating. If you
cultivate, what are you afraid of? You do not fear
a thing. From the time I was small, I have never
been afraid of anything. I used to go climbing in
the mountains where there were all kinds of wild
beasts: wolves, bears, panthers, leopards. I made
friends with them and played with them and had no
fear. I have never been afraid from the time I was
born.

SUTRA:

"AND WHY? IT IS BECAUSE THESE BODHISATTVAS
ARE FREE FROM THE THOUGHT OF SELF. THEY DO NOT
EVEN CHERISH THEIR OWN BODIES, HOW MUCH THE LESS
WEALTH AND POSSESSIONS. THEREFORE, THEY HAVE NO
FEAR OF NOT STAYING ALIVE. THEY DO NOT SEEK OFFER-
INGS FROM OTHERS, BUT ONLY GIVE TO OTHER LIVING
BEINGS. THEREFORE, THEY HAVE NO FEAR OF A BAD RE-
PUTATION. THEY HAVE LEFT THE VIEW OF SELF FAR BE-
HIND, AND HAVE NO THOUGHT OF SELF. THEREFORE, THEY
HAVE NO FEAR OF DEATH. THEY THEMSELVES KNOW THAT
AFTER DEATH THEY CERTAINLY WILL NOT BE APART FROM
THE BUDDHAS AND BODHISATTVAS. THEREFORE, THEY HAVE
NO FEAR OF THE EVIL DESTINIES. THEIR INTENT AND
INCLINATIONS IN ALL WORLDS ARE UNEQUALLED, HOW MUCH
THE LESS SURPASSED. THEREFORE, THEY HAVE NO FEAR
OF THE AWESOME VIRTUE OF THE GREAT ASSEMBLY. BO-
DHISATTVAS IN THAT WAY LEAVE ALL ALARMING, HAIR-
RAISING EXPERIENCES FAR BEHIND.

"DISCIPLES OF THE BUDDHA, THESE BODHISATTVAS
TAKE GREAT COMPASSION AS FOREMOST. THEY HAVE VAST,
GREAT INTENT AND INCLINATIONS WHICH CANNOT BE DES-
TROYED. THEY INTENSELY AND DILIGENTLY CULTIVATE
ALL GOOD-ROOTS, WHICH BECOME ACCOMPLISHED.

COMMENTARY:

"Why do Bodhisattvas have no fear of not staying alive, no fear of a bad reputation, no fear of death, no fear of the evil destinies, and no fear of the great assembly? It is because they have left all alarming, hair-raising experiences far behind. *AND WHY?/* Why is it like that? *IT IS BE-CAUSE THESE BODHISATTVAS* who bring forth the thought for Bodhi, practice the Bodhisattva Way, and certify to the Ground of Happiness, *ARE FREE FROM THE THOUGHT OF SELF/* They have no self. Not only that, they never think about whether they have a self or not. *THEY DO NOT EVEN CHERISH THEIR OWN BODIES/* Their attitude towards their bodies is that they have already given them away to living beings to serve and work for them. Therefore, they are not selfish about their bodies, nor do they seek benefits for them, *HOW MUCH THE LESS WEALTH AND POSSESSIONS/* Since they do not even cherish their own bodies, how much the less do they cherish things external to the body? They even less cherish gold, silver, jewels, countries,, cities, wives, and children. They have attained real freedom. *THEREFORE, THEY HAVE NO FEAR OF NOT STAYING ALIVE/* They do not scheme for themselves. They are not afraid of their own lives being in jeopardy. They are not afraid of starving to death. Consequently they don't have the fear that they will not stay alive.

"*THEY DO NOT SEEK OFFERINGS FROM OTHERS, BUT ONLY GIVE TO OTHER LIVING BEINGS/* Bodhisattvas don't want to benefit themselves and aren't selfish, and so they seek nothing. As it is said:

> When you reach the point of seeking
> nothing,
> Then you have no worries.

The reason you have worries is that you have greed and longing for something. Bodhisattvas don't long for anything. They don't seek fame or fortune, sex, sleep, or food. These Bodhisattvas have already seen these five objects of desire as flavorless, and so they are not greedy for good offerings. They don't say, 'Who will be good to me and give me some fine food, some nice clothes,

some things that are useful or pleasing to look
at?' They concentrate on giving to other living
beings. They specialize in the practice of giving.
Whatever they have, they give away to other living
beings. THEREFORE, THEY HAVE NO FEAR OF A BAD REP-
UTATION/ They are not greedy for anything, nor do
they fear taking a loss or not getting a bargain
for themselves, and so it is not important to them
if they have a good name or not. Bodhisattvas are
incapable of being greedy for a false name or an
empty title, nor do they constantly put up a false
front so that people will praise them. Because
Bodhisattvas have gone beyond good and bad, if you
say they're good, they aren't pleased, and if you
call them by a bad name, they don't get upset.
That is what it means to have no fear of a bad
name."

They are not afraid of people slandering them.
I regularly tell you that, although I am not a Bodhisattva, still I am not afraid of people slandering me. They are afraid they won't have anything to eat, and so they talk about what's wrong
with other people. Their talking about others'
faults is designed to show what is right about
themselves. That is why I'm always telling you
that if people can get food to eat by slandering
me, then I am, indirectly, giving it to them. If
they can get people to give them food to eat, or
if they gain some other advantage by slandering me
a little, then I have indirectly given it to them.
As long as it is to their benefit, let them slander me all they want. I'm not afraid of it.

"THEY HAVE LEFT THE VIEW OF SELF FAR BEHIND
AND HAVE NO THOUGH, OF SELF. THEREFORE, THEY HAVE
NO FEAR OF DEATH/ Bodhisattvas have no self, no ego,
and so they have no view of self. Without even a
view, they also have no thought of self and are not
looking out for themselves, thinking, 'What's in
it for me?' Therefore, they do not fear death.
If they have no self, then who dies? That is why
they do not fear death, because THEY THEMSELVES
KNOW THAT AFTER DEATH THEY CERTAINLY WILL NOT BE
APART FROM THE BUDDHAS AND BODHISATTVAS/ They know
they won't fall into the hells or turn into hungry
ghosts, or become animals. Because all they've
done is practice the Bodhisattva Way, they certainly

will not be separated from the Buddhas and Bodhisattvas. *THEREFORE, THEY HAVE NO FEAR OF THE EVIL
DESTINIES/* Because they know they won't fall into
the three evil destinies, they have no fear of becoming hell-beings, hungry ghosts, or animals.

"*THEIR INTENT AND INCLINATIONS,* the vows and
what the Bodhisattvas like, *IN ALL WORLDS ARE UN-
EQUALLED/* Their wishes and their purpose are not
equalled by anything in all worlds, *HOW MUCH THE
LESS SURPASSED. THEREFORE, THEY HAVE NO FEAR OF
THE AWESOME VIRTUE OF THE GREAT ASSEMBLY/* They
have no fear of and are not scared of the Great Assembly's awesome virtue, because these Bodhisattvas know that they surpass the Great Assembly."

You may ask, "If they think that way, then
aren't Bodhisattvas very arrogant, thinking that
no one in the world can compare with them?" The
Bodhisattvas aren't thinking this. It's Vajra
Treasury Bodhisattva speaking the *Flower Adornment
Sutra* and explaining the kinds of states certified
to by Bodhisattvas on the Ten Grounds. The Bodhisattvas don't say it of themselves. Vajra Treasury
Bodhisattva is describing the kind of resultant
position held by Bodhisattvas on the Ground of Happiness. It is definitely not the case that the
Bodhisattvas arrogantly consider that no one in the
world can compare to them. It's simply that when
they speak Dharma and explain Sutras within the
Great Assembly, they are very much at ease and unafraid.

"*BODHISATTVAS IN THAT WAY LEAVE ALL ALARMING,
HAIR-RAISING EXPERIENCES FAR BEHIND/* That is how
Bodhisattvas leave behind the five fearsome mat-
ters:

1. fear of not staying alive,
2. fear of a bad reputation,
3. fear of death,
4. fear of the four evil destinies,
5. fear of the awesome virtue of the
   Great Assembly.

Those are all experiences which are frightening
and make one's hair stand on end. *DISCIPLES OF
THE BUDDHA"/* Vajra Treasury Bodhisattva calls out
again, "All of you disciples of the Buddha, *THESE
BODHISATTVAS TAKE GREAT COMPASSION AS FOREMOST/*

Compassion can pull one out of suffering. Being
greatly compassionate is their most important duty.
They HAVE VAST, GREAT INTENT AND INCLINATIONS WHICH
CANNOT BE DESTROYED/ No heavenly demons or those
of externalist ways could destroy, obstruct, or
ruin them. THEY INTENSELY AND DILIGENTLY CULTI-
VATE, working harder every day at developing ALL
GOOD ROOTS, WHICH BECOME ACCOMPLISHED/ They are
able to perfect and bring to accomplishment the
roots of Bodhi. That is why these Bodhisattvas
have none of the five types of fears."

All of you should use your own wisdom to contemplate the principles I have spoken. If they
are reasonable, cultivate according to them. If
they are not reasonable, you can forget them. That
is:

Select the good and repeat it.

If it's not right, then change it. Don't follow
blindly thinking that whatever I say has to be
right. In that way you yourself will discover
your own inherent wisdom, and the true principles
that are yours to start with. Therefore, people
who cultivate absolutely cannot follow blindly. If
something is not right, it doesn't matter who said
it, you cannot believe it. If something is right,
then no matter who said it, we should believe it.

SUTRA:

"THAT IS, THROUGH INCREASING FAITH; THROUGH
AUGMENTING PURE FAITH; THROUGH PURE UNDERSTANDING;
THROUGH DECISIVE FAITH; THROUGH BECOMING SYMPA-
THETIC; THROUGH ACCOMPLISHING GREAT KINDNESS;
THROUGH HAVING NO WEARINESS OR LAZINESS OF MIND;
THROUGH ADORNMENT WITH REPENTANCE AND REFORM;
THROUGH ACCOMPLISHING FORBEARANCE; THROUGH RESPECT-
FULLY HEEDING THE BUDDHAS' INSTRUCTIONS; THROUGH
CULTIVATING AND ACCUMULATING GOOD ROOTS DAY AND
NIGHT WITHOUT BECOMING TIRED; THROUGH DRAWING NEAR
GOOD KNOWING ADVISORS; THROUGH CONSTANT DELIGHT IN
THE DHARMA; THROUGH SEEKING LEARNING WITHOUT SATIA-
TION; THROUGH PROPERLY CONTEMPLATING IN ACCORD WITH
THE DHARMA ONE HAS HEARD; THROUGH HAVING NO RE-
LIANCE OR ATTACHMENT OF MIND; THROUGH NOT HANKERING

AFTER PROFIT, FAME, OR RESPECT; THROUGH NOT SEEK-
ING THE NECESSITIES OF LIFE; THROUGH BRINGING FORTH
THE JEWEL-LIKE THOUGHT WITHOUT SATIATION; THROUGH
SEEKING THE GROUND OF ALL KNOWLEDGE; THROUGH SEEK-
ING THE THUS COME ONES' POWERS, FEARLESSNESSES, AND
THE DHARMAS SPECIAL TO A BUDDHA.

COMMENTARY:

"When the Bodhisattva of the Ten Grounds has
certified to the Ground of Happiness, he is happy
all the time, and all of the good roots that he
diligently cultivates very quickly are brought to
maturity. THAT IS, THROUGH INCREASING FAITH/ He
has faith which does not decrease but only increases. THROUGH AUGMENTING PURE FAITH/ At the beginning, although he had faith, it was still defiled,
but as his faith increases it becomes purer day by
day. Eventually he is pure, and has returned to
the origin and gone back to the source. THROUGH
PURE UNDERSTANDING/ Furthermore, he understands
that the reason he has obtained that state of purity is because his faith has increased. THROUGH
DECISIVE FAITH/ He never doubts, but absolutely
believes in the Buddhas of the ten directions, in
the Dharma they have spoken, and that all of the
sagely Sangha members of the ten directions are
his friends.
    "THROUGH BECOMING SYMPATHETIC/ He himself is
one of the Three Jewels, and so he wishes to become sympathetic towards living beings and save
all of them. THROUGH ACCOMPLISHING GREAT KINDNESS/
His thoughts are very kind and compassionate:

> Kindness can bestow happiness;
> Compassion can pull one out of
>   suffering.

THROUGH HAVING NO WEARINESS OR LAZINESS OF MIND/
His resolve to cultivate the Buddhadharma is more
vigorous and more courageous every day. He is absolutely never lazy or tired.
    "THROUGH ADORNMENT WITH REPENTANCE AND REFORM/

> Repenting of previous offenses,
> Reforming future mistakes.

He uses all of his merit and virtue of repentai ce
and reform to adorn the countries of the ten directions. *THROUGH ACCOMPLISHING FORBEARANCE/* He
brings the Paramita of Patience to accomplishment.
No matter what people say, he is able to endure it
all. Whether things go against him or for him, he
does not become intractable and fight for victory.
He does not contend or argue with people. *THROUGH
CULTIVATING AND ACCUMULATING GOOD ROOTS. DAY AND
NIGHT WITHOUT BECOMING TIRED/*

"*THROUGH DRAWING NEAR GOOD-KNOWING ADVISORS/*
He always likes to draw near great, good, and wise
advisors, and is able to offer up his conduct in
accord with their teachings. *THROUGH CONSTANT DE-
LIGHT IN THE DHARMA; THROUGH SEEKING LEARNING WITH-
OUT SATIATION/* He always wants to increase his
wisdom. He doesn't say, 'I've studied enough. I
understand everything.' Bodhisattvas don't think
that way. They at all times diligently cultivate
precepts, samadhi, and wisdom, and put to rest
greed, hatred, and stupidity. *THROUGH PROPERLY
CONTEMPLATING IN ACCORD WITH THE DHARMA ONE HAS
HEARD/* It is through properly contemplating the
proper Dharma that he himself has heard in the
presence of all Buddhas. He is constantly able to
contemplate the true mark of all dharmas.

"*THROUGH HAVING NO RELIANCE OR ATTACHMENT OF
MIND/* Within his mind there is nothing to which
he is attached or upon which he relies. He is not
attached to self or to dharmas. *THROUGH NOT HANK-
ERING AFTER PROFIT, FAME, OR RESPECT/* He is unable
to be greedy and say, 'I have Dharma protectors.
I have a lot of gains.' Most people want to be
believed in order to become wealthy and famous.
Bodhisattvas don't hanker after that, are not attached to that, and do not seek it; nor do they
want people to be respectful to them. *THROUGH NOT
SEEKING THE NECESSITIES OF LIFE/* He also does not
seek out all the things that sustain life. *THROUGH
BRINGING FORTH THE JEWEL-LIKE THOUGHT WITHOUT SA-
TIATION/* He brings forth the jewel-like thought--
similar to precious jewels and very valuable--
without weariness. He could never grow tired or
think he has had enough. That is, he himself cultivates and seeks jewel-like thought--the thought
for Bodhi--which is as solid as vajra.

"*THROUGH SEEKING THE GROUND OF ALL-KNOWLEDGE/*
He wants to attain all-knowledge and all-wisdom.
*THROUGH SEEKING THE THUS COME ONES' POWERS, FEAR-
LESSNESSES AND THE DHARMAS SPECIAL TO A BUDDHA/* He
seeks and obtains the benefits of the Ten Powers,
the Four Fearlessnesses, and the Eighteen Dharmas
Special to a Buddha, which are not shared by those
of the Two Vehicles."

SUTRA:

"*THROUGH SEEKING ALL PARAMITAS, DHARMAS THAT
AID THE WAY; THROUGH FREEDOM FROM ALL FLATTERY AND
DECEIT; THROUGH BEING ABLE TO PRACTICE AS IS SPO-
KEN; THROUGH ALWAYS GUARDING TRUE SPEECH; THROUGH
NOT DEFILING THE THUS COME ONES' HOUSEHOLD; THROUGH
NOT RENOUNCING THE BODHISATTVA PRECEPTS; THROUGH
BRINGING FORTH THE THOUGHT FOR ALL KNOWLEDGE, UN-
MOVING LIKE THE KING OF MOUNTAINS; THROUGH NOT
ABANDONING ALL WORLDLY MATTERS, YET ACCOMPLISHING
THE WAY OF WORLD-TRANSCENDENCE; THROUGH ACCUMULAT-
ING ASSISTING BODHI-SHARE DHARMAS WITHOUT WEARI-
NESS; THROUGH CONSTANTLY SEEKING THE SUPERIORLY
SUPERIOR, ESPECIALLY SUPREME WAY.*

COMMENTARY:

"*THROUGH SEEKING ALL PARAMITAS/* The Bodhisattva who cultivates the practices of a Bodhisattva seeks all of the Paramitas, *DHARMAS THAT AID
THE WAY,* those methods of assistance to the Way.
THROUGH FREEDOM FROM ALL FLATTERY AND DECEIT/ He
is also free of all flattery and deceptions and
does not fawn upon the rich or tell lies. *THROUGH
BEING ABLE TO PRACTICE AS IS SPOKEN/* He can really
cultivate the Dharmas the Buddhas' explain. *THROUGH
ALWAYS GUARDING TRUE SPEECH/* He is watchful of
his own speech to be sure it is true, not false,
and he never tells any lies. *THROUGH NOT DEFILING
THE BUDDHAS' HOUSEHOLD/* He himself has been born
as a disciple of the Buddha. This Bodhisattva is
the most pure and lofty kind of person, and so he
is incapable of defiling the household of the Buddhas, that is, of defiling the Bodhimanda. *THROUGH
NOT RENOUNCING THE BODHISATTVA PRECEPTS/* He could

not cast aside the precepts and regulations that a
Bodhisattva should cultivate. *THROUGH BRINGING
FORTH THE THOUGHT FOR ALL-KNOWLEDGE, UNMOVING LIKE
THE KING OF MOUNTAINS/* He brings forth the resolve
for all-wisdom, which is like Mount Sumeru and
never moves. *THROUGH NOT ABANDONING ALL WORLDLY
MATTERS, YET ACCOMPLISHING THE WAY OF WORLD-TRANS-
CENDENCE/* One does not need to put down all worldly matters to be able to realize dharmas for transcending the world. *THROUGH ACCUMULATING ASSISTING
BODHI-SHARE DHARMAS WITHOUT WEARINESS/* He could
not at times say, 'I've already accumulated and
perfected enough of these dharmas.' He is incapable of thinking that way. *THROUGH CONSTANTLY
SEEKING THE SUPERIORLY SUPERIOR, ESPECIALLY SUPREME
WAY/* He always seeks and hopes to accomplish the
most superior among the superior, most especially
supreme Way--which is constantly to seek the Buddha Way."

SUTRA:

"*DISCIPLES OF THE BUDDHA, WHEN THE BODHISAT-
TVA ACCOMPLISHES SUCH PURIFICATION AND REGULATION
OF THE GROUNDS, THAT IS CALLED SECURELY DWELLING
ON THE BODHISATTVA'S GROUND OF HAPPINESS. DISCI-
PLES OF THE BUDDHA, THE BODHISATTVA WHO DWELLS
UPON THIS GROUND OF HAPPINESS IS ABLE TO ACCOM-
PLISH SUCH GREAT VOWS, SUCH GREAT VIGOR, SUCH GREAT
EFFICACY. THAT IS, HE BRINGS FORTH VAST, GREAT,
PURE, DECISIVE UNDERSTANDING AND USES ALL KINDS
OF OBJECTS AS OFFERINGS TO WORSHIP AND MAKE OFFER-
INGS TO ALL BUDDHAS, OMITTING NONE--VAST AND GREAT
AS THE DHARMA REALM, ULTIMATE AS EMPTY SPACE, EX-
HAUSTING THE BOUNDARIES OF THE FUTURE, THROUGHOUT
ALL NUMBERS OF KALPAS, WITHOUT CEASE.*
    "*HE FURTHER MAKES GREAT VOWS, VOWING TO RE-
CEIVE ALL BUDDHAS' DHARMA WHEEL, VOWING TO GATHER
IN ALL BUDDHAS' BODHI, VOWING TO PROTECT ALL BUD-
DHAS' TEACHINGS, VOWING TO MAINTAIN ALL BUDDHAS'
DHARMAS--VAST AND GREAT AS THE DHARMA REALM, ULTI
MATE AS EMPTY SPACE, EXHAUSTING THE BOUNDARIES OF
THE FUTURE, THROUGHOUT ALL NUMBERS OF KALPAS,
WITHOUT CEASE.*
    "*HE FURTHER MAKES GREAT VOWS, VOWING THAT IN
ALL WORLDS, WHEN A BUDDHA APPEARS IN THE WORLD,*

DESCENDING FROM THE TUSHITA HEAVEN, ENTERING THE WOMB, DWELLING IN THE WOMB, BEING BORN, LEAVING HOME, ACCOMPLISHING THE WAY, SPEAKING DHARMA, AND MANIFESTING NIRVANA, HE WILL GO TO ALL OF THEM, DRAW NEAR AND MAKE OFFERINGS, ACT AS THE HEAD OF THE ASSEMBLY, AND RECEIVE AND PRACTICE THE PROPER DHARMA, IN EVERY PLACE AT ONE TIME TURNING--VAST AND GREAT AS THE DHARMA REALM, ULTIMATE AS EMPTY SPACE, EXHAUSTING THE BOUNDARIES OF THE FUTURE, THROUGHOUT ALL NUMBERS OF KALPAS, WITHOUT CEASE.

COMMENTARY:

"DISCIPLES OF THE BUDDHA, WHEN THE BODHISATTVA ACCOMPLISHES SUCH PURIFICATION AND REGULATION OF THE GROUNDS/ When the Bodhisattva practices the Grounds as was previously described, he purifies and cultivates all the Dharma-doors of the Ten Grounds, and THAT IS CALLED SECURELY DWELLING ON THE BODHISATTVA'S GROUND OF HAPPINESS/ That is what is meant by a Bodhisattva's always certifying to the fruit position of the Ground of Happiness. DISCIPLES OF THE BUDDHA, THE BODHISATTVA WHO DWELLS UPON THIS GROUND OF HAPPINESS/ When a Bodhisattva cultivates and certifies to this Ground of Happiness, he IS ABLE TO ACCOMPLISH SUCH GREAT VOWS/ What sorts of great vows? That is to say, SUCH GREAT VIGOR/ What most people are unable to do, he can do, which is called great vigor. SUCH GREAT EFFICACY/ What most people cannot accomplish, he can accomplish, which is called great efficacy. THAT IS, HE BRINGS FORTH VAST, GREAT, PURE, DECISIVE UNDERSTANDING, AND HE USES ALL KINDS OF OBJECTS AS OFFERINGS, TO WORSHIP AND MAKE OFFERINGS TO ALL BUDDHAS, OMITTING NONE/ He makes offerings to all Buddhas, no matter which Buddha it is--VAST AND GREAT AS THE DHARMA REALM/ How great is the dharma of making offerings? It is as vast and great as the Dharma Realm. How ultimate is it? ULTIMATE AS EMPTY SPACE, EXHAUSTING THE BOUNDARIES OF THE FUTURE/ It is that way not just one time; to the exhaustion of the limits of future kalpas it is that way, THROUGHOUT ALL NUMBERS OF KALPAS, in all numbers of aeons, WITHOUT CEASE/ He never stops and rests.

"*HE FURTHER MAKES GREAT VOWS, VOWING TO RECEIVE ALL BUDDHAS' DHARMA WHEEL/* He vows to receive the wheel of Dharma turned by all Buddhas and to continue to turn it. *VOWING TO GATHER IN ALL BUDDHAS' BODHI/* He vows to constantly cultivate the Enlightenment of all Buddhas, and to gather in, maintain, and protect it. He makes a further vow, *VOWING TO PRO-TECT ALL BUDDHAS' TEACHINGS/* He further makes a vow, *VOWING TO MAINTAIN ALL BUDDHAS' DHARMAS/* He vows to constantly receive and uphold the Dharma spoken by all Buddhas--*VAST AND GREAT AS THE DHARMA REALM/* This great Dharma is as vast and great as the Dharma Realm, and this Dharma is cultivated to the ultimate, which is as *ULTIMATE AS EMPTY SPACE, EXHAUSTING THE BOUNDARIES OF THE FUTURE THROUGHOUT ALL NUMBERS OF KALPAS WITHOUT CEASE/* In all the numbers of aeons, at no time does he rest.

"*HE FURTHER MAKES GREAT VOWS, VOWING THAT IN ALL WORLDS, WHEN A BUDDHA APPEARS IN THE WORLD/* In all the places where a Buddha is appearing in the world: *DESCENDING FROM THE TUSHITA HEAVEN* to be born; and afterwards *ENTERING THE WOMB, DWELLING IN THE WOMB, BEING BORN* into the world, and then *LEAVING HOME* are part of his vows. Then, *ACCOM-PLISHING THE WAY, SPEAKING DHARMA, AND MANIFESTING NIRVANA*--he will manifest those Eight Marks. *HE WILL GO TO ALL OF THEM, DRAW NEAR, AND MAKE OFFER-INGS,* and *ACT AS THE HEAD OF THE ASSEMBLY/* Al-though he is still in his mother's womb, the Bo-dhisattva's basic substance still goes to all Bud-dhas' Way Places, draws near all Buddhas, makes offerings to all Buddhas, and universally acts as the head of the assemblies in all Buddhas' Way places. *AND RECEIVE AND PRACTICE THE PROPER DHAR-MA/* There he constantly cultivates and practices the Proper Dharma Eye Treasury. *IN EVERY PLACE AT ONE TIME TURNING/* In all places at one and the same time he turns the great Dharma Wheel. The *VAST AND GREAT* Dharma, again, is as great *AS THE DHARMA REALM/* Again it is *ULTIMATE AS EMPTY SPACE/* And it also is *EXHAUSTING THE BOUNDARIES OF THE FUTURE, THROUGHOUT ALL NUMBERS OF KALPAS, WITHOUT CEASE/* There is no time of rest."

SUTRA:

"HE FURTHER MAKES GREAT VOWS, VOWING THAT THE
BODHISATTVA PRACTICES: VAST, GREAT, LIMITLESS, UN-
BREAKABLE, AND UNMIXED, INCLUDING ALL PARAMITAS, PURIFYING
AND REGULATING ALL GROUNDS, CHARACTERIZED BY GENERAL-
ITY, CHARACTERIZED BY PARTICULARITY, CHARACTERIZED
BY IDENTITY, CHARACTERIZED BY DIFFERENCE, CHARAC-
TERIZED BY PRODUCTION, AND CHARACTERIZED BY EXTINC-
TION--ALL THE BODHISATTVA PRACTICES--BE SPOKEN AS
THEY TRULY ARE, TO TEACH AND TRANSFORM ALL, CAUS-
ING THEM TO ACCEPT AND PRACTICE, AND THEIR THOUGHT
TO INCREASE AND GROW--VAST AND GREAT AS THE DHARMA
REALM, ULTIMATE AS EMPTY SPACE, EXHAUSTING THE
BOUNDARIES OF THE FUTURE, THROUGHOUT ALL NUMBERS
OF KALPAS, WITHOUT CEASE.
    "HE FURTHER MAKES GREAT VOWS, VOWING THAT
'ALL THE REALMS OF LIVING BEINGS: THOSE WITH FORM,
WITHOUT FORM, WITH THOUGHT, WITHOUT THOUGHT, NEI-
THER WITH THOUGHT NOR WITHOUT THOUGHT, EGG-BORN,
WOMB-BORN, MOISTURE-BORN, TRANSFORMATIONALLY BORN,
BOUND IN THE THREE REALMS, WHO HAVE ENTERED THE
SIX DESTINIES, IN ALL SUCH PLACES OF REBIRTH, COM-
PRISED OF NAME AND FORM--ALL SUCH CATEGORIES--I
SHALL TEACH AND TRANSFORM, CAUSING THEM TO ENTER
THE BUDDHADHARMA, CAUSING THEM ONCE AND FOR ALL TO
CUT OFF ALL WORLDLY DESTINIES, AND CAUSING THEM TO
DWELL IN THE WAY OF ALL WISDOM--VAST AND GREAT AS
THE DHARMA REALM, ULTIMATE AS EMPTY SPACE, EXHAUST
ING THE BOUNDARIES OF THE FUTURE, THROUGHOUT ALL
NUMBERS OF KALPAS, WITHOUT CEASE.'

COMMENTARY:

    "HE FURTHER MAKES GREAT VOWS/ The Bodhisattva
vows again, VOWING THAT ALL THE BODHISATTVA PRAC-
TICES: VAST, GREAT, LIMITLESS, UNBREAKABLE, AND
UNMIXED/ It's not known how many Bodhisattva prac-
tices there are, and no heavenly demons or those
of externalist paths are able to destroy them; nor
is there evil mixed in with the good. This is IN-
CLUDING ALL PARAMITAS, as well as PURIFYING AND
REGULATING ALL GROUNDS--that is, the Dharma-doors
of the Ten Grounds. All of these are CHARACTER-
IZED BY GENERALITY, CHARACTERIZED BY PARTICULARITY,
CHARACTERIZED BY IDENTITY, CHARACTERIZED BY DIF-

FERENCE, CHARACTERIZED BY PRODUCTION, AND CHARAC-
TERIZED BY EXTINCTION, the six characteristics.
The Bodhisattva vows that ALL THE BODHISATTVA PRAC-
TICES SHALL BE SPOKEN AS THEY TRULY ARE, TO TEACH
AND TRANSFORM ALL living beings, CAUSING THEM TO
ACCEPT AND PRACTICE them.   They accept these Dharma
doors and cultivate in accord with them.   AND THEIR
THOUGHT TO INCREASE AND GROW/   The Bodhisattva en-
ables living beings' thought for Bodhi to grow
greater every day.   These vows are VAST AND GREAT
AS THE DHARMA REALM, ULTIMATE AS EMPTY SPACE, EX-
HAUSTING THE BOUNDARIES OF THE FUTURE, THROUGHOUT
ALL NUMBERS OF KALPAS, WITHOUT CEASE/   At no time
does he rest.
      "HE FURTHER MAKES GREAT VOWS, VOWING THAT 'ALL
THE REALMS OF LIVING BEINGS, whether those beings
are THOSE WITH FORM, WITHOUT FORM, WITH THOUGHT,
WITHOUT THOUGHT, NEITHER WITH NOR WITHOUT THOUGHT!'/
And, he also vows on behalf of beings 'EGG-BORN,
WOMB BORN, MOISTURE BORN, AND those TRANSFORMA-
TIONALLY BORN'/   All the different categories of
living beings are 'BOUND IN THE THREE REALMS': the
Desire Realm, the Form Realm, and the Formless
Realm.   He also vows on behalf of those 'WHO HAVE
ENTERED THE SIX DESTINIES'/   They have gone off to
rebirth among the six paths, going 'IN ALL PLACES
OF REBIRTH' and being COMPRISED OF NAME AND FORM/
The Bodhisattva vows that 'ALL SUCH CATEGORIES--I
SHALL TEACH AND TRANSFORM/   I shall teach and
transform them, CAUSING THEM TO ENTER THE BUDDHA-
DHARMA, CAUSING THEM ONCE AND FOR ALL TO CUT OFF
ALL WORLDLY DESTINIES, AND CAUSING THEM TO DWELL
IN THE WAY OF ALL WISDOM/   The Way of the wisdom
of the One of All Wisdom--this, too, is VAST AND
GREAT AS THE DHARMA REALM, and ULTIMATE AS EMPTY
SPACE, EXHAUSTING THE BOUNDARIES OF THE FUTURE,
THROUGHOUT ALL NUMBERS OF KALPAS, WITHOUT CEASE.'

SUTRA:

      "HE FURTHER MAKES GREAT VOWS, VOWING THAT ALL
WORLDS: VAST, GREAT, LIMITLESS; GROSS, SUBTLE, DIS-
ARRAYED, UPSIDE-DOWN, ORDERLY; WHETHER ENTERING,
MOVING, OR GOING OUT; WITH DISTINCTIONS LIKE SHAK-
RA'S NET; IN THE TEN DIRECTIONS OF LIMITLESS DIS-
SIMILAR VARIETIES--HIS WISDOM WILL UNDERSTAND THEM

ALL, WITH DIRECT KNOWLEDGE AND PERCEPTION--VAST AND
GREAT AS THE DHARMA REALM, ULTIMATE AS EMPTY SPACE,
EXHAUSTING THE BOUNDARIES OF THE FUTURE, THROUGH-
OUT ALL NUMBERS OF KALPAS, WITHOUT CEASE.

COMMENTARY:

"HE FURTHER MAKES GREAT VOWS/ The Bodhisattva
makes another great vow. He vows, VOWING THAT ALL
WORLDS, whether upwards or inverted worlds, rec-
tangular or square worlds--all worlds--are VAST,
GREAT, LIMITLESS/ One does not know how many there
are. Among them are GROSS ones and SUBTLE ones,
and those that are DISARRAYED with no order to
them, as well as ones that are UPSIDE-DOWN/ There
are ORDERLY ones, all well-arranged and according
to the rules. WHETHER ENTERING, perhaps they are
entering, MOVING, constantly in motion, OR GOING
OUT--they may be undergoing a kind of transforma-
tion--WITH DISTINCTIONS LIKE SHAKRA'S NET/ Just
like the net banner of Shakra, Lord of gods, some
are horizontal, some perpendicular, with all kinds
of differences. IN THE TEN DIRECTIONS OF LIMITLESS
DISSIMILAR VARIETIES,--each direction has its own
shapes and appearances, all not the same. HIS WIS-
DOM WILL UNDERSTAND THEM ALL/ The wisdom of the
Bodhisattva will understand the shapes and appear-
ances of those worlds, WITH DIRECT KNOWLEDGE AND
PERCEPTION/ His empirical wisdom of direct percep-
tion will understand all of those dissimilarities--
VAST AND GREAT AS THE DHARMA REALM, ULTIMATE AS
EMPTY SPACE, EXHAUSTING THE BOUNDARIES OF THE FU-
TURE, THROUGHOUT ALL NUMBERS OF KALPAS, WITHOUT
CEASE."

SUTRA:

"HE FURTHER MAKES GREAT VOWS, VOWING THAT ALL
COUNTRIES ENTER ONE COUNTRY, AND THAT ONE COUNTRY
ENTER ALL COUNTRIES; THAT LIMITLESS BUDDHALANDS
UNIVERSALLY BE PURIFIED; THAT LIGHT AND MULTITUDES
OF ORNAMENTS ADORN THEM; THAT THEY BE FREE FROM
ALL AFFLICTIONS; THAT THEY ACCOMPLISH THE WAY OF
PURITY; THAT LIMITLESS WISE LIVING BEINGS FILL
THEM; THAT THEY UNIVERSALLY ENTER ALL BUDDHAS'

VAST, GREAT STATES; THAT THEY APPEAR IN ACCORDANCE
WITH THE MINDS OF LIVING BEINGS, CAUSING THEM ALL
TO BE HAPPY--VAST AND GREAT AS THE DHARMA REALM,
ULTIMATE AS EMPTY SPACE, EXHAUSTING THE BOUNDARIES
OF THE FUTURE, THROUGHOUT ALL NUMBERS OF KALPAS,
WITHOUT CEASE.

"HE FURTHER MAKES GREAT VOWS, VOWING TO BE
CONNECTED WITH ALL BODHISATTVAS IN RESOLUTION AND
PRACTICE, WITHOUT RESENTMENT OR JEALOUSY; TO AC-
CUMULATE ALL GOOD ROOTS; TO BE OF ONE AND THE SAME
CONDITION WITH ALL BODHISATTVAS; CONSTANTLY TO AS-
SEMBLE TOGETHER AND NEVER LEAVE EACH OTHER; TO
MAKE APPEAR AT WILL VARIOUS KINDS OF BUDDHA BODIES;
ALWAYS TO BEAR IN HIS OWN MIND THE ABILITY TO KNOW
ALL THUS COME ONES' STATES, THEIR AWESOME POWERS,
AND THEIR WISDOM; TO ATTAIN TO IRREVERSIBILITY AND
SPIRITUAL PENETRATIONS ACCORDING TO INTENT; FREELY
TO ROAM TO ALL WORLDS AND APPEAR IN ALL ASSEMBLIES;
UNIVERSALLY TO ENTER ALL PLACES OF BIRTH; TO ACCOM-
PLISH THE INCONCEIVABLE GREAT VEHICLE; TO CULTI-
VATE THE PRACTICES OF BODHISATTVAS--VAST AND GREAT
AS THE DHARMA REALM, ULTIMATE AS EMPTY SPACE, EX-
HAUSTING THE BOUNDARIES OF THE FUTURE, THROUGHOUT
ALL NUMBERS OF KALPAS, WITHOUT CEASE.

COMMENTARY:

"HE FURTHER MAKES GREAT VOWS/ The Bodhisattva
makes yet another great vow, VOWING THAT ALL COUN-
TRIES ENTER ONE COUNTRY AND THAT ONE COUNTRY ENTER
ALL COUNTRIES/ This is mutual fusion without ob-
struction, mutual identity, and mutual entry. He
vows THAT LIMITLESS BUDDHALANDS UNIVERSALLY BE
PURIFIED and THAT LIGHTS AND MULTITUDES OF ORNA-
MENTS ADORN THEM/ He vows THAT THEY BE FREE FROM
ALL AFFLICTIONS--without the three poisons of
greed, hatred, and stupidity. He vows THAT THEY
ACCOMPLISH THE WAY OF PURITY, that they all dili-
gently cultivate precepts, samadhi, and wisdom.
He vows THAT LIMITLESS WISE LIVING BEINGS FILL
THEM/ All Bodhisattvas have limitless wisdom, and
the living beings fill up the lands. He vows THAT
THEY UNIVERSALLY ENTER ALL BUDDHAS' VAST, GREAT
STATES--that they will all be able to realize the
states which all Buddhas have. He further vows
THAT THEY APPEAR IN ACCORDANCE WITH THE MINDS OF

LIVING BEINGS--that is, that they, constantly in
accord with all the thoughts of living beings, will
manifest all states, thereby *CAUSING THEM TO BE
HAPPY/* His vow to cause all living beings to be-
come happy is *VAST AND GREAT AS THE DHARMA REALM,
ULTIMATE AS EMPTY SPACE, EXHAUSTING THE BOUNDARIES
OF THE FUTURE, THROUGHOUT ALL NUMBERS OF KALPAS,
WITHOUT CEASE.*

   "HE FURTHER MAKES GREAT VOWS/ The Bodhisattva makes another great vow, *VOWING TO BE CONNECTED
WITH ALL BODHISATTVAS IN RESOLUTION AND PRACTICE/*
That is, that he will always cultivate together
with all Bodhisattvas, *WITHOUT RESENTMENT OR JEAL-
OUSY/* While cultivating, they will have mutual regard and support for one another, not mutual dis-
like or resentment. Nor will they have any thoughts
of jealousy. He vows *TO ACCUMULATE ALL GOOD ROOTS*
and *TO BE OF ONE AND THE SAME CONDITION WITH ALL
BODHISATTVAS*--that is, to be the same and identical with all Bodhisattvas. He vows that all Bodhisattvas will *CONSTANTLY ASSEMBLE TOGETHER AND NEV-
ER LEAVE EACH OTHER/* They will never be separated
from each other. He vows *TO MAKE APPEAR AT WILL*--
according to his mind's wishes--*VARIOUS KINDS OF
BUDDHA BODIES; ALWAYS TO BEAR IN HIS OWN MIND THE
ABILITY TO KNOW ALL THUS COME ONES' STATES/* In
his own mind, he himself knows all the states of
all Buddhas, the Thus Come Ones, *THEIR AWESOME
POWERS, AND THEIR WISDOM/* He vows *TO ATTAIN TO
IRREVERSIBILITY* in spiritual penetrations and in
wisdom, *AND* to attain *SPIRITUAL PENETRATIONS AC-
CORDING TO INTENT/* He vows to have spiritual pene-
trations of inexhaustibly multiple transformations
in accordance with his mind's intent. He vows
*FREELY TO ROAM TO ALL WORLDS AND APPEAR IN ALL AS-
SEMBLIES,* to go to all the multitudes of Dharma
Assemblies. He vows *UNIVERSALLY TO ENTER ALL PLA-
CES OF BIRTH,* to go to all places where there are
beings, and *TO ACCOMPLISH THE INCONCEIVABLE GREAT
VEHICLE/* He intends to accomplish all the incon-
ceivable Great Vehicle Dharma-doors. He vows *TO
CULTIVATE THE PRACTICES OF BODHISATTVAS*--the ten
thousand practices--*VAST AND GREAT AS THE DHARMA
REALM, ULTIMATE AS EMPTY SPACE, EXHAUSTING THE
BOUNDARIES OF THE FUTURE, THROUGHOUT ALL NUMBERS
OF KALPAS, WITHOUT CEASE."*

SUTRA:

"HE FURTHER MAKES GREAT VOWS, VOWING TO MOUNT
THE IRREVERSIBLE WHEEL; TO CULTIVATE THE BODHISAT-
TVA PRACTICES; THAT THE KARMAS OF BODY, SPEECH,
AND MIND BE NOT IN VAIN; THAT ANYONE WHO BRIEFLY
SEES HIM WILL THEN CERTAINLY BECOME FIXED IN THE
BUDDHADHARMA; THAT ANYONE WHO BRIEFLY HEARS THE
SOUND OF HIS VOICE WILL THEN OBTAIN JEWEL-LIKE WIS-
DOM; THAT ANYONE WHO HAS JUST BROUGHT FORTH PURE
FAITH WILL THEN FOREVER CUT OFF AFFLICTIONS; TO
OBTAIN A BODY LIKE THE GREAT MEDICINE KING TREE;
TO OBTAIN A BODY LIKE THE AS-YOU-WILL JEWEL; TO
CULTIVATE ALL BODHISATTVAS' PRACTICES--VAST AND
GREAT AS THE DHARMA REALM, ULTIMATE AS EMPTY SPACE,
EXHAUSTING THE BOUNDARIES OF THE FUTURE, THROUGH-
OUT ALL NUMBERS OF KALPAS, WITHOUT CEASE.
    "HE FURTHER MAKES GREAT VOWS, VOWING WITHIN
ALL WORLDS TO ACHIEVE ANUTTARASAMYAKSAMBODHI, WITH-
OUT LEAVING THE PLACE OF THE TIP OF A SINGLE HAIR;
IN EVERY PLACE OF A HAIR-TIP, TO MAKE APPEAR BEING
BORN, LEAVING HOME, GOING TO THE WAY PLACE, ACCOM-
PLISHING PROPER ENLIGHTENMENT, TURNING THE DHARMA
WHEEL, AND ENTERING NIRVANA; TO OBTAIN THE BUD-
DHA'S STATE AND THE POWER OF GREAT WISDOM; IN
THOUGHT AFTER THOUGHT, IN ACCORD WITH THE MINDS OF
LIVING BEINGS, TO DISPLAY THE ACCOMPLISHMENT OF
BUDDHAHOOD, AND CAUSE THEM TO OBTAIN STILL EXTINC-
TION; WITH EVERY SAMBODHI TO KNOW ALL DHARMA REALMS
ARE CHARACTERIZED BY NIRVANA; WITH A SINGLE SOUND
TO SPEAK DHARMA AND CAUSE LIVING BEINGS TO BE DE-
LIGHTED AT HEART; TO DISPLAY ENTRY INTO GREAT NIR-
VANA, YET NOT CUT OFF THE BODHISATTVA CONDUCT; TO
DISPLAY THE GROUND OF GREAT WISDOM, AND THE ESTAB-
LISHMENT OF ALL DHARMAS; WITH THE PENETRATION OF
DHARMA WISDOM, THE PENETRATION OF SPIRITUAL FUL-
FILLMENTS, THE PENETRATION OF ILLUSIONS, AND COM-
FORTABLE CHANGES AND TRANSFORMATIONS, COMPLETELY
TO FILL THE DHARMA REALM--VAST AND GREAT AS THE
DHARMA REALM, ULTIMATE AS EMPTY SPACE, EXHAUSTING
THE BOUNDARIES OF THE FUTURE, THROUGHOUT ALL NUM-
BERS OF KALPAS, WITHOUT CEASE.

COMMENTARY:

    "HE, the Bodhisattva, FURTHER MAKES GREAT
VOWS, VOWING TO MOUNT THE IRREVERSIBLE WHEEL and

TO CULTIVATE THE BODHISATTVA PRACTICES--the Dharma
doors that Bodhisattvas practice. He vows THAT THE
KARMAS OF BODY, SPEECH, AND MIND all be pure, and
that they NOT BE IN VAIN/ None of them can create
bad karma; they have not the slightest bit of of-
fense. He vows THAT ANYONE WHO BRIEFLY SEES HIM
THEN CERTAINLY BECOME FIXED IN THE BUDDHADHARMA/
If someone sees this Bodhisattva for a short interval of time, he or she will certainly plant good
roots and understand the Buddhadharma. He vows
THAT ANYONE WHO BRIEFLY HEARS THE SOUND OF HIS
VOICE WILL THEN OBTAIN JEWEL-LIKE WISDOM/ He or
she attains to wisdom that is like a jewel. Again,
he vows THAT ANYONE WHO HAS JUST BROUGHT FORTH
TRUE FAITH, pure faith, WILL THEN FOREVER CUT OFF
AFFLICTIONS/ Afflictions will be gone. He vows
TO OBTAIN A BODY LIKE THE GREAT MEDICINE KING TREE
which can cure all living beings' illnesses, and
TO OBTAIN A BODY LIKE THE AS-YOU-WILL JEWEL/ He
vows TO CULTIVATE ALL BODHISATTVAS' PRACTICES--the
Dharma-doors that Bodhisattvas cultivate--VAST AND
GREAT AS THE DHARMA REALM, ULTIMATE AS EMPTY SPACE,
EXHAUSTING THE BOUNDARIES OF THE FUTURE, THROUGHOUT
ALL NUMBERS OF KALPAS, WITHOUT CEASE.
    "HE FURTHER MAKES GREAT VOWS, VOWING WITHIN
ALL WORLDS TO ACHIEVE ANUTTARASAMYAKSAMBODHI, the
unsurpassed, right and equal, proper enlightenment,
WITHOUT LEAVING THE PLACE OF THE TIP OF A SINGLE
HAIR/ Right on the tip of a hair he accomplishes
right and equal, proper enlightenment. IN EVERY
PLACE OF A HAIR-TIP, in all the places of hair-
tips, in every single hair-tip, he vows TO MAKE
APPEAR BEING BORN, descending from the Tushita
Heaven, dwelling in the womb, and being born; LEAV-
ING HOME; GOING TO THE WAY PLACE, the Bodhimanda;
ACCOMPLISHING PROPER ENLIGHTENMENT, Right and
Equal, Proper Enlightenment, that is, becoming a
Buddha; TURNING THE DHARMA WHEEL; AND ENTERING
NIRVANA, Parinirvana--the various events of the
Eight Marks of Accomplishing the Way. He vows TO
OBTAIN THE BUDDHA'S STATE AND THE POWER OF GREAT
WISDOM/ He vows IN THOUGHT AFTER THOUGHT, within
each instant of thought, IN ACCORD WITH THE MINDS
OF LIVING BEINGS, TO DISPLAY THE ACCOMPLISHMENT
OF BUDDHAHOOD AND CAUSE THEM TO OBTAIN STILL EX-
TINCTION/ He wants to enable all living beings
also to attain to still extinction.

"He vows WITH EVERY SAMBODHI, that is, using one kind of proper enlightenment, TO KNOW ALL DHARMA REALMS, that is, to know the proper enlightenments of all Buddhas of the Dharma Realms ARE CHARACTERIZED BY NIRVANA/ He vows WITH A SINGLE SOUND TO SPEAK DHARMA AND CAUSE ALL LIVING BEINGS TO BE DELIGHTED AT HEART/ He vows TO DISPLAY ENTRY INTO GREAT NIRVANA, YET NOT CUT OFF THE BODHISATTVA CONDUCT/ He has manifested the entry into great Nirvana, but he still is in the world cultivating the Bodhisattva Way. He vows TO DISPLAY THE GROUND OF GREAT WISDOM/ He displays it for living beings so they can know about the ground of great wisdom. And he vows to display THE ESTABLISHMENT OF ALL DHARMAS of the Buddhas. He vows he will display them WITH THE PENETRATION OF DHARMA WISDOM, THE PENETRATION OF SPIRITUAL FULFILLMENTS, THE PENETRATION OF ILLUSIONS, that is, of changes and transformations, AND COMFORTABLE CHANGES AND TRANSFORMATIONS, COMPLETELY TO FILL THE DHARMA REALM--VAST AND GREAT AS THE DHARMA REALM, ULTIMATE AS EMPTY SPACE, EXHAUSTING THE BOUNDARIES OF THE FUTURE, THROUGHOUT ALL NUMBERS OF KALPAS, WITHOUT CEASE."

SUTRA:

"DISCIPLES OF THE BUDDHA, THE BODHISATTVA DWELLING ON THE GROUND OF HAPPINESS BRINGS FORTH SUCH GREAT VOWS, SUCH GREAT VIGOR, SUCH GREAT EFFICACY. USING THOSE TEN KINDS OF VOW-DOORS AS FOREMOST, HE FULFILLS A MILLION ASAMKHYEYAS OF GREAT VOWS.
"DISCIPLES OF THE BUDDHA, THESE GREAT VOWS THROUGH TEN PROPOSITIONS OF FINALITY COME TO ACCOMPLISHMENT. WHAT ARE THE TEN? THEY ARE: THE END OF THE REALM OF LIVING BEINGS; THE END OF THE WORLD-REALMS; THE END OF THE REALM OF EMPTY SPACE; THE END OF THE DHARMA REALM; THE END OF THE REALM OF NIRVANA; THE END OF THE REALM OF BUDDHAS' APPEARINGS; THE END OF THE REALM OF WISDOM OF THUS COME ONES; THE END OF THE REALM OF WHAT IS THOUGHT BY MIND; THE END OF THE REALM OF STATES ENTERED BY THE BUDDHA'S WISDOM; THE END OF THE REALM OF WORLDLY TURNINGS, DHARMA TURNINGS, AND KNOWLEDGE TURNINGS.

"'IF THE REALM OF LIVING BEINGS IS ENDED, THEN
MY VOWS ARE ENDED. IF WORLD-REALMS, UP TO AND IN-
CLUDING THE REALM OF WORLDLY TURNINGS, DHARMA TURN-
INGS, AND KNOWLEDGE TURNINGS ARE ENDED, THEN MY
VOWS ARE ENDED. BUT, THE REALM OF LIVING BEINGS
UP TO AND INCLUDING THE REALM OF WORLDLY TURNINGS,
DHARMA TURNINGS, AND KNOWLEDGE TURNINGS, CANNOT BE
ENDED. THEREFORE, THESE GREAT VOWS AND GOOD ROOTS
OF MINE HAVE NO END.'

COMMENTARY:

    Vajra Treasury Bodhisattva, afraid the Bodhi-
sattvas might become lax and not pay attention to
him speaking the Dharma of the *Avatamsaka Sutra*, then
said again, "DISCIPLES OF THE BUDDHA, all of you
great Buddhist disciples, do you know? THE BODHI-
SATTVA DWELLING ON THE GROUND OF HAPPINESS certified to this Ground of Happiness from having cultivated all kinds of good roots and accomplished
the position of the Paramitas for crossing to the
other shore. He at all times produces great happiness and BRINGS FORTH SUCH GREAT VOWS/ He makes
the various kinds of great vows that were previously described. He brings forth SUCH GREAT VIGOR--
courageous vigor. The Dharma-doors living beings
do not dare to cultivate, he goes and cultivates.
He dares to do what living beings do not dare to
do. He brings forth SUCH GREAT EFFICACY--great
activity and great functioning such as was previously described. USING THOSE TEN KINDS OF VOW-
DOORS AS FOREMOST, HE FULFILLS A MILLION ASAMKHYE-
YAS OF GREAT VOWS/ The other great vows all come
out of those great vows, and, because those great
vows are fulfilled, all the limitlessly many remaining great vows are fulfilled, too.
    "DISCIPLES OF THE BUDDHA," Vajra Treasury Bodhi-
sattva said again, "THESE GREAT VOWS THROUGH TEN
PROPOSITIONS OF FINALITY COME TO ACCOMPLISHMENT"/
He said that great vows made by the Bodhisattva
who certifies to the Ground of Happiness are
brought to success by ten kinds of disappearances
of realms.
    "WHAT ARE THE TEN? What are the ten kinds of
disappearances? THEY ARE THE END OF THE REALM OF
LIVING BEINGS/ All living beings disappear. THE

END OF WORLD-REALMS/ World-realms, as well, all
disappear. THE END OF THE REALM OF EMPTY SPACE/
Make the realm of empty space disappear, too. THE
END OF THE DHARMA REALM/ Basically, the Dharma
Realm is inexhaustible. Still, take it as non-
existent: that is, no realm of living beings, no
world-realm, no realm of empty space, no Dharma
Realm. THE END OF THE REALM OF NIRVANA/ It's
also gone. THE END OF THE BUDDHAS' APPEARINGS/
In addition, no Buddhas appear in the world. THE
END OF THE REALM OF THE WISDOM OF THE THUS COME
ONES/ The Thus Come Ones' wisdom also does not
exist. THE END OF THE REALM OF WHAT IS THOUGHT BY
MIND/ What is climbed upon and thought about in
the mind also ceases to exist. THE END OF THE
REALM OF STATES ENTERED BY THE BUDDHA'S WISDOM/
The states that the Buddha's wisdom understands,
realizes, and comprehends--all of those states--
vanish, too. THE END OF THE REALMS OF WORLDLY
TURNINGS, DHARMA TURNINGS, AND KNOWLEDGE TURNINGS/
Everything worldly can turn and move. Dharma can
also turn, and knowledge can turn as well. Those
kinds of realms all disappear. Basically, all of
those realms cannot be non-existent, but suppose
we say they cease to exist.

      "So the Bodhisattva says, 'IF THE REALM OF
LIVING BEINGS IS ENDED, THEN MY VOWS ARE ENDED/
Should it come to be possible for the realm of
living beings to cease to exist, then and only
then can these great vows that I have made cease
to exist. If the realm of living beings cannot
cease to exist, then my vows will always remain.
IF WORLD-REALMS UP TO AND INCLUDING THE REALM OF
WORLDLY TURNINGS, DHARMA TURNINGS, AND KNOWLEDGE
TURNINGS ARE ENDED, THEN MY VOWS ARE ENDED/ All
worlds turn, Dharma turns, and knowledge turns,
as well. If all those realms become non-existent
then the vows I have made will cease to exist.
BUT THE REALM OF LIVING BEINGS CANNOT BE ENDED/
However, you should be aware that the realm of
living beings cannot end; and, therefore, my vows
cannot come to an end. World-realms can't come to
an end, so my vows can't end. The Dharma Realm
can't end, so my vows can't end. The realm of
Nirvana can't end, so my vows can't end. The
realm of the states of wisdom of Thus Come Ones
also will not end, and so my vows will eternally

remain. Were the realm of what is thought in the
mind to cease to exist... However, it cannot cease
to exist, and so, too, my vows will never cease to
exist. Were the realm of the states entered by
the Buddha's wisdom to cease to exist... However,
it cannot go out of existence. Therefore, my vows
too, will exist forever. Should worldly turnings,
Dharma turnings, and knowledge turnings all become
non-existent... However, they cannot go out of
existence. Therefore, my vows, too, will always
remain. *UP TO AND INCLUDING THE REALM OF WORLDLY
TURNINGS, DHARMA TURNINGS, AND KNOWLEDGE TURNINGS
CANNOT BE ENDED. THEREFORE, THESE GREAT VOWS AND
GOOD ROOTS OF MINE HAVE NO END/* "Therefore, the
great vows that I have made and the good roots that
I have cultivated are also inexhaustible.'"

SUTRA:

"*DISCIPLES OF THE BUDDHA, AFTER THE BODHISAT-
TVA HAS MADE SUCH GREAT VOWS, HE THEN OBTAINS A
BENEFICIENT MIND, A COMPLIANT MIND, AN ACCORDANT
MIND, A QUIET MIND, A SUBDUED MIND, A STILL AND
EXTINCT MIND, A HUMBLE MIND, A MOISTENED MIND, AN
UNMOVING MIND, A NON-TURBID MIND.*
"*HE BECOMES ONE OF PURE FAITH AND HAS THE OP-
ERATIVE USE OF FAITH. HE CAN BELIEVE IN THE THUS
COME ONE'S ORIGINAL PRACTICES WHICH ARE ENTERED:
BELIEVING IN THE ACCOMPLISHMENT OF ALL THE PARA-
MITAS; BELIEVING IN THE ENTRY TO ALL THE SUPREME
GROUNDS; BELIEVING IN THE ACCOMPLISHMENT OF THE
POWERS; BELIEVING IN THE PERFECTION OF THE FEAR-
LESSNESSES; BELIEVING IN THE GROWTH OF THE INDES-
TRUCTIBLE UNCOMMON BUDDHA DHARMAS; BELIEVING IN
THE INCONCEIVABLE BUDDHA DHARMAS; BELIEVING IN
THE PRODUCTION OF THE BUDDHA'S STATES WHICH ARE
NOT TO EITHER SIDE OF MIDDLE; BELIEVING IN THE EN-
TRY TO THE LIMITLESS STATES OF A THUS COME ONE;
BELIEVING IN THE ACCOMPLISHMENT OF THE FRUIT. TO
MENTION THE ESSENTIAL, IT IS BECAUSE HE BELIEVES
IN ALL BODHISATTVAS' PRACTICES UP TO AND INCLUD-
ING THE DESCRIPTION OF ALL POWERS OF THE THUS COME
ONE'S WISDOM GROUND.*

COMMENTARY:

"DISCIPLES OF THE BUDDHA"/ Vajra Treasury
Bodhisattva again says, "All of you disciples of
the Buddha, do you know? AFTER THE BODHISATTVA
HAS MADE SUCH GREAT VOWS, HE THEN OBTAINS A BENE-
FICIENT MIND"/ Before having made such great vows,
he'd wanted to benefit living beings but couldn't
manage to decide to do so. He wanted to be of
some advantage to living beings, but could never
find a way. But, since he has these vows to aid
him, his beneficient mind comes forth, too. He
also obtains "A COMPLIANT MIND"/ Before he made
those vows, he was like most living beings: stubborn and not easy to tame and subdue--really ob-
stinate. But, since he has made those vows,
through those vows' aid, his mind is compliant,
and he has great patience and no afflictions.
"He obtains AN ACCORDANT MIND"/ Before he had
brought forth the thought for Bodhi or had the intention to cultivate the Bodhisattva Way, this
person was always trying to get people to go along
with him, to follow him. He was unwilling to obey
other people's instructions. That is, he was:

> Able neither to lead,
> Nor to take orders.

On the one hand, he was incapable of issuing orders commanding people to do something, and yet
on the other hand, he wouldn't follow the instructions of other people. He wouldn't take orders
from anyone. When someone told him to do something, he wouldn't do it. But, since having made
the vows, he had resolved to forever accord with
living beings. He has no ego: 'Who is me? I am
who? You ask me? I ask who?' He accords with
living beings and has no self. Therefore, because
he has made those vows, he just accords, and he
doesn't tell people to accord with him.
"He obtains A QUIET MIND"/ This quietness is
constantly having no afflictions and being at
peace. This quiet mind is being happy. Quietness
does not mean, "I like it quiet. You should all
go along with me and be quiet." It's not that
way. It means that right in the middle of a place
whose atmosphere is not quiet, if you can be quiet,
as the saying goes:

> The middle of a noisy marketplace
> Is good for cultivation.

If you can be quiet in a noisy marketplace, then that's real *gung fu*. If you go off someplace where there isn't a soul, saying that you want peace and quiet, once you've run off to some solitary mountain forest, what ends up happening? You quarrel with yourself. You exhale one breath of air and say, "Hey, you're not being quiet!" You inhale the next breath of air and say, "Hey, *you're* not being quiet!" And you get afflicted. This quietness means that if you are someone who can apply their skill, then any place will be quiet. If you are someone who is unable to apply his or her skill, then even if you try to find a quiet place, you won't be able to. Why not? It's because you haven't made vows. If you had made vows, then what was not quiet would be quiet. That's the quiet mind.

"He obtains *A SUBDUED MIND*"/ In the Saha world, all the living beings are stubborn, difficult to tame, and difficult to subdue. Not to speak of taming and subduing other people, they can't even tame and subdue themselves. You sit there and without rhyme or reason become afflicted, get angry.

> The eyes and ears don't hit it off.

The eyes say the nose is too high, and the nose says the eyes are too low. The eyes tell the mouth, "You can only eat, you can't see," and the tongue tells it, "You can only eat, you can't taste." The ears say, "You eyes can see, but you can't hear. I can hear." The nose tells the ears, "You can only hear, but you can't smell the way I can." Is this trouble or not? The eyes and the nose don't get along, and the nose tells the mouth, "You can only eat candy, but you can't smell its odor." You can't get tamed and subdued; you can't tame and subdue your mind.

"He obtains *A STILL AND EXTINCT MIND*"/ This mind is still and extinct:

> All dharmas in their origin of
>   themselves,
> Are characterized by still extinction.

If you can calm your mind down to still extinction then that is good. He obtains A HUMBLE MIND/ Before he made vows, he was very haughty and arrogant. After making the vows, he obtained a humble mind.

"He obtains A MOISTENED MIND/ In his mind it is never dry or parched. It is always as if moistened by water. He obtains AN UNMOVING MIND/ His mind also does not move.

> When thought moves,
> The thousand matters exist;
> When thought stops,
> The myriad matters vanish.

If you do not move your mind, then your basic wisdom manifests. He obtains A NON-TURBID MIND/ In his mind there are no defiled thoughts.
"HE BECOMES ONE OF PURE FAITH/ Once he has obtained those various kinds of minds, then he becomes one who can purely believe, AND HAS THE OPERATIVE USE OF FAITH. HE HAS FAITH IN THE THUS COME ONES' ORIGINAL PRACTICES/ He can believe in the doors of practice which the Buddhas originally cultivated, WHICH ARE ENTERED/ What is entered? BELIEVING IN THE ACCOMPLISHMENT OF ALL THE PARAMITAS/ He believes and so can accomplish ten kinds of paramitas. BELIEVING IN THE ENTRY TO ALL SUPREME GROUNDS/ Being able to believe, he is then able to enter the Ten Grounds, these most supreme ground-positions. BELIEVING IN THE ACCOMPLISHMENT OF THE POWERS/ Believing, he can accomplish the powers of spiritual penetrations. BELIEVING IN THE PERFECTION OF THE FEARLESSNESSES/ With this attitude of faith, he then can perfect the fearlessnesses. As it is said:

> Faith is the source of the Way,
> The mother of merit and virtue,
> That nurtures all good dharmas.

BELIEVING IN THE GROWTH OF THE INDESTRUCTIBLE, UNCOMMON BUDDHA DHARMAS/ Believing, he can make grow the indestructible Dharmas Special to a Buddha.
"BELIEVING IN THE INCONCEIVABLE BUDDHA DHARMAS. BELIEVING IN THE PRODUCTION OF THE BUDDHA'S STATES WHICH ARE NOT TO EITHER SIDE OF MIDDLE/

Believing, he can produce the states of a Buddha, which are such that they have nothing to the side of middle. The Buddha's states are all of the Middle Way, with no extremes. They do not fall to either side. What is the Middle? The Middle Way is:

> Not falling into emptiness,
> Not falling into existence.

BELIEVING IN ACCORDING ENTRY TO THE LIMITLESS STATES OF A THUS COME ONE/ Believing, he can accord with and enter the limitless states of a Buddha *BELIEVING IN THE ACCOMPLISHMENT OF THE FRUIT/* Believing, he can accomplish all of the fruit-positions. *TO MENTION THE ESSENTIAL, IT IS BECAUSE HE BELIEVES IN ALL THE BODHISATTVA'S PRACTICES UP TO AND INCLUDING THE DESCRIPTION OF ALL POWERS OF THE THUS COME ONE'S WISDOM GROUND."*

SUTRA:

"*DISCIPLES OF THE BUDDHA, THIS BODHISATTVA FURTHER MAKES THE FOLLOWING REFLECTIONS: 'ALL BUDDHAS' POWER PROPER DHARMAS ARE SO PROFOUND, SO QUIET, SO STILL AND EXTINCT, SO EMPTY, SO MARKLESS SO WISHLESS, SO UNDEFILED, SO LIMITLESS, SO VAST AND GREAT, WHILE ORDINARY BEINGS IN THEIR MINDS FALL INTO DEVIANT VIEWS. THEY ARE COVERED BY THE FILM OF IGNORANCE. THEY ERECT THE BANNER OF PRIDE AND ARROGANCE. THEY ENTER INTO THE NET OF THIRSTY LOVE, AND COURSE IN THE DENSE FOREST OF FLATTERY AND DECEIT, UNABLE TO EXTRICATE THEMSELVES. THEIR MINDS ARE CONJOINED WITH STINGINESS AND JEALOUSY WHICH THEY NEVER ABANDON. THEY CONSTANTLY CREATE THE CAUSAL CONDITIONS FOR UNDERGOING BIRTH IN THE DESTINIES. WITH GREED, HATRED, AND STUPIDITY, THE ACCUMULATE ALL KARMA, WHICH DAY AND NIGHT INCREASES AND GROWS. WITH THE WIND OF RESENTMENT THEY FAN THE FIRE OF MIND-CONSCIOUSNESS, WHOSE BLAZE NEVER CEASES. ALL OF THE KARMA THEY CREATE IS CONJOINED WITH INVERSION. IN THE FLOW OF DESIRE, THE FLOW OF EXISTENCE, THE FLOW OF IGNORANCE, AND THE FLOW OF VIEWS, THE SEEDS OF MIND-CONSCIOUSNESS CONTINUALLY ARISE. WITHIN THE FIELD OF THE THREE REALMS THE SPROUTS OF SUFFERING ARE REPEATEDLY PRODUCED.'*

COMMENTARY:

"*DISCIPLES OF THE BUDDHA*"/ Vajra Treasury
Bodhisattva again called out, "All of you disci-
ples of the Buddha, do you know or not that *THIS
BODHISATTVA* who certifies to the Ground of Happi-
ness *FURTHER MAKES THE FOLLOWING REFLECTIONS*/ He
also has these thoughts: '*ALL BUDDHAS' PROPER
DHARMAS*--all Buddhas' Proper Dharma Eye Treasuries
--*ARE SO PROFOUND*'/ He says they are:

> So deep the bottom can't be seen,
> Just like the great sea.

'They are *SO QUIET*/ The basic substance of their
Dharmas is tranquil and quiet, without any move-
ment. They are *SO STILL AND EXTINCT*, without shape
or characteristics. *SO EMPTY*/ They are *SO MARK-
LESS*/ They also have no appearance. They are *SO
WISHLESS*/ Everything is empty. They are *SO UNDE-
FILED*/ They are free of defiled attachments. The
Proper Dharmas spoken by all Buddhas are *SO LIMIT-
LESS*/ They also have no calculable measure, and
they are *SO VAST AND GREAT*.'
    "'*WHILE ORDINARY BEINGS IN THEIR MINDS FALL
INTO DEVIANT VIEWS*/ All ordinary living beings
are very lazy. They all have deviant knowledge
and deviant views, and do not cultivate. *THEY ARE
COVERED BY THE FILM OF IGNORANCE*/ Ignorance covers
them over like clouds in the sky. *THEY ERECT THE
BANNER OF PRIDE AND ARROGANCE*/ They always think
of themselves as very great, and wear their pride,
arrogance, and conceit like a banner. *THEY ENTER
INTO THE NET OF THIRSTY LOVE*/ They enter into the
net of love--love which is like being very hungry
and thirsty and from which they never get out. *AND
THEY COURSE IN THE DENSE FOREST OF FLATTERY AND DE-
CEIT, UNABLE TO EXTRICATE THEMSELVES*/ They are
unable to get themselves out of the net of love
and desire and the dense forest of flattery and
deceit. *THEIR MINDS ARE CONJOINED WITH STINGINESS
AND JEALOUSY WHICH THEY NEVER ABANDON*.'
    "'*THEY CONSTANTLY CREATE THE CAUSAL CONDITIONS
FOR UNDERGOING BIRTH IN THE DESTINIES*/ They keep
being born and dying, dying and being reborn, in
the four evil destinies--asuras, hell-beings, hungry ghosts, and animals--and keep creating the

causal conditions for being reborn there again.
*WITH GREED, HATRED, AND STUPIDITY, THEY ACCUMULATE
ALL KARMA'"/* Ignorance, that is, stupidity, is pro-
duced, and then, because they are stupid, they
create all sorts of karma; and, so it says, "They
accumulate all karma," *"'WHICH DAY AND NIGHT IN-
CREASES AND GROWS. WITH THE WIND OF RESENTMENT,
THEY FAN THE FIRE OF MIND-CONSCIOUSNESS/* They
blow within mind consciousness, that kind of fire,
WHOSE BLAZE NEVER CEASES/ They feel it's blazing
hot. *ALL OF THE KARMA THEY CREATE IS CONJOINED
WITH INVERSION/* Everything they do is interactive
with upside-downness. *IN THE FLOW OF DESIRE, THE
FLOW OF EXISTENCE, THE FLOW OF IGNORANCE, AND THE
FLOW OF VIEWS, THE SEEDS OF MIND-CONSCIOUSNESS
CONTINUALLY ARISE/* Their karma is interactive
with the flow of love and desire. Within the
Three Realms—the Desire Realm, the Form Realm,
and the Formless Realm—they undergo the flow of
existence. They flow along with ignorance or else
they flow along with views. The seeds of mind-
consciousness continually and uninterruptedly come
forth. *WITHIN THE FIELD OF THE THREE REALMS THE
SPROUTS OF SUFFERING ARE REPEATEDLY PRODUCED.'"*

SUTRA:

    *"'THAT IS, NAME AND FORM ARISE TOGETHER AND
DO NOT SEPARATE. BECAUSE NAME AND FORM INCREASE,
THE ASSEMBLAGE OF THE SIX PLACES ARISES. AMIDST
THEIR JUNCTURES, CONTACT ARISES: BECAUSE OF CON-
TACT, FEELING ARISES. BECAUSE OF FEELING, LOVE
ARISES. LOVE INCREASES, THEREFORE GRASPING ARISES.
GRASPING INCREASES, THEREFORE EXISTENCE ARISES.
BECAUSE EXISTENCE ARISES, BIRTH, OLD AGE, ANXIETY,
SORROW, SUFFERING, AND VEXATION COME TO EXIST. SUCH
LIVING BEINGS AS THOSE PRODUCE AND INCREASE THE
MASS OF SUFFERING. WITHIN IT, ALL IS EMPTY: FREE
OF SELF AND WHAT BELONGS TO SELF, DEVOID OF KNOWING
AND AWARENESS, WITH NO DOER AND NO RECEIVER, LIKE
GRASS AND WOOD, LIKE ROCKS AND WALLS, AND ALSO
LIKE REFLECTIONS. STILL, LIVING BEINGS ARE UN-
AWARE AND DO NOT KNOW.' THE BODHISATTVA SEES ALL
LIVING BEINGS WITHIN THIS MASS OF SUFFERING, UNABLE
TO GET OUT. THEREFORE, HE IMMEDIATELY BRINGS FORTH
WISDOM OF GREAT COMPASSION AND MAKES THE FOLLOWING*

REFLECTIONS: 'ALL THESE LIVING BEINGS I SHOULD
RESCUE AND SAVE AND SET IN THE PLACE OF ULTIMATE
PEACE AND JOY.'   THEREFORE, HE IMMEDIATELY BRINGS
FORTH BRIGHT WISDOM OF GREAT KINDNESS."

COMMENTARY:

"'THAT IS, NAME AND FORM ARISE TOGETHER'"/
This discusses the Twelve Links of Causal Conditions, the first of which is ignorance. Because
of the upside-downness of ignorance, there arise
activities--the activities of love and desire.
Once there are activities, the seeds of mind-consciousness are planted within the field of the Three
Realms, and the sprouts of suffering are produced.
These sprouts of suffering are the name and form
under discussion. Once there is name and form,
one says, "Perhaps this is a boy." "Perhaps this
is a girl." Once there is form, a name arises together with it and they "DO NOT SEPARATE. BECAUSE
NAME AND FORM INCREASE, THE ASSEMBLAGE OF THE SIX
PLACES ARISES/ The assemblage of the six places
is the arisal of the six faculties of eyes, ears,
nose, tongue, body, and mind. They are also called
the six entrances, as well as the six places, and
their assemblage means their collectivity. AMIDST
THEIR JUNCTURES, CONTACT ARISES/ In the midst of
this, the junctures of the six entrances within
the mother's womb, the dust-objects of the sense
of touch is produced. BECAUSE OF CONTACT, FEELING
ARISES/ Since there are objects of touch, there
then arises feeling, receptivity. BECAUSE OF FEEL-
ING, LOVE ARISES/ Due to the arisal of receptivity, from that feeling there arises love; love and
desire arise. LOVE INCREASES, THEREFORE GRASPING
ARISES/ Because grasping increases and grows,
existence comes about. BECAUSE EXISTENCE ARISES,
BIRTH, OLD AGE, ANXIETY, SORROW, SUFFERING, AND
VEXATION COME TO EXIST/ Because existence increases, therefore there arises birth. Once there
is birth, there is death; and all the rest come
along with it.
    "'SUCH LIVING BEINGS AS THOSE PRODUCE AND IN-
CREASE THE MASS OF SUFFERING. WITHIN IT, ALL IS
EMPTY/ However, although these causal conditions
are explained as suffering, nonetheless you should

understand that it is all empty and all extin-
guished. *FREE OF SELF AND WHAT BELONGS TO SELF.
DEVOID OF KNOWING AND AWARENESS/* Within these
twelve causal conditions, there basically is no
knowing and no awareness. *WITH NO DOER AND NO RE-
CEIVER, LIKE GRASS AND WOOD, LIKE, ROCKS AND WALLS/*
Like insentient things such as grass and wood,
rocks and walls, *AND ALSO LIKE REFLECTIONS/* That
is the way things really are. If you understand,
they are like reflections. *STILL LIVING BEINGS
ARE UNAWARE AND DO NOT KNOW/* They have noT become
enlightened, and they do not know that basically
all of this is empty.'
  "THE BODHISATTVA SEES ALL LIVING BEINGS bob-
bing up and down within the twelve causal condi-
tions, *WITHIN THIS MASS OF SUFFERING, UNABLE TO
GET OUT/* They never wake up; they are always
bound up in the net of love, desire, and craving.
*THEREFORE, HE IMMEDIATELY BRINGS FORTH WISDOM OF
GREAT COMPASSION AND MAKES THE FOLLOWING REFLEC-
TIONS: 'ALL THESE LIVING BEINGS I SHOULD RESCUE
AND SAVE AND SET IN THE PLACE OF ULTIMATE PEACE
AND JOY/* I should settle them in the place where
they will obtain the utmost, ultimate peace and
happiness.' *THEREFORE HE IMMEDIATELY BRINGS FORTH
BRIGHT WISDOM OF GREAT KINDNESS/* For that reason
he then gives rise to a mind of great kindness
and brings forth bright wisdom."

SUTRA:

  *"DISCIPLES OF THE BUDDHA, THE BODHISATTVA MA-
HATSATTVA ACCORDS WITH SUCH GREAT COMPASSION AND
GREAT KINDNESS. USING DEEP, PROFOUND THOUGHT, AT
THE TIME OF DWELLING ON THE FIRST GROUND, HE GIVES
AWAY ALL OBJECTS WITHOUT GRUDGING OR STINGINESS.
SEEKING THE BUDDHA'S GREAT WISDOM, HE CULTIVATES
GREAT RENUNCIATION. WHATEVER HE POSSESSES, HE IS
ABLE TO GIVE AWAY COMPLETELY. THAT IS, SUCH OB-
JECTS AS WEALTH AND GRANARIES, GOLD, SILVER, MANI,
PEARLS, LAPIS LAZULI, SHELLS, JADE, AND CORAL;
JEWELLED ORNAMENTAL ARTICLES TO DECORATE THE BODY;
ELEPHANTS, HORSES, CHARIOTS AND CONVEYANCES; SER-
VANTS AND CITIZENS; CITIES, TOWNS, AND VILLAGES;
PARKS, GROVES, PAVILLIONS WITH VISTAS; WIVES, CON-
CUBINES, SONS, DAUGHTERS; THE INNER AND OUTER RETI-*

NUES, AND ALL REMAINING ENJOYABLE POSSESSIONS; HIS
HEAD, EYES, HANDS, AND FEET; HIS BLOOD, FLESH,
MARROW AND ALL THE PARTS OF HIS BODY, BEGRUDGING
NONE OF THEM, IN ORDER TO SEEK ALL BUDDHAS' VAST,
GREAT WISDOM. THAT IS CALLED THE BODHISATTVA WHO
DWELLS UPON THE FIRST GROUND'S ACCOMPLISHMENT OF
GREAT RENUNCIATION

COMMENTARY:

Vajra Treasary Bodhisattva, since he fears
the Bodhisattvas are always in samadhi and not pay-
ing attention to the Dharma he is speaking, at
that time decides to call out, "All of you disciples of the Buddha, do you know? THE BODHISATTVA
MAHASATTVA ACCORDS WITH SUCH GREAT COMPASSION AND
GREAT KINDNESS/ The great Bodhisattva who cultivates the Bodhisattva Way and accumulates all kinds
of good roots always accords with that kind of
great compassion which can pluck out living beings'
sufferings, and great kindness which can bestow
happiness upon living beings. USING DEEP, PRO-
FOUND THOUGHT, AT THE TIME OF DWELLING ON THE FIRST
GROUND/ He uses thought so very deep and profound
that it cannot be fathomed, at the time of dwelling on the First Ground, and HE GIVES AWAY ALL
OBJECTS, WITHOUT GRUDGING OR STINGINESS/ Upon
certifying to the attainment of this First Ground,
the Ground of Happiness, there are no objects
which he is unable to renounce. There is no object, however valuable, with which he is unable
to part, or which he begrudges giving away to
others. He would never be that way. He has no
greed or stinginess, no inability to part with
things. SEEKING THE BUDDHA'S GREAT WISDOM, HE
CULTIVATES GREAT RENUNCIATION/ The Buddha has ultimate, great wisdom, and the Bodhisattva seeks
the ultimate wisdom of a Buddha. So, he cultivates
this kind of giving.
"WHATEVER HE POSSESSES HE IS ABLE TO GIVE
AWAY COMPLETELY/ He can give all the inner wealth
and outer wealth he may posses away to living beings. THAT IS, SUCH OBJECTS AS WEALTH AND GRA-
NARIES/ He can renounce all kinds of articles,
such as all his wealth, his inner and outer wealth
--along with all his granaries, all of his GOLD,

and all his SILVER, his MANI jewels, his precious
PEARLS, his precious LAPIS LAZULI, his precious
SHELLS, his precious JADE, his precious CORAL, and
all the rest. He can give JEWELLED ORNAMENTAL
ELEPHANTS, all his HORSES, all his CHARIOTS AND
CONVEYANCES." Nowadays he could give all his cars
and boats, along with his airplanes. "He can re-
nounce SERVANTS, or those who work for him, AND
CITIZENS of his country. He can give up CITIES,
TOWNS, AND VILLAGES, or his PARKS and his GROVES,
PAVILLIONS WITH VISTAS/ He can give his pavil-
lions, towers--all those things which afford fine
views. He can renounce his WIVES, CONCUBINES,
SONS, AND DAUGHTERS/ He can give up his INNER AND
OUTER RETINUES, that is, both close and distant
relatives, AND ALL REMAINING ENJOYABLE POSSESSIONS/
He can also give HIS HEAD, or else his EYES, or
his HANDS AND FEET, or HIS BLOOD, FLESH, MARROW,
AND ALL THE PARTS OF HIS BODY, including all the
objects inside his body and all objects external
to the body, BEGRUDGING NONE OF THEM/ There are
none of these which he is unable to give up, IN
ORDER TO SEEK ALL BUDDHAS' VAST, GREAT WISDOM/ He
can do this because he wants to seek all the Buddhas' vast, great wisdom. THAT IS CALLED THE BO-
DHISATTVA WHO DWELLS UPON THE FIRST GROUND'S AC-
COMPLISHMENT OF GREAT RENUNCIATION/ This is called
the kind of great renunciation, the accomplishment of the merit and virtue of all good roots, of
the Bodhisattva who dwells upon this Ground of
Happiness."

SUTRA:

    "DISCIPLES OF THE BUDDHA, THE BODHISATTVA,
USING THIS KIND OF COMPASSIONATE MIND OF GREAT RE-
NUNCIATION, WISHING TO RESCUE AND PROTECT ALL LIV-
ING BEINGS, FURTHER ENLARGES THE SCOPE OF HIS
SEARCH FOR ALL WORLDLY AND WORLD-TRANSCENDING BENE-
FICIAL MATTERS, NEVER BEING TIRED OR WEARY. THERE-
FORE, HE IMMEDIATELY ATTAINS TO THE ACCOMPLISHMENT
OF AN UNTIRING, UNWEARIED MIND. ONCE HE HAS OB-
TAINED AN UNTIRING, UNWEARIED MIND, CONCERNING ALL
SUTRAS AND SHASTRAS, HIS MIND IS NOT NERVOUS OR
AFRAID. BECAUSE HE IS NOT NERVOUS OR AFRAID, HE
IMMEDIATELY ATTAINS TO THE ACCOMPLISHMENT OF THE

WISDOM OF ALL SUTRAS AND SHASTRAS. ONCE HE HAS
ACQUIRED THAT WISDOM, HE IS SKILLED AT ESTIMATING
WHAT SHOULD BE DONE AND WHAT SHOULD NOT BE DONE.
TOWARDS ALL SUPERIOR, AVERAGE, AND INFERIOR LIVING
BEINGS, AS IS APPROPRIATE AND ACCORDING TO HIS
STRENGTH, IN ACCORD WITH WHAT THEY LIKE, HE ACTS
IN THAT WAY. THEREFORE, THIS BODHISATTVA ATTAINS
TO THE ACCOMPLISHMENT OF WORLDLY WISDOM. ONCE HE
HAS ACCOMPLISHED WORLDLY WISDOM, HE KNOWS THE TIMES
AND HE KNOWS THE CAPACITIES, AND, USING THE ADORN-
MENTS OF REPENTANCE AND REFORM, HE DILIGENTLY CUL-
TIVATES THE PATH OF BENEFITTING SELF WHILE BENE-
FITTING OTHERS. THEREFORE, HE ACCOMPLISHES THE
ADORNMENTS OF REPENTANCE AND REFORM. IN THE MIDST
OF THESE PRACTICES, HE DILIGENTLY CULTIVATES ES-
CAPE, WITHOUT RETREATING OR DEFLECTING, AND ACCOMP-
LISHES THE POWER OF SOLIDITY. ONCE HE HAS ACQUIRED
THE POWER OF SOLIDITY, HE DILIGENTLY MAKES OFFER-
INGS TO ALL BUDDHAS. WITH REGARD TO THE BUDDHAS'
TEACHING DHARMAS, HE IS ABLE THUS TO SPEAK AND
PRACTICE.

COMMENTARY:

"DISCIPLES OF THE BUDDHA, THE BODHISATTVA on
the Ground of Happiness, USING THIS KIND OF COM-
PASSIONATE MIND OF GREAT RENUNCIATION, WISHING TO
RESCUE AND PROTECT ALL LIVING BEINGS, FURTHER EN-
LARGES THE SCOPE OF HIS SEARCH"/ Vajra Treasury
Bodhisattva again calls out, "All of you Buddhist
disciples, the Bodhisattva uses compassionate giving and loving protection towards all living beings. After practicing giving, he has the further
intention of deepening his search FOR ALL WORLDLY
AND WORLD-TRANSCENDING BENEFICIAL MATTERS/ He
looks for each and every beneficial means to help
living beings, as well as being concerned about
how to benefit living beings on the world-transcending plane. NEVER BEING TIRED OR WEARY, he
constantly cultivates Bodhisattva conduct, and at
no time does he retreat saying, 'I've cultivated
enough. I'm tired of it. I'm weary.' THEREFORE,
HE IMMEDIATELY ATTAINS TO THE ACCOMPLISHMENT OF AN
UNTIRING, UNWEARIED MIND/ Right then he accomplishes an unflagging attitude, and at no time
would he say he didn't want to cultivate the Bodhisattva Way.

"ONCE HE HAS OBTAINED UN UNTIRING, UNWEARIED
MIND, CONCERNING ALL SUTRAS AND SHASTRAS HIS MIND
IS NOT NERVOUS OR AFRAID/ After he has perfected
this attitude of never being tired or weary, he
studies all the Sutras, Vinaya, and Shastras which
the Buddhas have spoken. He would never say, 'Oh,
this Sutra is so long, so difficult to understand!'
or, 'There's too much to this Shastra, and it's
not easy to investigate.' BECAUSE HE IS NOT NER-
VOUS OR AFRAID, HE IMMEDIATELY ATTAINS TO THE AC-
COMPLISHMENT OF THE WISDOM OF ALL SUTRAS AND SHAS-
TRAS/ Because he is not afraid that the Buddhadharma, being like the great sea, is not easy to
cultivate, he gains wisdom from the Sutras and
Shastras. As soon as they pass by his eyes, he
understands all Buddhadharmas, illumines the real
mark of all dharmas. He:

> Deeply enters the Sutra store,
> And has wisdom like the sea.

"ONCE HE HAS ACQUIRED THAT WISDOM, HE IS
SKILLED AT ESTIMATING/ He is good at evaluating,
and figuring out WHAT SHOULD BE DONE AND WHAT
SHOULD NOT BE DONE/ He can distinguish all things
that should be done from all the things that should
not be done. TOWARDS ALL SUPERIOR, AVERAGE, AND
INFERIOR LIVING BEINGS, AS IS APPROPRIATE AND AC-
CORDING TO HIS STRENGTH, HE ACTS IN THAT WAY/ Towards living beings with superior good roots, living beings with average faculties and average wisdom, and towards the most stupid kinds of living
beings he appears as needed.

> Whatever body is needed to cross
> them over,
> He manifests that kind of body and
> speaks Dharma for them.

In accordance with what living beings like and with
what they understand, he cultivates in that way to
teach and transform them. THEREFORE, THIS BODHI-
SATTVA ATTAINS TO THE ACCOMPLISHMENT OF WORLDLY
WISDOM.
"ONCE HE HAS ACCOMPLISHED WORLDLY WISDOM, HE
KNOWS THE TIMES AND HE KNOWS THE CAPACITIES/ He
knows for any time whether a given living being's

opportunities have matured or not. He knows which
living beings should be saved and which living beings are not due to be saved, which is to know
their capacities. AND, USING THE ADORNMENTS OF
REPENTANCE AND REFORM, HE DILIGENTLY CULTIVATES/
He uses his cultivation of repentance and reform
to adorn his own blessings and virtue. He is dili-
gent in his cultivation of blessings and wisdom,
as well. HE DILIGENTLY CULTIVATES THE PATH OF
BENEFITTING SELF WHILE BENEFITTING OTHERS/ The
path he cultivates is that of benefitting himself
and benefitting others, and he is able to benefit
and aid living beings. THEREFORE, HE ACCOMPLISHES
THE ADORNMENTS OF REPENTANCE AND REFORM, and the
adornments of merit and virtue.
    "IN THE MIDST OF THESE PRACTICES, within these
doors of cultivation, HE DILIGENTLY CULTIVATES ES-
CAPE from the Three Realms, WITHOUT RETREATING OR
DEFLECTING/ He does not retreat from Anuttarasam-
yaksambodhi, AND ACCOMPLISHES THE POWER OF SOLID-
ITY/_ In cultivation, he has a mind of non-retreat.
ONCE HE HAS ACQUIRED THE POWER OF SOLIDITY, HE
DILIGENTLY MAKES OFFERINGS TO ALL BUDDHAS. WITH
REGARD TO THE BUDDHAS' TEACHING DHARMAS, HE IS
ABLE THUS TO SPEAK AND PRACTICE/ As to the teach-
ing Dharmas pronounced by the Buddhas, he can
speak them thus, and thus can he practice them."

SUTRA:

    "DISCIPLES OF THE BUDDHA, THE BODHISATTVA IN
THAT WAY ACCOMPLISHES TEN KINDS OF DHARMAS OF PURI-
FICATION OF ALL GROUNDS. THAT IS: FAITH, COMPAS-
SION, KINDNESS, RENUNCIATION, NON-WEARINESS, KNOW-
ING ALL SUTRAS AND SHASTRAS, SKILL AT UNDERSTANDING
WORLDLY DHARMAS, REPENTANCE AND REFORM, THE POWER
OF SOLIDITY, MAKING OFFERINGS TO ALL BUDDHAS, RE-
LYING ON THE TEACHINGS TO CULTIVATE. DISCIPLES OF
THE BUDDHA, WHEN THE BODHISATTVA HAS COME TO DWELL
ON THIS GROUND OF HAPPINESS, BY MEANS OF THE POWER
OF GREAT VOWS, HE COMES TO SEE MANY BUDDHAS. THAT
IS: HE SEES MANY HUNDREDS OF BUDDHAS, MANY THOUS-
ANDS OF BUDDHAS, MANY HUNDREDS OF THOUSANDS OF
BUDDHAS, MANY MILLIONS OF BUDDHAS, MANY HUNDREDS
OF MILLIONS OF BUDDHAS, MANY THOUSANDS OF MILLIONS
OF BUDDHAS, MANY HUNDREDS OF THOUSANDS OF MILLIONS

O.F BUDDHAS, MANY MILLIONS OF NAYUTAS OF BUDDHAS,
MANY HUNDREDS OF MILLIONS OF NAYUTAS OF BUDDHAS,
MANY THOUSANDS OF MILLIONS OF NAYUTAS OF BUDDHAS,
MANY HUNDREDS OF THOUSANDS OF MILLIONS OF NAYUTAS
OF BUDDHAS, AND COMPLETELY, WITH A GREAT AND PRO-
FOUND MIND, HE WORSHIPS AND REVERES THEM, ATTENDS
UPON AND MAKES OFFERINGS TO THEM, USING CLOTHING,
FOOD AND DRINK, BEDDING AND MEDICINES--ALL OF THE
NECESSITIES OF LIFE--COMPLETELY OFFERING THEM UP.
HE MAKES OFFERINGS AS WELL TO ALL MEMBERS OF THE ·
SANGHA, AND TAKING THOSE GOOD ROOTS, HE TRANSFERS
THEM ALL TO UNSURPASSED BODHI.

COMMENTARY:

   "*DISCIPLES OF THE BUDDHA*"/ When Vajra Treasury Bodhisattva had spoken to this point, he again
called out saying, "All of you Buddhist disciples,
*THE BODHISATTVA IN THAT WAY ACCOMPLISHES TEN KINDS
OF DHARMAS OF PURIFICATION OF ALL GROUNDS*/ He accomplishes Dharma-doors for purifying and regulating the Grounds. *THAT IS: FAITH, COMPASSION,
KINDNESS, RENUNCIATION*/ One must believe in all
the Buddhadharmas, pluck out all the sufferings of
living beings, bestow all happiness on living beings, and practice great giving. *NON-WEARINESS*/
He cultivates those various kinds of dharmas with-
out becoming weary or tired. *KNOWING ALL SUTRAS
AND SHASTRAS*/ He is able to deeply enter the Sutra
Store and have wisdom like the sea. He has *SKILL
AT UNDERSTANDING WORLDLY DHARMAS* and *REPENTANCES
AND REFORM*/ He has *THE POWER OF SOLIDITY* of re-
pentance and reform. The last two Dharmas of puri-
fication are *MAKING OFFERINGS TO ALL BUDDHAS AND
RELYING ON THE TEACHINGS TO CULTIVATE.*
   "*DISCIPLES OF THE BUDDHA, WHEN THE BODHISATTVA
HAS COME TO DWELL UPON THIS GROUND OF HAPPINESS*,
this First Ground, *BY MEANS OF THE POWER OF GREAT
VOWS, HE COMES TO SEE MANY BUDDHAS. THAT IS* to
say: *HE SEES MANY HUNDREDS OF BUDDHAS, MANY THOU-
SANDS OF BUDDHAS*, as well as seeing *MANY HUNDREDS
OF THOUSANDS OF BUDDHAS*/ He can also see *MANY
MILLIONS OF BUDDHAS*, and see *MANY HUNDREDS OF MIL-
LIONS OF BUDDHAS*/ He can see *MANY THOUSANDS OF
MILLIONS OF BUDDHAS*, too, in addition to seeing ·
MANY HUNDREDS OF THOUSANDS OF MILLIONS OF BUDDHAS/

He can also see MANY MILLIONS OF NAYUTAS OF BUD-
DHAS, MANY HUNDREDS OF MILLIONS OF NAYUTAS OF BUD-
DHAS, along with seeing MANY THOUSANDS OF MILLIONS
OF NAYUTAS OF BUDDHAS.

"He can also see MANY HUNDREDS OF THOUSANDS
OF MILLIONS OF NAYUTAS OF BUDDHAS, AND COMPLETELY
WITH A GREAT MIND AND A PROFOUND MIND HE WORSHIPS
AND REVERES THEM, ATTENDS UPON AND MAKES OFFERINGS
TO THEM, USING CLOTHING, FOOD AND DRINK, BEDDING
AND MEDICINES--the Four Requisites--to make offer-
ings of ALL OF THE NECESSITIES OF LIFE, COMPLETELY
OFFERING THEM UP/ He offers them all up complete-
ly. HE MAKES OFFERINGS AS WELL TO ALL MEMBERS OF
THE SANGHA/ He makes offerings to all the Sagely
Sangha members, AND, TAKING THOSE GOOD ROOTS, HE
TRANSFERS THEM ALL TO UNSURPASSED BODHI, to the
unsurpassed fruit position of Wonderful Enlighten-
ment."

SUTRA:

"DISCIPLES OF THE BUDDHA, THIS BODHISATTVA,
BECAUSE OF MAKING OFFERINGS TO ALL BUDDHAS, OB-
TAINS THE DHARMAS FOR ACCOMPLISHING LIVING BEINGS
USING THE FORMER TWO ATTRACTIONS, HE ATTRACTS AND
GATHERS IN LIVING BEINGS, THAT IS, GIVING AND KIND
WORDS. AS TO THE LATTER TWO DHARMAS OF ATTRACTION,
BECAUSE HE ONLY USES THE POWER OF FAITH AND UNDER-
STANDING, HIS PRACTICE HAS NOT YET WELL-PENETRATED
THESE. THAT BODHISATTVA, AMONG THE TEN PARAMITAS,
EMPHASIZES THE PARAMITA OF GIVING. IT IS NOT THAT
HE FAILS TO CULTIVATE THE REMAINING PARAMITAS, BUT
HE ONLY DOES SO ACCORDING TO HIS STRENGTH AND PRO-
PORTIONATELY.

"WHAT THIS BODHISATTVA DILIGENTLY CULTIVATES
--THE MAKING OF OFFERINGS TO ALL BUDDHAS, THE
TEACHING AND TRANSFORMING OF LIVING BEINGS, AND
ALL OF THE GOOD ROOTS FROM CULTIVATING THE DHARMAS
OF PURIFICATION OF THE GROUNDS--HE COMPLETELY TRANS-
FERS TO THE GROUND OF ALL-WISDOM, BECOMING PROGRES-
SIVELY MORE BRIGHT AND PURE, SUBDUED, COMPLIANT
AND ACCOMPLISHED, AND CAPABLE OF ACTING IN ACCORD
WITH HIS INTENT.

COMMENTARY:

Vajra Treasury Bodhisattva again said to all the Bodhisattvas, "All of you *DISCIPLES OF THE BUDDHA, THIS BODHISATTVA* who has certified to the Ground of Happiness, *BECAUSE OF MAKING OFFERINGS TO ALL BUDDHAS, OBTAINS THE DHARMAS FOR ACCOMPLISHING LIVING BEINGS/* Due to his vastly cultivating the giving of offerings to all Buddhas, he obtains the meritorious virtues of the Four Dharmas of Attraction. *USING THE FORMER TWO ATTRACTIONS, HE GATHERS IN LIVING BEINGS. THAT IS* to say: *GIVING AND KIND WORDS/* The Bodhisattva vastly cultivates the practice of giving--giving all of his own wealth and treasures to living beings--and kind words, always caring about and being protective of living beings in his words and saying what they like to hear. He uses kindness and compassion to care for and protect all living beings. Even if it is the very worst sort of living being, he still brings forth the Bodhi resolve to save that being and teach it.

"*AS TO THE LATTER TWO DHARMAS OF ATTRACTION,* that is, beneficial conduct and similarity in deeds *--BECAUSE HE ONLY USES THE POWER OF FAITH AND UNDERSTANDING, HIS PRACTICE HAS NOT YET WELL-PENETRATED THESE/* He cultivates them, but has not yet perfected that kind of Bodhisattva conduct. *THAT BODHISATTVA, AMONG THE TEN PARAMITAS EMPHASIZES THE PARAMITA OF GIVING/* The Ten Paramitas are:

1. Giving.
2. Holding Precepts.
3. Patience.
4. Vigor.
5. Dhyana-Samadhi.
6. Wisdom.
7. Expedients.
8. Vows.
9. Powers.
10. Knowledge.

The perfection of giving is most stressed. *IT IS NOT THAT HE FAILS TO CULTIVATE THE REMAINING PARAMITAS/* It's not that he does not use the other nine Paramitas to cultivate, *BUT HE ONLY DOES SO ACCORDING TO HIS STRENGTH AND PROPORTIONATELY/* He

does as much with them as he can, according to what
his strength permits and does as much as possible
in proportion to the causes and conditions.
   "WHAT THIS BODHISATTVA DILIGENTLY CULTIVATES
--THE MAKING OF OFFERINGS TO ALL BUDDHAS in accord-
ance with what his strength permits him to do,
THE TEACHING AND TRANSFORMING OF LIVING BEINGS,
AND ALL OF THE GOOD ROOTS FROM CULTIVATING THE
DHARMAS OF PURIFICATION OF THE GROUNDS, the Ten
Grounds--HE COMPLETELY TRANSFERS TO THE GROUND OF
ALL-WISDOM, that fruit position, BECOMING PROGRES-
SIVELY MORE BRIGHT AND PURE. He makes more pro-
gress in his cultivation every day and becomes
more and more SUBDUED, COMPLIANT, AND ACCOMPLISHED,
AND CAPABLE OF ACTING IN ACCORD WITH HIS INTENT/
He causes his mind and nature constantly to be
yielding, patient, and accomplished. In accord-
ance with his own wishes, he is capable of putting
all Buddhadharmas into action and using them to
teach and transform living beings.

SUTRA:

   "DISCIPLES OF THE BUDDHA, FOR INSTANCE, WHEN
A GOLDSMITH WELL-SKILLED AT SMELTING GOLD REPEAT-
EDLY PUTS IT THROUGH THE FIRE, IT BECOMES PROGRES-
SIVELY MORE BRIGHT AND PURE, SUPPLE, PLIANT, AND
ACCOMPLISHED, AND CAPABLE OF BEING WORKED IN AC-
CORD WITH HIS INTENT. THE BODHISATTVA IS ALSO LIKE
THIS. HE MAKES OFFERINGS TO ALL BUDDHAS AND TEA-
CHES AND TRANSFORMS LIVING BEINGS, ALL OF WHICH
IS CULTIVATION OF THE DHARMAS OF PURIFICATION OF
THE GROUNDS. THEN HE TAKES ALL OF THOSE GOOD
ROOTS AND COMPLETELY TRANSFERS THEM TO THE GROUND
OF ALL-WISDOM. THUS, HE BECOMES PROGRESSIVELY
MORE BRIGHT AND PURE, SUBDUED, COMPLIANT, AND AC-
COMPLISHED, AND CAPABLE OF ACTING IN ACCORD WITH
HIS INTENT.
   "DISCIPLES OF THE BUDDHA, THE BODHISATTVA MA-
HASATTVA, WHEN DWELLING UPON THIS, THE FIRST
GROUND, SHOULD FROM WHERE ALL BUDDHAS, BODHISAT-
TVAS, AND GOOD, WISE ADVISORS ARE, SEARCH OUT AND
REQUEST WITHIN THESE GROUNDS THE MARKS AND THE
FRUIT OBTAINED, WITH NO WEARINESS OR SATIATION,
IN ORDER TO ACCOMPLISH THE DHARMAS OF THESE
GROUNDS. HE SHOULD ALSO FROM WHERE ALL BUDDHAS,

BODHISATTVAS, AND GOOD, WISE ADVISORS ARE, SEARCH
OUT AND REQUEST WITHIN THE SECOND GROUND THE MARKS
AND THE FRUIT OBTAINED, WITH NO WEARINESS OR SA-
TIATION, IN ORDER TO ACCOMPLISH THE DHARMAS OF THAT
GROUND. HE SHOULD ALSO IN THAT WAY SEARCH OUT AND
REQUEST WITHIN THE THIRD, THE FOURTH, THE FIFTH,
THE SIXTH, THE SEVENTH, THE EIGHTH, THE NINTH, AND
THE TENTH GROUNDS, THE MARKS AND THE FRUIT OBTAIN-
ED, WITH NO WEARINESS OR SATIATION, IN ORDER TO
ACCOMPLISH THE DHARMAS OF THOSE GROUNDS.
    "THIS BODHISATTVA IS GOOD AT KNOWING REMEDIES
FOR ALL OBSTRUCTIONS TO THE GROUNDS, GOOD AT KNOW-
ING THE ACCOMPLISHMENT AND DESTRUCTION OF THE
GROUNDS, GOOD AT KNOWING THE MARKS AND FRUITS OF
THE GROUNDS.

Commentary:

    Vajra Treasury Bodhisattva again said to all
the Bodhisatvas, "All of you DISCIPLES OF THE BUD_
DHA, FOR INSTANCE, I'll give you an analogy for
this principle. What is it like? It is just as
WHEN A GOLDSMITH WELL-SKILLED AT SMELTING GOLD RE-
PEATEDLY PUTS IT THROUGH THE FIRE/ A goldsmith
uses all kinds of clever and skillful methods to
smelt gold and refine it. Time after time he uses
fire on it and IT BECOMES PROGRESSIVELY MORE BRIGHT
AND PURE/ When it has been through the fire once,
the gold is just that much more purified. After
repeated smeltings, it becomes unalloyed gold,
without the least admixture, and is SUPPLE, PLIANT,
AND ACCOMPLISHED, AND CAPABLE OF BEING WORKED IN
ACCORD WITH HIS INTENT/ When the gold has been
fired to the point of being very soft and pliant,
so there is no way it could break, it is pliant
and accomplished. You can make whatever you want
out of it, in accord with your intent. One can
use the gold to make all kinds of ornaments to
adorn one's person.
    "THE BODHISATTVA IS ALSO LIKE THIS. HE MAKES
OFFERINGS TO ALL BUDDHAS/ The Bodhisattva, in cultivating all of the dharmas of regulating the
Grounds, is also like that. First of all, he vastly
cultivates the giving of offerings. AND he TEACHES
AND TRANSFORMS LIVING BEINGS/ He uses kindness,
compassion, joy, renunciation, patience, vigor--

those Paramitas--to teach and transform living beings. ALL OF WHICH IS CULTIVATION OF THE DHARMAS
OF PURIFICATION OF THE GROUNDS/ He enables all
living beings to be able to cultivate the Dharma
doors of purification of the Ten Grounds. THEN
HE TAKES ALL OF THOSE GOOD ROOTS AND COMPLETELY
TRANSFERS THEM/ The good roots that have been
amassed from cultivation he completely uses to
make transference TO THE GROUND OF ALL-WISDOM, the
dharmas of the Ten Grounds. THUS HE BECOMES PRO-
GRESSIVELY MORE BRIGHT AND PURE/ Every day he understands the Dharma-doors of the Ten Grounds better, and each day he is more pure, SUBDUED, COM-
PLIANT, AND ACCOMPLISHED/ That he is subdued and
compliant means this Bodhisattva hasn't the least
bit of temper, and not the slightest affliction.
At all times he is very kind, compassionate, joyous, and renouncing, and accomplishes the door of
practice of patience; AND is CAPABLE OF ACTING IN
ACCORD WITH HIS INTENT/ Whatever Dharma-door he
wants to employ he is able to employ.
      "DISCIPLES OF THE BUDDHA"/ Vajra Treasury
Bodhisattva again said to the Bodhisattvas, "All
of you disciples of the Buddha, THE BODHISATTVA
MAHASATTVA, WHEN DWELLING UPON THE FIRST GROUND,
SHOULD FROM WHERE ALL BUDDHAS AND BODHISATTVAS
AND GOOD, WISE ADVISORS ARE, SEARCH OUT AND RE-
QUEST WITHIN THESE GROUNDS/ When the Great Bodhisattva who cultivates the Bodhisattva conduct
and amasses all kinds of good roots certifies to
the position of the Ground of Happiness, he should
from where all Buddhas and Great Bodhisattvas and
all Good-Knowing Advisors are, investigate the
Dharma-doors of all the Grounds. If there are
places one does not understand, one asks the Buddhas, the Bodhisattvas, the Good, Wise Advisors
within these Ten Grounds about THE MARKS AND THE
FRUIT OBTAINED, about the characteristics one experiences in cultivating them, along with what the
fruit-positions to be obtained in the future are
like. He does this WITHOUT WEARINESS OR SATIA-
TION/ One does the seeking-out oneself, and the
requesting is that of requesting all the Buddhas,
the Bodhisattvas, and all Good-knowing Advisors.
It's that way every day; it's all the time that
way, with no weariness or satiation. There's no
saying, "I've cultivated enough," and then not

investigating or being lazy. He is vigorous all
the time. *IN ORDER TO ACCOMPLISH THE DHARMAS OF
THESE GROUNDS/* The reason is that he wants to
bring the dharmas of the Ten Grounds to accomplishment.

"*HE SHOULD ALSO, FROM WHERE ALL BUDDHAS, BO-
DHISATTVAS, AND GOOD, WISE ADVISORS ARE, SEARCH
OUT AND REQUEST WITHIN THE SECOND GROUND THE MARKS
AND THE FRUIT OBTAINED/* The First Ground is that
way, and if one wishes to cultivate the dharmas
of the second of the Ten Grounds, one should again
request them from where the Buddhas, the Bodhisat-
tvas, and the Good-Knowing Advisors are. One
should seek them out and investigate them. If
there are places one does not understand, one requests the characteristics of what one experiences,
along with the fruit-positions one obtains, *WITH
NO WEARINESS OR SATIATION. IN ORDER TO ACCOMPLISH
THE DHARMAS OF THAT GROUND, HE SHOULD ALSO IN THAT
WAY SEARCH OUT AND REQUEST WITHIN THE THIRD, THE
FOURTH, THE FIFTH, THE SIXTH, THE SEVENTH, THE
EIGHTH, THE NINTH, AND THE TENTH GROUND, THE MARKS
AND THE FRUIT OBTAINED/* When one intends to bring
to accomplishment the dharmas of the Third Ground,
the Fourth Ground, up to and including the dharmas
of the Tenth Ground, one should investigate and
ask all the Buddhas, all Bodhisattvas, and all
Good-Knowing Advisors the characteristics of what
one goes through on each of these grounds and the
fruit-positions one obtains. One should do this
WITH NO WEARINESS OR SATIATION/ This, too, is
without growing tired, *IN ORDER TO ACCOMPLISH THE
DHARMAS OF THOSE GROUNDS/* This is also because
of wanting to accomplish the dharmas of the Ten
Grounds.

"*THIS BODHISATTVA IS GOOD AT KNOWING REMEDIES
FOR ALL OBSTRUCTIONS TO THE GROUNDS/* He is skilled
in the knowledge of what obstacles arise on each
Ground, and what methods to employ to counteract
them. He is *GOOD AT KNOWING THE ACCOMPLISHMENT
AND DESTRUCTION OF THE GROUNDS/* He is skilled in
knowing how the Dharma-doors of the Ten Grounds
are accomplished, and how they are not accomplished; and *GOOD AT KNOWING THE MARKS AND FRUITS
OF THE GROUNDS/* He is also skilled in the knowledge of the characteristics of the Ten Grounds
and how one attains to their fruit-positions."

SUTRA:

"GOOD AT KNOWING THE ATTAINMENT AND CULTIVA-
TION OF THE GROUNDS, GOOD AT KNOWING THE PURIFICA-
TION OF THE DHARMAS OF THE GROUNDS, GOOD AT KNOW-
ING THE PRACTICES IN TURN FOR EACH GROUND, GOOD AT
KNOWING WHAT HOLDS AND DOES NOT HOLD FOR EACH
GROUND, GOOD AT KNOWING THE MOST SUPREME WISDOM
FOR EACH GROUND, GOOD AT KNOWING THE IRREVERSIBIL-
ITIES OF EACH GROUND, GOOD AT KNOWING HOW TO PURI-
FY AND REGULATE ALL THE BODHISATTVAS' GROUNDS, UP
TO AND INCLUDING IN TURN ENTERING THE GROUND OF
THE THUS COME ONE.

"DISCIPLES OF THE BUDDHA, THE BODHISATTVA, IN
THAT WAY, IS GOOD AT KNOWING THE MARKS OF THE
GROUNDS. STARTING WITH THE FIRST GROUND, HE GIVES
RISE TO PRACTICE WHICH IS UNINTERRUPTED. HE CON-
TINUES IN THAT WAY UNTIL HE ENTERS THE TENTH
GROUND, WITHOUT INTERRUPTION. DUE TO THE LIGHT
OF WISDOM OF ALL THOSE GROUNDS, HE ACCOMPLISHES
THE THUS COME ONE'S LIGHT OF WISDOM.

"DISCIPLES OF THE BUDDHA, HE IS LIKE A MER-
CHANT LEADER WHO IS SKILLED IN EXPEDIENT METHODS.
WHEN HE IS ABOUT TO LEAD A GROUP OF MERCHANTS TO
VISIT A GREAT CITY, BEFORE THEY HAVE SET OUT, HE
FIRST INQUIRES ABOUT THE MERITS AND DRAWBACKS OF
THE ROUTE, THE HALTING PLACES ALONG IT, AND WHETH-
ER IT IS SAFE OR NOT. AFTERWARDS, EQUIPPED WITH
PROVISIONS FOR THE ROAD, HE DOES WHAT NEEDS TO BE
DONE. DISCIPLES OF THE BUDDHA, THAT GREAT MER-
CHANT LEADER, ALTHOUGH HE HAS NOT YET TAKEN A
STEP, IS ABLE TO KNOW ALL MATTERS CONCERNING SAFE-
TY ON THE ROAD. HE SKILLFULLY USES WISDOM TO PLAN,
ESTIMATE, AND CONSIDER, AND PREPARES WHAT IS RE-
QUIRED SO THAT THEY WILL NOT RUN SHORT. HE THEN
LEADS THE GROUP OF MERCHANTS UNTIL THEY SAFELY
REACH THAT GREAT CITY. HE AND THE GROUP OF PEO-
PLE COMPLETELY AVOID ALL DISASTERS.

"DISCIPLES OF THE BUDDHA, THE BODHISATTVA,
THAT MERCHANT LEADER, IS ALSO THAT WAY. WHILE
DWELLING ON THE FIRST GROUND, HE IS GOOD AT KNOW-
ING REMEDIES FOR OBSTRUCTIONS TO ALL GROUNDS, UP
TO AND INCLUDING BEING GOOD AT KNOWING HOW TO PURI-
FY ALL THE BODHISATTVA GROUNDS, AND IN TURN ENTER
THE GROUND OF THE THUS COME ONE. AFTERWARDS,
EQUIPPED WITH THE PROVISIONS OF BLESSINGS AND WIS-
DOM, HE LEADS ALL LIVING BEINGS THROUGH THE WIL-

DERNESS OF BIRTH AND DEATH WITH ITS PLACES OF DAN-
GER UNTIL THEY SAFELY ARRIVE AT THE CITY OF SAR-
VAJNA. HE AND ALL THE LIVING BEINGS DO NOT EXPER-
IENCE DISASTERS.

"THEREFORE, THE BODHISATTVA SHOULD NEVER BE
L'AX, AND SHOULD CULTIVATE THE MOST SUPREME, PURE
KARMA OF ALL GROUNDS, UP TO AND INCLUDING TENDING
TOWARDS AND ENTERING THE GROUND OF THE THUS COME
ONES' WISDOM.

"DISCIPLES OF THE BUDDHA, THIS IS CALLED A
SUMMARY DISCUSSION OF THE BODHISATTVA MAHASATTVA'S
ENTRY TO THE DOOR OF THE FIRST BODHISATTVA GROUND.
IF DISCUSSED AT-LENGTH, THERE ARE LIMITLESS AND
BOUNDLESS HUNDREDS OF THOUSANDS OF ASAMKHYEYAS OF
PARTICULARS.

COMMENTARY:

"The Bodhisattva is GOOD AT KNOWING THE AT-
TAINMENT AND CULTIVATION OF THE GROUNDS/ A Bodhi-
sattva who has certified to the First Ground, the
Ground of Happiness, is good at knowing how to
cultivate each Ground. He is GOOD AT KNOWING THE
PURIFICATION OF THE DHARMAS OF THE GROUNDS and
GOOD AT KNOWING THE PRACTICES IN·TURN FOR EACH
GROUND/ He is also good at knowing for all the
Ten Grounds how one goes in turn from the First
Ground to the Second Ground, from the Second Ground
to the Third Ground, up to and including how to
cultivate the Tenth Ground. He is GOOD AT KNOWING
WHAT HOLDS AND DOES NOT HOLD FOR EACH GROUND/ He
is skilled as well at knowing what is right and
what is wrong for each Ground. He is GOOD AT KNOW-
ING THE MOST SUPREME WISDOM FOR EACH GROUND/ Each
Ground has its own particular wisdom, its own par-
ticular doors of practice. He is GOOD AT KNOWING
THE IRREVERSIBILITIES OF EACH GROUND and GOOD AT
KNOWING HOW TO PURIFY AND REGULATE ALL THE BODHI-
SATTVA GROUNDS, UP TO AND INCLUDING IN TURN ENTER-
ING THE GROUND OF THE THUS COME ONE/ He knows it
all, up to and including what one goes through in
order to obtain entry to certification to the fruit
of the Ground of the Thus Come One.

"DISCIPLES OF THE BUDDHA"/ Vajra Treasury
Bodhisattva again calls out, "All of you disciples
of the Buddha,.THE BODHISATTVA IN THAT WAY IS GOOD

AT KNOWING THE MARKS OF THE GROUNDS/ He is good at
knowing the characteristics of each Ground. START-
ING WITH THE FIRST GROUND, HE GIVES RISE TO PRAC-
TICE WHICH IS UNINTERRUPTED. HE CONTINUES IN THAT
WAY UNTIL HE ENTERS THE TENTH GROUND WITHOUT IN-
TERRUPTION. DUE TO THE LIGHT OF WISDOM OF ALL
THOSE GROUNDS, HE ACCOMPLISHES THE THUS COME ONES'
LIGHT OF WISDOM/ He is able to obtain the light
of wisdom of a Buddha."

Vajra Treasury Bodhisattva again calls out,
"All you DISCIPLES OF THE BUDDHA, HE IS LIKE A
MERCHANT LEADER"/ He says, "Now I'll give you an
analogy. He is like a merchant leader WHO IS
SKILLED IN EXPEDIENT METHODS/ He is skilled in
knowing all expedient Dharma-doors. WHEN HE IS
ABOUT TO LEAD A GROUP OF MERCHANTS TO VISIT A
GREAT CITY, BEFORE THEY HAVE SET OUT, HE FIRST
INQUIRES ABOUT THE MERITS AND DRAWBACKS OF THE
ROUTE/ When he is going to head up a party of
merchants to visit a metropolis on business, in
advance of their trip he finds out in which places
the road is easy to traverse and in which places
passage is not easy. He determines which places
are dangerous and which places are safe. He learns
it all. He also ascertains THE HALTING PLACES
ALONG IT, that is, what places there are where one
can stop for the night, AND WHETHER IT IS SAFE OR
NOT/ He finds out which situations are safe and
which are not. AFTERWARDS, EQUIPPED WITH PROVI-
SIONS FOR THE ROAD, HE DOES WHAT HAS TO BE DONE/
Afterwards they all prepare the provisions, that
is, the money to be used, and he goes about doing
his job.

"DISCIPLES OF THE BUDDHA," Vajra Treasury
again says, "THAT GREAT MERCHANT LEADER, ALTHOUGH
HE HAS NOT YET TAKEN A STEP, IS ABLE TO KNOW ALL
MATTERS CONCERNING SAFETY ON THE ROAD/ That great
entrepreneur who does business on a large scale,
even though he has not yet set out on the road,
already knows all the safety factors and dangers
along the route. HE SKILLFULLY USES WISDOM TO
PLAN, ESTIMATE, AND CONSIDER, AND PREPARES WHAT
IS REQUIRED/ He prepares a sufficient quantity
of things that they will need to use SO THAT THEY
WILL NOT RUN SHORT. HE THEN LEADS THE GROUP OF
MERCHANTS UNTIL THEY SAFELY REACH THAT GREAT CITY.
They arrive at the great metropolis to which they

want to go. *HE AND THE GROUP OF PEOPLE COMPLETELY AVOID ALL DISASTERS/* They safely reach the place to which they want to go.

"DISCIPLES OF THE BUDDHA"/ Vajra Treasury Bodhisattva again says, "All you disciples of the Buddha, *THE BODHISATTVA, THAT MERCHANT LEADER, IS ALSO THAT WAY/* The Bodhisattva is like a merchant leader. *WHILE DWELLING ON THE FIRST GROUND,* the Ground of Happiness, *HE IS GOOD AT KNOWING THE REMEDIES FOR OBSTRUCTIONS TO ALL GROUNDS/* He is good at knowing what methods to use to counteract any obstacles to cultivation that may arise on any one of the Grounds, *UP TO AND INCLUDING BEING GOOD AT KNOWING HOW TO PURIFY ALL THE BODHISATTVA GROUNDS/* He knows how all of the Bodhisattvas of the Ten Grounds can attain to purity, *AND IN TURN ENTER THE GROUND OF THE THUS COME ONE. AFTERWARDS, EQUIPPED WITH THE PROVISIONS OF BLESSINGS AND WISDOM, HE LEADS ALL LIVING BEINGS THROUGH THE WILDERNESS OF BIRTH AND DEATH/* He guides all living beings through the wilderness of the revolving wheel of birth and death *WITH ITS PLACES OF DANGER, UNTIL THEY SAFELY ARRIVE AT THE CITY OF SARVAJNA/* They arrive at the City of All Wisdom. *HE AND ALL THE LIVING BEINGS DO NOT EXPERIENCE DISASTERS/* The Bodhisattva himself, and all the living beings with him, have no disasters.

"THEREFORE, THE BODHISATTVA SHOULD NEVER BE LAX/ As a consequence of this, the Bodhisattva should at all times never be lax, *AND SHOULD CULTIVATE THE MOST SUPREME, PURE KARMA OF ALL GROUNDS/* He should diligently cultivate the Dharma-doors of the Ten Grounds, that pure and most supreme Way karma, *UP TO AND INCLUDING TENDING TOWARDS AND ENTERING THE GROUND OF THE THUS COME ONE'S WISDOM/* He should do so until he reaches the fruit-position of Buddhahood.

"DISCIPLES OF THE BUDDHA"/ Vajra Treasury Bodhisattva again says, "All you disciples of the Buddha, *THAT IS CALLED A SUMMARY DISCUSSION OF THE BODHISATTVA MAHASATTVA'S ENTRY TO THE DOOR OF THE FIRST BODHISATTVA GROUND/* This is the Bodhisattva Mahasattva's entry to the Dharma-door of the First Ground. *IF DISCUSSED AT LENGTH, THERE ARE LIMITLESS AND BOUNDLESS HUNDREDS OF THOUSANDS OF ASAMKHYEYAS OF PARTICULARS/* If expanded upon, it has a great many different aspects."

SUTRA:

"*DISCIPLES OF THE BUDDHA, THE BODHISATTVA WHO DWELLS UPON THIS, THE FIRST GROUND, FOR THE MOST PART ACTS AS KING OF JAMBUDVIPA. HE IS POWERFUL, HONORED, AND SOVEREIGN, AND CONSTANTLY PROTECTS THE PROPER DHARMA. HE IS ABLE TO USE GREAT GIVING TO GATHER IN LIVING BEINGS. HE IS SKILLED AT RIDDING LIVING BEINGS OF THE DEFILEMENT OF STINGINESS. HE CONSTANTLY PRACTICES GREAT GIVING WITHOUT EXHAUSTION OR END. GIVING, PLEASING WORDS, BENEFICIAL PRACTICE, AND IDENTITY IN ACTIONS--ALL SUCH KARMA THAT IS CREATED IS NOT SEPARATE FROM MINDFULNESS OF THE BUDDHA, NOT SEPARATE FROM MINDFULNESS OF THE DHARMA, NOT SEPARATE FROM MINDFULNESS OF THE SANGHA, NOT SEPARATE FROM MINDFULNESS OF THE BODHISATTVAS OF IDENTICAL PRACTICE, NOT SEPARATE FROM MINDFULNESS OF THE BODHISATTVA PRACTICES, NOT SEPARATE FROM MINDFULNESS OF THE PARAMITAS, NOT SEPARATE FROM MINDFULNESS OF ALL GROUNDS, NOT SEPARATE FROM MINDFULNESS OF THE POWERS, NOT SEPARATE FROM MINDFULNESS OF THE FEARLESSNESSES, NOT SEPARATE FROM MINDFULNESS OF THE UNCOMMON BUDDHA DHARMAS, UP TO AND INCLUDING NOT SEPARATE FROM MINDFULNESS OF ENDOWMENT WITH THE WISDOM OF ALL WISDOMS OF ALL MODES.*

COMMENTARY:

Vajra Treasury Bodhisattva again called out and said, "All you *DISCIPLES OF THE BUDDHA, THE BODHISATTVA MAHASATTVA WHO DWELLS UPON THIS, THE FIRST GROUND, FOR THE MOST PART ACTS AS KING OF JAMBUDVIPA*"/ The Great Bodhisattva who cultivates the Bodhisattva conduct and amasses all kinds of good roots regularly becomes the king of Jambudvipa when he accomplishes the First Ground, that of Happiness. *HE IS POWERFUL, HONORED, AND SOVEREIGN*/ He either is someone with a great deal of money, or extremely sovereign and at ease, *AND CONSTANTLY PROTECTS THE PROPER DHARMA. HE IS ABLE TO USE GREAT GIVING TO GATHER IN LIVING BEINGS* and cause them to bring forth the great thought of Bodhi. *HE IS SKILLED AT RIDDING LIVING BEINGS OF THE DEFILEMENT OF STINGINESS*/ He is able to get rid of living beings' bad habit, the fault of 'stinginess. *HE CONSTANTLY PRACTICES GREAT GIVING WITHOUT EXHAUSTION OR END/* He is always practicing giving on a large scale, and his giving never ends.

"GIVING, PLEASING WORDS, BENEFICIAL PRACTICE, AND IDENTITY IN ACTIONS--ALL SUCH KARMA THAT IS CREATED, IS NOT SEPARATE FROM MINDFULNESS OF THE BUDDHA, NOT SEPARATE FROM MINDFULNESS OF THE DHARMA, NOT SEPARATE FROM MINDFULNESS OF THE SANGHA/ No matter what good karma is created, it is never separate from mindfulness of the Triple Jewel: the Buddha, the Dharma, and the Sangha. It is *NOT SEPARATE FROM MINDFULNESS OF THE BODHISATTVAS OF IDENTICAL PRACTICE/* Not to separate from mindfulness of the Bodhisattvas of identical practice is also mindfulness of the Sangha. It is *NOT SEPARATE FROM MINDFULNESS OF THE BODHISATTVA PRACTICES* which are cultivated. It is *NOT SEPARATE FROM MINDFULNESS OF THE PARAMITAS,* the dharmas of Arrival at the Other Shore. It is *NOT SEPARATE FROM MINDFULNESS* of the wisdom *OF ALL GROUNDS/* It is *NOT SEPARATE FROM MINDFULNESS OF THE POWERS--* the Buddha's Ten Powers. It is *NOT SEPARATE FROM MINDFULNESS OF THE FEARLESSNESSES--*the Four Fearlessnesses. It is *NOT SEPARATE FROM MINDFULNESS OF THE UNCOMMON BUDDHA DHARMAS--*the Eighteen Dharmas Special to a Buddha, *UP TO AND INCLUDING* it is *NOT SEPARATE FROM MINDFULNESS OF ENDOWMENT WITH THE WISDOM OF ALL WISDOMS OF ALL MODES--*all the wisdoms of a Buddha."

SUTRA:

"HE FURTHER MAKES THE FOLLOWING REFLECTION: 'I SHOULD, AMONG ALL LIVING BEINGS, BE A LEADER, BE SUPREME, BE ESPECIALLY SUPREME, BE WONDERFUL, BE SUBTLE AND WONDERFUL, BE SUPERIOR, BE UNSURPASSED, BE A GUIDE, BE A GENERAL, BE A CHIEF, UP TO AND INCLUDING BEING ONE WITH THE WISDOM OF ALL WISDOMS UPON WHOM ONE MAY RELY.'

"THIS BODHISATTVA, IF HE WANTS TO RENOUNCE THE HOME LIFE, WITHIN THE BUDDHADHARMA DILIGENTLY CULTIVATES WITH VIGOR AND THEN CAN LEAVE THE HOME, HIS WIFE AND CHILDREN, AND THE FIVE DESIRES. HE RELIES UPON THE THUS COME ONES' TEACHING, LEAVES THE HOME LIFE, AND STUDIES THE WAY.

COMMENTARY:

"*HE FURTHER MAKES THE FOLLOWING REFLECTION:*
The Bodhisattva of the First Ground, the Ground
of Happiness, also makes the following contemplation, saying, '*I SHOULD, AMONG ALL LIVING BEINGS,
BE A LEADER.*' '*I*' is the Bodhisattva referring
to himself. '*I* should *BE SUPREME, BE ESPECIALLY
SUPREME/* I should be an especially outstanding
and superior person. I should *BE WONDERFUL/* Among
living beings, I should be an inconceivable person. I should *BE SUBTLE AND WONDERFUL/* Among
living beings, I should be an unsurpassed, deep,
profound, subtle, and wonderfully inconceivable
person. I should *BE SUPERIOR/* I should be a lofty and superior person. I should *BE UNSURPASSED/*
Among living beings, I should be an unsurpassed
person. I should *BE A GUIDE/* I should, in the
midst of all living beings, act as their guide.
I should *BE A GENERAL/* Among living beings, I
should be a great general. I should *BE A CHIEF/*
I should be a principal among living beings. *UP
TO AND INCLUDING BEING ONE OF THE WISDOM OF ALL
WISDOMS UPON WHOM ONE MAY RELY/* I should be someone who has the wisdom of a Buddha upon whom liv-
ing beings can rely.
    "*THIS BODHISATTVA, IF HE WANTS TO RENOUNCE
THE HOME LIFE*--if he wants to leave home--*WITHIN
THE BUDDHADHARMA DILIGENTLY CULTIVATES WITH VIGOR
AND THEN* he *CAN LEAVE THE HOME LIFE/* He can give
up his family, *HIS WIFE AND CHILDREN AND THE FIVE
DESIRES*--wealth, sex, fame, food, and sleep. *HE
RELIES UPON THE THUS COME ONES' TEACHING/* He re-
lies upon the teaching dharmas spoken by the Bud-
dhas, *LEAVES THE HOME LIFE, AND STUDIES THE WAY*"/
He:

    1. Leaves the home of afflictions,
    2. leaves the worldly home, and
    3. leaves the home of the Three Realms.

SUTRA:

    "*THEREUPON, AFTER LEAVING HOME, HE DILIGENTLY
CULTIVATES WITH VIGOR. WITHIN THE SPACE OF A
THOUGHT, HE ATTAINS A HUNDRED SAMADHIS. HE COMES*

TO SEE A HUNDRED BUDDHAS. HE IS ABLE TO KNOW A
HUNDRED BUDDHAS' SPIRITUAL POWERS. HE IS ABLE TO
QUAKE A HUNDRED BUDDHA LANDS. HE IS ABLE TO GO BE-
YOND A HUNDRED BUDDHA LANDS. HE IS ABLE TO ILLU-
MINE A HUNDRED BUDDHA LANDS. HE IS ABLE TO TEACH
AND TRANSFORM THE LIVING BEINGS OF A HUNDRED
WORLDS. HE IS ABLE TO LIVE FOR A HUNDRED KALPAS.
HE IS ABLE TO KNOW THE BOUNDARIES OF BEFORE AND
AFTERWARDS, THE EVENTS OF A HUNDRED KALPAS FOR
EACH. HE IS ABLE TO ENTER A HUNDRED DHARMA DOORS.
HE IS ABLE TO MANIFEST A HUNDRED BODIES. WITH
EVERY BODY HE IS ABLE TO MANIFEST A HUNDRED BODHI-
SATTVAS AS HIS RETINUE.
        "IF HE EMPLOYS ESPECIALLY SUPREME POWER OF
BODHISATTVA VOWS TO MANIFEST AT EASE, HE SURPASSES
THAT NUMBER. IN A HUNDRED KALPAS, A THOUSAND KAL-
PAS, A HUNDRED THOUSAND KALPAS, UP TO AND INCLUD-
ING A HUNDRED THOUSAND MILLION NAYUTAS OF KALPAS,
THE NUMBER COULD NOT BE COUNTED OR KNOWN."
        AT THAT TIME, VAJRA TREASURY BODHISATTVA,
WISHING TO RESTATE HIS MEANING, SPOKE VERSES,
SAYING:

COMMENTARY:

        "THEREUPON, AFTER LEAVING HOME, HE DILIGENTLY
CULTIVATES WITH VIGOR/ After the Bodhisattva has
brought forth the thought for Bodhi, renounced
the world, and left the home life, in order to seek
the unsurpassed Way, he very diligently and earn-
estly cultivates with courageous vigor. WITHIN
THE SPACE OF A THOUGHT, HE ATTAINS A HUNDRED SA-
MADHIS/ Within the interval of a single thought,
he obtains more than a hundred kinds of proper
receptions, proper concentrations, that kind of
wisdom. HE COMES TO SEE A HUNDRED BUDDHAS/ When
in a single interval of thought he is able to attain a hundred kinds of samadhis, then he is able
to see a hundred Buddhas of a hundred worlds. HE
IS ABLE TO KNOW A HUNDRED BUDDHAS' SPIRITUAL POW-
ERS/ He is able to know all of the powers of
spiritual penetrations of a hundred Buddhas of a
hundred worlds. HE IS ABLE TO QUAKE A HUNDRED
BUDDHA LANDS/ The Bodhisattva is able to use
spiritual penetrations and cause a hundred Buddha
lands to tremble and quake in six ways. HE IS

ABLE TO GO BEYOND A HUNDRED BUDDHA LANDS/ The
power of his spiritual penetrations is able to
transcend a hundred Buddha lands. HE IS ABLE TO
ILLUMINE A HUNDRED BUDDHA LANDS/ His light, too,
is able to light up as many as a hundred Buddha
lands.

"HE IS ABLE TO TEACH AND TRANSFORM THE LIVING
BEINGS OF A HUNDRED WORLDS/ Within a single interval of thought, he can teach and transform as
many as a hundred Buddha lands' living beings.
HE IS ABLE TO LIVE FOR A HUNDRED KALPAS/ He is
able to maintain his life for a hundred great kalpas. HE IS ABLE TO KNOW THE BOUNDARIES OF BEFORE
AND AFTERWARDS and THE EVENTS OF A HUNDRED KALPAS
FOR EACH/ He knows a hundred kalpas before, and
he knows a hundred kalpas afterwards, knowing all
of the events within them. HE IS ABLE TO ENTER
A HUNDRED DHARMA DOORS. HE IS ABLE TO MANIFEST A
HUNDRED BODIES/ Within this very world he can
make appear a hundred bodies and go to other
worlds to teach and transform living beings. WITH
EVERY BODY HE IS ABLE TO MANIFEST A HUNDRED BODHI-
SATTVAS/ He can use spiritual penetrations to
make appear by transformation a hundred Bodhisattvas AS HIS RETINUE/ They act as his retainers.

"IF HE EMPLOYS ESPECIALLY SUPREME POWER OF
BODHISATTVA VOWS TO MANIFEST AT EASE, HE SURPASSES
THAT NUMBER. IN A HUNDRED KALPAS, A THOUSAND KAL-
PAS, A HUNDRED THOUSAND KALPAS, UP TO AND INCLUD-
ING A HUNDRED THOUSAND MILLION NAYUTAS OF KALPAS/
Should it be the case that the Bodhisattva has extraordinary and especially supreme vow-power and
manifests at ease, he goes beyond that number, up
to and including going beyond as many as a hundred
thousand million nayutas of kalpas. THE NUMBER
COULD NOT BE COUNTED OR KNOWN/ From this it can
be seen that if a Bodhisattva has extraordinary
vow-power, his merit and virtue exceed those of
the previously described Bodhisattva to the point
that they cannot be counted or known."

AT THAT TIME, VAJRA TREASURY BODHISATTVA,
WISHING TO RESTATE HIS MEANING, SPOKE VERSES, SAY-
ING/ Wanting to repeat those principles, he used
verses to speak for everyone.

SUTRA:

> "SHOULD SOMEONE ASSEMBLE MULTITUDES OF
>   GOOD,
> HE BECOMES ENDOWED WITH WHITE, PURE DHARMAS,
> HE MAKES OFFERINGS TO THE HONORED ONE OF
>   GODS AND HUMANS,
> AND FOLLOWS THE PATH OF KINDNESS AND
>   COMPASSION.
>
> "HIS FAITH AND UNDERSTANDING ARE MOST
>   VAST AND GREAT
> HIS RESOLUTIONS AND INCLINATIONS, TOO,
>   ARE PURE.
> INTENT UPON THE SEARCH FOR A BUDDHA'S
>   WISDOM,
> HE BRINGS FORTH THIS THOUGHT UNSURPASSED.
>
> "HAVING PURIFIED ALL THE POWERS OF
>   KNOWLEDGE,
> ALONG WITH THE FEARLESSNESSES AS WELL,
> AND HAVING ACCOMPLISHED ALL THE BUDDHA
>   DHARMAS;
> HE SAVES AND GATHERS IN THE FLOCKS OF
>   BEINGS.
>
> "IN ORDER TO OBTAIN GREAT KINDNESS AND
>   COMPASSION,
> AND TO TURN THE SUPREME DHARMA WHEEL,
> TO ADORN AND PURIFY THE BUDDHA-COUNTRIES,
> HE BRINGS FORTH THIS THOUGHT MOST SUPREME

COMMENTARY:

"SHOULD SOMEONE ASSEMBLE MULTITUDES OF GOOD/ HE BECOMES ENDOWED WITH WHITE, PURE DHARMAS", This says, "If a Bodhisattva cultivates the doors of practice cultivated by Bodhisattvas and accumulates various kinds of good roots, because of having a great deal of merit and virtue from good roots, he eliminates all defiled dharmas, so that all that remain are pure dharmas. HE MAKES OFFERINGS TO THE HONORED ONE OF GODS AND HUMANS/ He is able to make offerings to all Buddhas, AND FOLLOWS THE PATH OF KINDNESS AND COMPASSION/ He constantly teaches and transforms living beings, using kindness, com-

passion, joy, and renunciation, those Four Limitless Minds, to teach and transform living beings.

"HIS FAITH AND UNDERSTANDING ARE MOST VAST
AND GREAT/   His faith along with the principles
that he understands are both extremely vast and
great.   HIS RESOLUTIONS AND HIS INCLINATIONS, TOO,
ARE PURE/   All of his resolutions, as well as what
he likes, are pure.   INTENT UPON THE SEARCH FOR A
BUDDHA'S WISDOM/ HE BRINGS FORTH THIS THOUGHT UN-
SURPASSED/   His determination is to seek wisdom
which is the same as that of a Buddha, so he
brings forth the thought for unsurpassed Bodhi.

"HAVING PURIFIED ALL THE POWERS OF KNOWLEDGE/
ALONG WITH THE FEARLESSNESSES AS WELL/ AND HAVING
ACCOMPLISHED ALL THE BUDDHA DHARMAS/ HE SAVES AND
GATHERS IN THE FLOCKS OF BEINGS/   He has purified
all the powers of all wisdom, in addition to the
freedoms from fear.   He has brought to accomplish-
ment all of the Dharma doors spoken by the Buddha.
He saves and protects all living beings.

"IN ORDER TO OBTAIN GREAT KINDNESS AND COM-
PASSION/ AND TO TURN THE SUPREME DHARMA WHEEL/ TO
ADORN AND PURIFY THE BUDDHA-COUNTRIES/ HE BRINGS
FORTH THIS THOUGHT MOST SUPREME/   In order to ac-
quire a mind of great kindness and compassion, and
also in order to turn the wheel of all the most
supreme Dharmas, and so that he may adorn and purify all Buddhas' lands, he brings forth this
thought for most supreme Bodhi."

SUTRA:

   "HE IN ONE THOUGHT KNOWS THE THREE
         PERIODS OF TIME,
   YET HE HAS NO DISCRIMINATIONS;
   THEIR VARIOUS TIMES WHICH ARE NOT
         THE SAME,
   HE EMPLOYS TO APPEAR WITHIN THE WORLD.

   "TO SPEAK IN SUMMARY, HE SEEKS ALL
         BUDDHAS'
   SUPREME MERIT AND VIRTUE, EACH AND ALL;
   HE BRINGS FORTH THE THOUGHT VAST AND
         GREAT,
   WHOSE MEASURE EQUALS REALMS OF EMPTY
         SPACE

"WITH COMPASSION FOREMOST, AND WISDOM
        PRINCIPAL,
AND EXPEDIENTS ALONG WITH INTERACTIVES,
HIS MIND OF FAITH AND UNDERSTANDING PURE,
HE HAS THE THUS COME ONE'S LIMITLESS
        POWERS.

"UNOBSTRUCTED WISDOM THEN APPEARS.
ENLIGHTENED OF HIMSELF, NOT DUE TO
        OTHERS.
IDENTICALLY ENDOWED AS THE THUS COME ONES,
HE BRINGS FORTH THIS THOUGHT MOST SUPREME.

"THE DISCIPLE OF THE BUDDHA WHO FIRST
        BRINGS FORTH,
THE WONDERFULLY PRECIOUS THOUGHT SUCH
        AS THIS,
THEN TRANSCENDS THE COMMONER'S POSITION,
ENTERING THE BUDDHAS' PLACE OF PRACTICE.

COMMENTARY:

   "HE IN ONE THOUGHT KNOWS THE THREE PERIODS OF
TIME, the past, the present, and the future. YET
HE HAS NO DISCRIMINATIONS/ He uses wisdom to know
them, not the discriminations of consciousness. He
knows THEIR VARIOUS TIMES WHICH ARE NOT THE SAME/
All of the times within the three periods of time
are not identical. HE EMPLOYS them TO APPEAR
WITHIN THE WORLD.
   "TO SPEAK IN SUMMARY, HE SEEKS ALL BUDDHAS'
unsurpassed Way, their SUPREME MERIT AND VIRTUE,
EACH AND ALL. HE BRINGS FORTH THE THOUGHT VAST
AND GREAT, WHOSE MEASURE EQUALS REALMS OF EMPTY
SPACE/ He brings forth the thought for Bodhi,
which is as vast as empty space.
   "WITH COMPASSION FOREMOST, AND WISDOM PRINCI-
PAL, AND EXPEDIENTS ALONG WITH INTERACTIVES, HIS
MIND OF FAITH AND UNDERSTANDING is PURE/ He makes
great compassion of foremost importance and relies
on wisdom as his principal necessity. He practices all clever and expedient dharmas, along with
all mutually interactive dharmas. He is able to
have a pure mind of faith and understanding. HE
HAS THE THUS COME ONE'S LIMITLESS POWERS/ He obtains the limitless powers of spiritual penetrations of a Buddha.

"*UNOBSTRUCTED WISDOM THEN APPEARS/*   He has
obtained unobstructed wisdom.   *ENLIGHTENED OF HIM-
SELF, NOT DUE TO OTHERS/*   He himself obtains the
hundreds of thousands of millions of samadhis, and
they are not bestowed upon him by anyone else.
IDENTICALLY ENDOWED AS THE THUS COME ONES/   Those
powers of spiritual penetrations--that unobstructed wisdom--are the same as those of the Buddha.
HE BRINGS FORTH THIS THOUGHT MOST SUPREME, this
thought for Bodhi.

"*THE DISCIPLE OF THE BUDDHA WHO FIRST BRINGS
FORTH THE WONDERFULLY PRECIOUS THOUGHT SUCH AS
THIS, THEN TRANSCENDS THE COMMONER'S POSITION, EN-
TERING THE BUDDHAS' PLACE OF PRACTICE/*   The dis-
ciple's initial thought for Bodhi is as solid as
vajra.   He is no longer the same as an ordinary
person.   He enters upon the Way travelled by the
Buddhas."

SUTRA:

"*HE IS BORN WITHIN THE THUS COME ONE'S
      HOUSEHOLD,
AND HIS LINEAGE HAS NO FLAWS;
HE IS THE SAME AS THE BUDDHA,
AND IS CERTAIN TO ACCOMPLISH UNSURPASSED
      BODHI.*

"*UPON PRODUCING THOUGHTS SUCH AS THOSE,
HE IMMEDIATELY COMES TO ENTER THE
      FIRST GROUND;
HIS RESOLVE AND INCLINATIONS ARE IMMOVABLE,
BEING LIKE THE GREAT KING OF MOUNTAINS.*

"*HE HAS MUCH HAPPINESS, MUCH LIKING,
AND MUCH PURE FAITH, AS WELL;
HE HAS COURAGEOUS VIGOR TO THE UTMOST,
ALONG WITH MUCH ELATION AND REJOICING.*

"*HE IS QUITE FREE FROM CONTENTION,
FROM TROUBLING AND HARMING, AND FROM
      HATRED;
HE KNOWS SHAME, RESPECT, AND RECTITUDE,
AND WELL PROTECTS AND GUARDS HIS FACULTIES.*

> *"HE SEEKS ALL THE MULTITUDES OF WISDOM,*
> *OF THE ONE INCOMPARABLE IN THE WORLD:*
> *'THIS PLACE IS ONE I SHOULD ACHIEVE,*
> *MINDFUL, GIVING RISE TO HAPPINESS.'*

COMMENTARY:

"*HE IS BORN WITHIN THE THUS COME ONE'S HOUSE-HOLD/* The Bodhisattva who has certified to the First Ground, the Ground of Happiness, has already been born in the household of the Thus Come One, *AND HIS LINEAGE HAS NO FLAWS/* His lineage, his descent, is entirely honorable and lofty. It is not despicable and has nothing reprehensible about it. It is not at all lowly or poverty stricken. *HE IS THE SAME AS THE BUDDHA/* He is just like the Buddha, *AND IS CERTAIN TO ACCOMPLISH UNSURPASSED BODHI/* It is for sure that he will become a Buddha in the future. *UPON PRODUCING THOUGHTS SUCH AS THOSE, HE IMMEDIATELY COMES TO ENTER THE FIRST GROUND/* As soon as he has brought forth the thoughts of great kindness and compassion, and the thoughts of great joy and renunciation, he then can enter the Ground of Happiness. *HIS RESOLVE AND INCLINATIONS ARE IMMOVABLE/* His resolutions and what he likes cannot be moved by anyone at all. That is, if you want to cultivate the Bodhisattva Way, no one will be able to break up your cultivation, *BEING LIKE THE KING OF MOUNTAINS/* He is just like Mount Sumeru.

"*HE HAS MUCH HAPPINESS, MUCH LIKING/* When he certifies to the First Ground, the Ground of Happiness, he has much happiness and much liking for all living beings, *AND MUCH FAITH, AS WELL/* He also cultivates the dharmas of pure faith and understanding. *HE HAS COURAGEOUS VIGOR TO THE UTMOST/* He also has ultimately great, courageous vigor, *ALONG WITH MUCH ELATION AND REJOICING/* His happiness is full of enthusiastic delight and rejoicing. *HE IS QUITE FREE FROM CONTENTION/* The Bodhisattva who has certified to this position has no contention. He doesn't strive or fight with anyone. He is also free *FROM TROUBLING AND HARMING AND FROM HATRED/* He has not the slightest wish to trouble or harm others, and not the least bit of hate for other people.

"*HE KNOWS SHAME, RESPECT, AND RECTITUDE/* He knows how to repent and reform, has reverence and respect, and rectitude of mind. Incapable of being evasive, shifty, or devious, his mind is straight and upright, *AND HE WELL PROTECTS AND GUARDS HIS FACULTIES/* He is good at guarding and protecting all his faculties. His eyes, ears, nose, tongue, body, and mind all follow the rules and are incapable of not following them. *HE SEEKS ALL THE MULTITUDES OF WISDOM OF THE ONE INCOMPARABLE IN THE WORLD/* He seeks all the wisdoms of the Buddha, to whom no one can compare. *'THIS PLACE IS ONE I SHOULD ACHIEVE, MINDFUL, GIVING RISE TO HAPPINESS/* I should certify to all the wisdoms of the Buddha. I am mindful of the Buddha, the Dharma and the Sangha--the Triple Jewel--and mindful of all living beings, and give rise to great joy.'"

SUTRA:

"*UPON INITIALLY ENTERING THE FIRST GROUND,*
HE IMMEDIATELY TRANSCENDS THE FIVE-FOLD
       FEARS:
NOT STAYING ALIVE, DYING, BAD REPUTATION,
EVIL DESTINIES AND THE ASSEMBLY'S AWESOME
       VIRTUE.

"*HE ATTACHES NEITHER TO SELF,*
NOR TO WHAT PERTAINS TO A SELF;
ALL OF THESE DISCIPLES OF THE BUDDHA,
LEAVE ALL FEARFULNESS FAR BEHIND.

"*ALWAYS PRACTICING GREAT KINDNESS AND*
       PITY,
HE CONSTANTLY HAS FAITH AS WELL AS
       REVERENCE;
HE IS REPLETE WITH MERIT AND VIRTUE OF
       REPENTANCE,
NIGHT AND DAY INCREASING WHOLESOME
       DHARMAS.

"*HE DELIGHTS IN DHARMA'S TRUE AND ACTUAL*
       BENEFITS,
AND DOES NOT LOVE THE RECEPTION OF DESIRES;
HE REFLECTS UPON THE DHARMAS HE HAS HEARD,
FAR FREE FROM THE PRACTICE OF GRASPING.

"HE HAS NO GREED FOR BENEFITS OR OFFERINGS,
AND HE ONLY DELIGHTS IN BUDDHA'S BODHI;
WITH ONE MIND HE SEEKS THE BUDDHA'S WISDOM,
CONCENTRATION UNDIVIDED WITH NO OTHER
THOUGHT.

COMMENTARY:

"UPON INITIALLY ENTERING THE FIRST GROUND,
HE IMMEDIATELY TRANSCENDS THE FIVE-FOLD FEARS/
When the Bodhisattva certifies to the Ground of
Happiness, he then leaves the Five Kinds of Fears
far behind: *NOT STAYING ALIVE, DYING, BAD REPU-*
TATION, EVIL DESTINIES, AND THE ASSEMBLY'S AWESOME
VIRTUE"/ In full, the list reads:

1. fear of not staying alive,
2. fear of a bad reputation,
3. fear of death,
4. fear of the evil destines,
5. fear of the awesome virtue of the Great
   Assembly.

Why does he leave these five kinds of fears far
behind? It is because *"HE ATTACHES NEITHER TO SELF*
NOR TO WHAT PERTAINS TO A SELF"/ He has no attachment to a self, and with no self what is there to
fear? What belongs to a self is gone, too. You
who are studying the Buddhadharma are afraid of
this and afraid of that. Why are you afraid? It
is because you are unable to be without a self.
You are greedily attached to "me" and greedily attached to "mine." But, if you had no self, and
if what belonged to self were empty, then what
could there be to fear? *"ALL OF THESE DISCIPLES*
OF THE BUDDHA LEAVE ALL FEARFULNESS FAR BEHIND/
"He is ALWAYS PRACTICING GREAT KINDNESS AND
PITY/ He always practices great kindness and
great compassion and pities and remembers all living beings. *HE CONSTANTLY HAS FAITH, AS WELL AS*
REVERENCE/ He always has genuine, pure faith in
and reverence and respect for the Triple Jewel.
HE IS REPLETE WITH MERIT AND VIRTUE OF REPENTANCE/
He is endowed with all the merit and virtue of re-
pentance and reform, *NIGHT AND DAY INCREASING*
WHOLESOME DHARMAS. HE DELIGHTS IN DHARMAS' TRUE

*AND ACTUAL BENEFITS AND DOES NOT LOVE THE RECEP-
TION OF DESIRES/* He does not love the five ob-
jects of desire. *HE REFLECTS UPON THE DHARMAS HE
HAS HEARD/* He is always pondering and contemplat-
ing the Buddhadharmas he has heard, *FAR FREE FROM
THE PRACTICE OF GRASPING/* He leaves grasping and
attaching behavior far behind. *HE HAS NO GREED
FOR BENEFITS OR OFFERINGS/* He is not greedy for
fame or profit, *AND HE ONLY DELIGHTS IN THE BUD-
DHA'S BODHI/* The only thing he delights in is the
Buddha's wonderful Dharma of Bodhi. *WITH ONE MIND
HE SEEKS THE BUDDHA'S WISDOM/* He is single-minded
in his quest for the wisdom of a Buddha alone,
CONCENTRATION UNDIVIDED WITH NO OTHER THOUGHT/ Intent and concentrated, he does not have two kinds
of thoughts; he only has the thought of seeking
the Buddha's wisdom."

SUTRA:

> *"HE CULTIVATES ALL OF THE PARAMITAS,
> FAR SEPARATES FROM FLATTERY AND DECEIT;
> AS IS SPOKEN, SO, TOO, DOES HE PRACTICE,
> AND IS SECURED IN TRUE AND ACTUAL SPEECH.*
>
> *"HE DOES NOT DEFILE THE BUDDHAS' HOUSEHOLD,
> NOR ABANDON BODHISATTVA PRECEPTS;
> TAKING NO DELIGHT IN WORLDLY MATTERS,
> CONSTANTLY HE BENEFITS THE WORLD.*
>
> *"HE CULTIVATES THE GOOD WITHOUT FATIGUE,
> HIS QUEST INTENSIFYING FOR THE WAY
>   SUPREME;
> SUCH, THEN, IS HIS LIKING FOR THE DHARMA,
> THAT MERIT AND VIRTUE INTERACT WITH
>   MEANINGS.*
>
> *"HE CONSTANTLY GIVES RISE TO A GREAT VOW-MIND,
> VOWING THAT ALL BUDDHAS HE WILL SEE,
> PROTECT AND HOLD ALL BUDDHAS' DHARMAS,
> AND GATHER IN THE GREAT IMMORTAL'S WAY.*
>
> *"ALWAYS BRINGING FORTH SUCH VOWS AS THESE,
> HE CULTIVATES THE PRACTICES SUPREME,
> MATURES AND RIPENS ALL THE FLOCKS OF
>   BEINGS,
> ADORNS AND PURIFIES ALL BUDDHAS' LANDS.*

COMMENTARY:

"HE CULTIVATES ALL OF THE PARAMITAS/   The Bodhisattva concentrates his mind and seeks the wisdom of a Buddha. If one wishes to obtain the wisdom of the Buddha, one must cultivate the Six
Crossings-over, or the Ten Crossings-over--the
Paramitas. One must also be FAR SEPARATE FROM
FLATTERY AND DECEIT/   One must leave flattery
and obsequiousness far behind, along with all fal-
sity and deceit. AS IS SPOKEN, SO, TOO, DOES HE
PRACTICE/ One must rely upon the Dharma spoken
by the Buddha to cultivate. AND he IS SECURED IN
TRUE AND ACTUAL SPEECH/ And at all times you
should cultivate the dharmas of true speech, actual speech, never engaging in false speech.
     "HE DOES NOT DEFILE THE BUDDHAS' HOUSEHOLD/
It is essential to cultivate the Dharma-doors spoken by the Buddha very, very well, and protect the
Dharma jewels spoken by the Buddha, never defiling
the household of all Buddhas. That is, one must
not make a bad impression for Buddhism by influenc-
ing people to have doubts. To start with, people
may want to believe in the Buddha, but if you do
not cultivate well, as soon as they see you they
lose their faith. You can't let that happen, NOR
ABANDON BODHISATTVA PRECEPTS/ He at all times
protects the ten heavy and forty-eight light precepts cultivated by Bodhisattvas, TAKING NO DELIGHT
IN WORLDLY MATTERS/ He has no greedy attachment
for worldly dharmas. That means he has no liking
for the world's wealth, sex, fame, food, and
sleep--matters concerned with the five objects of
desire. CONSTANTLY HE BENEFITS THE WORLD/ It is
his constant wish to benefit the living beings of
the world.
     "HE CULTIVATES THE GOOD WITHOUT FATIGUE/ In
practicing giving and doing wholesome deeds,
there never comes a time when he feels he's had
enough, HIS QUEST INTENSIFYING FOR THE WAY SUPREME/
He is more vigorous each day, daily becoming more
courageous in his search for the unsurpassed, most
supreme fruit of the Way. SUCH, THEN, IS HIS LIK-
ING FOR THE DHARMA THAT MERIT AND VIRTUE INTERACT
WITH MEANINGS/
     "HE CONSTANTLY GIVES RISE TO A GREAT VOW-MIND/
He is constantly bringing forth a great mind of

vows and resolutions, *VOWING THAT ALL BUDDHAS HE
WILL SEE/* He constantly makes the vow that he
will see all the Buddhas of the ten directions and
the three periods of time, and *PROTECT AND HOLD
ALL BUDDHAS' DHARMAS/* He vows to protect and maintain all dharmas spoken by the Buddhas, *AND* to
GATHER IN THE GREAT IMMORTAL'S WAY, that is, the
Buddha Way. *ALWAYS BRINGING FORTH SUCH VOWS AS
THESE/ HE CULTIVATES THE PRACTICES SUPREME/ MA-
TURES AND RIPENS ALL THE FLOCKS OF BEINGS/* He
brings all the flocks of beings to maturity, causing all living beings to become ripened and in the
future to become Buddhas. He *ADORNS AND PURIFIES
ALL BUDDHAS' LANDS/* He adorns and purifies the
countries of all of the Buddhas of the ten directions and the three periods of time."

In studying the Buddhadharma and listening
to Sutras, it is not the case that after one has
listened to the Sutra that is all there is to it.
It is necessary to base oneself upon the teachings
and cultivate. If you listen and then fail to put
what you have heard into actual practice, then
that is equivalent to talking about food and counting other people's money. You can talk all you
want about how good this or that food is to eat,
and about what a fine flavor it has, however, if
you never get around to eating it, you still will
not actually know what it tastes like. Day after
day, in the bank you may count out money to others
counting out as much as a thousand, ten thousand,
a hundred thousand, a million, or even ten million.
Yet, when the bank closes, you yourself haven't a
penny--none of it is yours. Therefore, when we
hear the Buddhadharma, we must put the Dharma into
practice. If the Bodhisattva cultivates the Six
Paramitas and the ten thousand practices, should
we be unable to cultivate so many, we should at
least cultivate three Paramitas, two Paramitas,
or one Paramita. We should cultivate either giving, or holding precepts, or patience, or vigor,
or dhyana-samadhi, or Prajna, or expedients, or
making vows, or using one's own strength to do all
kinds of good deeds, or using one's own wisdom to
perform various kinds of fine acts. For it to
count, one must at all times and very actually
practice. If you do not put it into practice, no
matter how much you hear, it will all be useless.

SUTRA:

     "ALL OF THE BUDDHAS' KSHETRA LANDS ,
     DISCIPLES OF THE BUDDHA FULLY FILL.
     IMPARTIAL, OF ONE SINGLE, EVEN MIND,
     NOTHING THAT THEY DO IS DONE IN VAIN.
     THEY, ON THE TIP OF EVERY SINGLE HAIR,
     AT ONE TIME, ACCOMPLISH RIGHT ENLIGHTENMENT.

     "VOWS LIKE THOSE OF THEIRS, WHICH ARE SO
            GREAT,
     ARE LIMITLESS, AND THEY HAVE NO BOUNDS:
     'EMPTY SPACE, ALONG WITH LIVING BEINGS,
     THE DHARMA REALM; TOGETHER WITH NIRVANA,

     "APPEARANCES OF BUDDHAS IN THE WORLD,
     BUDDHA'S WISDOM AND HIS STATES OF MIND,
     WHAT THE WISDOM OF THUS COME ONES ENTERS,
     AND THE EXHAUSTION OF THE TURNINGS THREE--

     "IF ALL OF THOSE SHOULD HAVE AN END,
     THEN ALL OF MY VOWS WOULD HAVE AN END.
     BUT, AS ALL OF THOSE CAN HAVE NO END,
     SO,   O, ARE MY VOWS JUST THAT WAY.'
     HAVING THUS MADE VOWS AS GREAT AS THOSE,
     THEIR MINDS BECOME COMPLIANT AND SUBDUED.

COMMENTARY:

     "ALL OF THE BUDDHAS' KSHETRA LANDS / DISCIPLES
OF THE BUDDHA FULLY FILL/ There is not just one
world; there are limitless and boundlessly many
worlds. All the Buddhalands are also limitless
and boundless. Disciples of the Buddha fill up
all of the worlds, all of the Buddhakshetras. IM-
PARTIAL, OF ONE SINGLE, EVEN MIND/ NOTHING THAT
THEY DO IS DONE IN VAIN/ These disciples of the
Buddha are all the Bodhisattvas. Everything those
Bodhisattvas cultivate is impartial and equal, and
they all with one even mind benefit living beings.
All of what they do and cultivate is not done in
vain. It is impossible for them to do something
that does not result in the slightest bit of merit
and virtue. In whatever they do, there is certain
to be some merit and virtue present. THEY, ON THE
TIP OF EVERY SINGLE HAIR/ AT ONE TIME, ACCOMPLISH

RIGHT ENLIGHTENMENT/ Those Bodhisattvas make the
vow that on the tip of every single hair they will
cultivate and will become Buddhas at one and the
same time. On a single hairtip, all Buddhas become Buddhas, and on all hairtips, too, all Buddhas simultaneously become Buddhas.

"VOWS LIKE THOSE OF THEIRS, WHICH ARE SO
GREAT/ ARE LIMITLESS, AND THEY HAVE NO BOUNDS/ The
vows such as those that they make are inconceiv-
ably great vows. There is no way you could measure the extent of those kinds of vows, nor do they
have any bounds. 'EMPTY SPACE, ALONG WITH LIVING
BEINGS/ Empty space and living beings are both
infinite. THE DHARMA REALM, TOGETHER WITH NIRVANA/
The Dharma realm and Nirvana are infinite, as
well--but, suppose they could come to an end. AP-
PEARANCES OF BUDDHAS IN THE WORLD, BUDDHA'S WIS-
DOM AND HIS STATES OF MIND/ WHAT THE WISDOM OF
THUS COME ONES ENTERS/ the kinds of states into
which the wisdom of a Buddha is able to enter, AND
THE EXHAUSTION OF THE TURNINGS THREE'--should the
realm of living beings come to an end, the realm of
empty space come to an end, and the realm of the
Dharma Realm come to an end, then the vows made by
the Bodhisattva would come to an end. If the Dharma
Realm, the realm of empty space, along with the Buddha's realm--all of those--have no time when they
come to an end, then the vows of the Bodhisattva
will have no exhaustion or end. That means that if
all that was listed above should come to an end,
then the vows made by the Bodhisattva would be over
and done with. Should they have no end, then the
Bodhisattva's vows will also never end.

"'IF ALL OF THOSE SHOULD HAVE AN END/ THEN
ALL MY VOWS WOULD HAVE AN END/ All the previously
described--empty space, living beings, afflictions,
the realm of Buddhas, and the Dharma Realm--if all
of those have a time when they come to an end,
then my vows will disappear. If it turns out not
to be that way, BUT, AS ALL OF THOSE CAN HAVE NO
END/ SO, TOO, ARE MY VOWS JUST THAT WAY/ My vows
too, can never come to an end.' HAVING THUS MADE
VOWS AS GREAT AS THOSE/ THEIR MINDS BECOME COMP-
LIANT AND SUBDUED/ Having in that way made such
inconceivable, vast, great, limitless, boundless,
inexhaustible, and infinite kinds of vows, their
minds are at all times supple and compliant, constantly tamed and subdued. Because the minds of

Bodhisattvas have no greed, hatred, or stupidity
within them, as a result they are always compliant
and subdued."

SUTRA:

> *"THEY CAN BELIEVE THE BUDDHA'S MERIT AND*
> *VIRTUE,*
> *AND CONTEMPLATE REGARDING LIVING BEINGS.*

> *"KNOWING THEY ARISE FROM CAUSES AND CON-*
> *DITIONS,*
> *THEY THEN GIVE RISE TO KINDLY MINDFULNESS;*
> *'SUCH SUFFERING LIVING BEINGS SUCH AS*
> *THESE,*
> *I NOW SHOULD LIBERATE AND SAVE.*

> *"'FOR THE SAKE OF THOSE LIVING BEINGS,*
> *I SHOULD CULTIVATE THE VARIOUS KINDS*
> *OF GIVING.*
> *POSITIONS AS A KING, ALL GEMS AND JEWELS,*
> *UP TO ELEPHANTS, HORSES, AND CONVEYANCES.*

> *"'HEAD, EYES, HANDS, AS WELL AS FEET,*
> *UP TO EVEN BODY, BLOOD, AND FLESH--*
> *EACH AND EVERY THING I CAN RENOUNCE.'*
> *THEIR MINDS HAVE NO WORRIES OR REGRETS.*

> *" SEEKING ALL THE VARIOUS SUTRA BOOKS,*
> *THEIR MINDS ARE NEVER WEARY OR FATIGUED.*
> *WELL CAN THEY UNDERSTAND THEIR DRIFT AND*
> *AND MEANING,*
> *ADAPTING THEM TO PRACTICES OF WORLDS.*

> *"REPENTANCE AND REFORM THEIR OWN ADORN-*
> *MENT,*
> *THEIR CULTIVATION IS PROGRESSIVELY*
> *MORE SOLID.*

COMMENTARY:

"*THEY CAN BELIEVE THE BUDDHA'S MERIT AND VIR-
TUE*"/ We who study the Buddhadharma should first
clearly recognize our tenets and convictions. We
should first ask ourselves, "Do I truly believe

in the Buddha? `Do I believe that the Buddha has
limitless merit and virtue?" Why is it that the
Buddha has limitless merit and virtue? It is because the Buddha in the past practiced giving on
a large scale, and he was able to give away all of
his wealth. He was able to take all of his inner
wealth--his head, eyes, brains, and marrow--and
his outer wealth--countries, cities, wives, and
children--and give it away without any attachment.
"THEY CONTEMPLATE REGARDING LIVING BEINGS"/   Since
we believe that the Buddha has limitless merit and
virtue, we should constantly follow the Buddha in
study and should also practice all kinds of giving.
Therefore, we should contemplate all living beings'
causes and conditions, *"KNOWING THEY ARISE FROM
CAUSES AND CONDITIONS"/*   All living beings are produced from the coming together of causes and conditions, and all have very deep relationships with
us. They may have been our parents from beginningless kalpas to the present, or they may have been
our elder or younger brothers, sisters, wives, or
friends from beginningless kalpas to the present,
so that they have the relationship of an intricate
network of karmas and turnings on the revolving
wheel with us. Because they are aware of that relationship, *"THEY THEN GIVE RISE TO KINDLY MINDFUL-
NESS/*   'I should bring forth a mind of kindness
and compassion and save and rescue all of those living beings who have relationships with me, so that
they leave suffering and attain bliss. I should
cause them to all be happy. *SUCH SUFFERING LIVING
BEINGS SUCH AS THESE/ I NOW SHOULD LIBERATE AND
SAVE/* If I do not save and rescue them, then there
is no way to know when their suffering can come to
an end. And so, those beings are turning on
the wheel of the six destinies, being born and then
dying, being reborn and then dying again; now that
I know, I should save them and cause them to be
liberated.
        *"'FOR THE SAKE OF THOSE LIVING BEINGS/ I
SHOULD CULTIVATE THE VARIOUS KINDS OF GIVING/ POSI-
TIONS AS A KING, ALL GEMS AND JEWELS/ UP TO ELE-
PHANTS, HORSES, AND CONVEYANCES/* I can give away
all of my royal positions to other people, and all
of my gems and jewels: my gold, silver, lapis lazuli, crystal, mother of pearl, red pearls, and car-
nelian--all of those seven precious things. I can

give away, as well, my most cherished great elephant, or my most beautiful horse, or my finest conveyances, whether it be my car, my train, my bus, or even the airplane I own--all of that I can give away to other living beings. Those are possessions external to the body. In addition, if someone required my *HEAD*, then I will give it to him. If someone requires my *EYES*, I'll give them to him. If someone needs my *HANDS*, they are his; *AS WELL AS IF* someone needs my *FEET*, he may have them. *UP TO EVEN BODY, BLOOD, AND FLESH/* Even to the point that if someone needs my body, it, too, will be given him.' Even one's own blood, the blood from one's own body, is bestowed as a gift upon all living beings. Even the flesh on one's own body can also be given to all living beings." Right now we should all look into ourselves and ask ourselves if we can do this. If we can, then we are Bodhisattvas who have brought forth the resolve of Bodhisattvas. If we are unable to do this, should we or should we not imitate the Bodhisattva? If we want to imitate the Bodhisattva, then we should, bit by bit, go forward and act in this way.

"'*EACH AND EVERY THING I CAN RENOUNCE/* I can give them all away. The external wealth of countries, cities, wives, and children, along with the internal wealth of head, eyes, brains, and marrow, I am completely able to give away.' *THEIR MINDS HAVE NO WORRIES OR REGRETS/* After they have performed such acts of giving, they are incapable of having regrets in their minds, saying, 'I should not have given them away! Such cherished possessions of mine--my countries, cities, wives, and children, my head, eyes, brains, and marrow--how could I have given them away to people? I should not have done that. It was too idiotic, too stupid!'" What the Bodhisattva wants to do is just what people are unable to do, the "stupid" things. He's not just always trying to get a bargain and come out on the long end of the stick when he gives. Therefore, when a Bodhisattva gives away all external and internal wealth, he is unable to regret it. "'*SEEKING ALL THE VARIOUS SUTRA BOOKS/* Furthermore, they find ways to study all of the books of Sutras spoken by the Buddha, and *THEIR MINDS ARE NEVER WEARY OR FATIGUED/* In their minds

there never comes a time when they would say, 'I've
looked at enough Sutras spoken by the Buddha, and
THEIR MINDS ARE NEVER WEARY OR FATIGUED/ In their
minds there never comes a time when they would say,
'I've looked at enough Sutras, and I've recited
this mantra enough; I would like to recite a new
and different one.' They could never be that way.
Bodhisattvas, in reading the Sutras, never weary of
a hundred recitations. Even if they have recited
one hundred times, they are never tired or weary
of it. In reciting mantras, too, they never weary
of a hundred recitations. They never become tired
of them."
         We people should realize why it is we need to
recite Sutras and hold mantras. It's not just because if you recite a certain Sutra you will have
a certain amount of merit and virtue. It is to
cure your false thinking. If you didn't have any
false thinking, then you could get away with not
reciting Sutras and holding mantras. But, if you
do have false thinking, then you have to recite
Sutras and hold mantras, which counteracts your
false thinking and helps your mind to become pure.
When we constantly strike up false thoughts in our
minds, always having unclean, defiled false thinking, so that as soon as you think, if you're not
thinking about how nice your girlfriend is, then
you're thinking about how handsome your boyfriend
is--all of that is false thinking. If all you are
doing is thinking, it's still not serious. However, if you keep on thinking like that, you'll
start to cry and will feel it's very painful. Due
to that, when we recite Sutras and hold mantras,
it's so we can expel the false and retain the true.
The mind is like a monkey. The monkey is always
looking for something to do. If you haven't any
work to give it, it runs off east and west. If
you do give the mind some work to do, such as reciting Sutras and holding mantras, then it will
strike up less false thinking, and the monkey won't
run off. "Their minds are never weary or fatigued." In reciting Sutras and holding mantras
--cultivating--they never could become tired or
weary.
         *"WELL CAN THEY UNDERSTAND THEIR DRIFT AND
MEANING/* In their recitation of the Sutras and
their holding of mantras, they understand the doc-

trines and purport of the Sutras and the principles of the mantras, *ADAPTING THEM TO PRACTICES OF
WORLDS/* Once you have understood the principles,
then you can apply them in the world to benefit
all living beings. *REPENTANCE AND REFORM THEIR
OWN ADORNMENT/* One should be very repentant and
reform the places where one made mistakes in past
behavior, and one should, oneself, use the merit
and virtue of repentance and reform to adorn one's
own resolve for Bodhi. *THEIR CULTIVATION IS PRO-
GRESSIVELY MORE SOLID/* If you yourself are able
greatly to repent and reform, bring forth the
thought for Bodhi, and cultivate the unsurpassed
Way of Bodhi, then day by day you will increase
in firmness and solidity."

SUTRA

> "THEY MAKE OFFERINGS TO BUDDHAS LIMITLESS,
> REVERE, DO REVERENCE, HONOR, AND RESPECT
>   THEM.

> "IN THAT WAY ALWAYS DO THEY PRACTICE,
> DAY AND NIGHT, NOT LAZY OR FATIGUED.
> GOOD ROOTS BRIGHTEN AND BECOME MORE PURE,
> LIKE GOLD WHICH HAS BEEN SMELTED IN
>   THE FIRE.

> "THE BODHISATTVA DWELLING IN THIS PLACE,
> PURELY CULTIVATES ALL OF THE TEN GROUNDS.
> IN WHAT HE DOES THERE IS NO OBSTRUCTION,
> HIS ENDOWMENTS CANNOT BE CUT OFF.

> "JUST AS WHEN A GREAT BUSINESS LEADER,
> TO BENEFIT THE HOSTS OF BUSINESS PEOPLE,
> ASKS AND KNOWS ROUTES' DANGERS AND
>   THEIR EASE,
> THEN ARRIVES IN SAFETY AT THE TOWN,

> "THE BODHISATTVA WHO DWELLS ON THE
>   FIRST GROUND,
> YOU SHOULD KNOW JUST ALSO IN THAT WAY,
> WITH COURAGEOUS VIGOR UNOBSTRUCTED,
> REACHES AND ARRIVES AT THE TENTH GROUND.

"WHILE HE DWELLS ON THIS, THE INITIAL
        GROUND,
HE ACTS AS KING OF MERIT AND GREAT
        VIRTUE.

COMMENTARY:

"The mind of the Bodhisattva daily increases
in solidity as he vastly cultivates the giving of
offerings. THEY MAKE OFFERINGS TO BUDDHAS LIMIT-
LESS/ REVERE, DO REVERENCE, HONOR, AND RESPECT
THEM/   Inasmuch as he makes limitless offerings to
limitless Buddhas, naturally he reveres and rever-
ences, honors and respects them.   IN THAT WAY AL-
WAYS DO THEY PRACTICE/   In praticing, one should
have an enduring mind.   One cannot achieve success
after a single day of practice.   Life after life
and time after time one must practice in this way,
cultivating the Bodhisattva Path, DAY AND NIGHT,
NOT LAZY OR FATIGUED/ Whether it's daytime or
nighttime, they are constantly practicing the Bodhisattva Way, never weary or fatigued.   Their
GOOD ROOTS BRIGHTEN AND BECOME MORE PURE/   As the
Bodhisattvas cultivate, they day by day accumulate
more good roots, their intelligence is daily greater, and they attain to their original purity, LIKE
GOLD WHICH HAS BEEN SMELTED IN THE FIRE/   It is
just the same as when a goldsmith uses fire to
smelt true gold.   Having put it through the fire
once, he again puts it through the fire.   When it
has been through the fire a great many times, the
gold becomes pure gold, without the least admixture.
        "THE BODHISATTVA DWELLING IN THIS PLACE/ PURE
LY CULTIVATES ALL OF THE TEN GROUNDS/   The Bodhisattva cultivating the Dharma-doors of the Ten
Grounds is also that way, being smelted in the
same manner as gold.   He purely cultivates the
states of the Ten Grounds.   IN WHAT HE DOES THERE
IS NO OBSTRUCTION/   When the Bodhisattva is cultivating the Bodhisattva Way, he cultivates all good
and eradicates all evil, and so he has no obstructions.   HIS ENDOWMENTS CANNOT BE CUT OFF/   He is
endowed with the light of all wisdoms, which cannot be cut off.

*"JUST AS WHEN A GREAT BUSINESS LEADER/ TO
BENEFIT THE HOSTS OF BUSINESS PEOPLE/ ASKS AND
KNOWS ROUTES' DANGERS AND THEIR EASE/ THEN ARRIVES
IN SAFETY AT THE TOWN"/* It is also like, in this
day and age, a great entrepreneur, perhaps a prominent corporate executive, in those days, a cara-
van leader, who, in order to do business and make
large profits, joins together a large number of
business people. He finds out clearly in advance
if the route to be traversed is dangerous or easy.
Then they arrive with no incident at the place to
which they wanted to go. In the same way, the Bodhisattva who is cultivating on the First Ground
should ask about the states of every single Ground,
along with the fruit positions to be obtained, all
the way to Buddhahood, just as the businessman going to the great city. *"THE BODHISATTVA WHO DWELLS
ON THE FIRST GROUND/ YOU SHOULD KNOW, JUST ALSO IS
IN THAT WAY/ WITH COURAGEOUS VIGOR UNOBSTRUCTED/
REACHES AND ARRIVES AT THE TENTH GROUND/* He is
just the same as the great business leader. He is
courageously vigorous, has no obstructions whatsoever, and from the First Ground, the Ground of
Happiness, he arrives at the Tenth Ground, the
Ground of the Dharma Cloud. *WHILE HE DWELLS ON
THIS, THE INITIAL GROUND/ HE ACTS AS A KING OF
MERIT AND GREAT VIRTUE/* While dwelling on the
Ground of Happiness, he is a king of great merit
and virtue and influences all the Bodhisattvas to
go forward and cultivate."

SUTRA:

> *"HE USES DHARMA TO TRANSFORM ALL BEINGS,
> COMPASSION-HEARTED, WITH NO TRACE OF
>   HARMING.*
>
> *"RULING AND DIRECTING JAMBUVIPA,
> IN TRANSFORMING CUSTOMS, NONE DOES HE
>   NOT REACH,
> MAKING ALL ESTABLISHED IN GREAT GIVING,
> ACCOMPLISHED BY THE WISDOM OF A BUDDHA.*
>
> *"IN HIS WISH TO SEEK THE WAY SUPREME,
> RENOUNCING THEN HIS OWN ROYAL POSITION,*

HE CAN, WITHIN THE MIDST OF THE BUDDHA'S
    TEACHING,
COURAGEOUS AND WITH DILIGENCE, CULTIVATE.

"HE THEN ATTAINS TO ONE HUNDRED SAMADHIS,
AND HE COMES TO SEE ALL HUNDRED BUDDHAS:
HE MAKES ONE HUNDRED WORLDS TREMBLE AND
    QUAKE:
HIS ILLUMINATION'S REACH IS ALSO THUS,

"HE TRANSFORMS AND SAVES A HUNDRED BEINGS,
TO ENTER IN ONE HUNDRED DHARMA-DOORS;
HE CAN KNOW ONE HUNDRED KALPAS' MATTERS,
AND APPEAR WITHIN ONE HUNDRED BODIES.

"THERE THEN APPEAR ONE HUNDRED BODHI-
    SATTVAS,
ACTING AS A RETINUE FOR HIM.

COMMENTARY:

"When the Bodhisattva acts as a king of great
merit and virtue, in Southern Jambudvipa he constantly becomes a wheel-turning king, in order to
teach and transform living beings. HE USES DHARMA
TO TRANSFORM ALL BEINGS/ He uses all the Buddhadharmas to save all living beings, by being COM-
PASSION-HEARTED, WITH NO TRACE OF HARMING/ In
transforming living beings, he constantly has a
mind of kindness and compassion, with no thought
of harming living beings. He firmly maintains the
practice of giving, RULING AND DIRECTING JAMBUD-
VIPA/ He acts as king of the region known as
Southern Jambudvipa and transforms and beautifies
its customs, causing the customs of each nation to
become wholesome ones. All countries hold the
Five Precepts:

    1. no killing,
    2. no stealing,
    3. no sexual misconduct,
    4. no false speech,
    5. no intoxicants.

The citizens of all countries hold the five precepts and practice the ten goods, and so IN TRANS-

FORMING CUSTOMS. NONE DOES HE NOT REACH, MAKING
ALL ESTABLISHED IN GREAT GIVING/ He causes all
living beings also to practice the Dharma-door of
great renunciation, to cultivate the Dharma-door
of giving, and ACCOMPLISHED IN THE WISDOM OF A
BUDDHA/ All living beings attain the true and actual wisdom of a Buddha.

"IN HIS WISH TO SEEK THE WAY SUPREME/ He himself seeks the most supreme Way, and he causes all
living beings to seek it, too. RENOUNCING THEN HIS
OWN ROYAL POSITION/ To start with, he is king of
a country, but he also gives away that kingly position to other people. HE CAN, WITHIN THE MIDST
OF THE BUDDHA'S TEACHING/ COURAGEOUS AND WITH DIL-
IGENCE, CULTIVATE/ What does he do after he has
renounced his royal position? He cultivates. He
leaves home and cultivates the Way, with courageous
vigor. In diligently cultivating precepts, samadhi, and wisdom and putting to rest, greed, hatred,
and stupidity, at no time is he lazy.

"HE THEN ATTAINS TO ONE HUNDRED SAMADHIS/ At
that time, the Bodhisattva in the interval of a
single instant of thought, attains to a hundred
kinds of samadhis, AND HE COMES TO SEE ALL HUNDRED
BUDDHAS/ Again, within the space of a single
thought, he can see all the Buddhas of a hundred
lands. HE MAKES ONE HUNDRED WORLDS TREMBLE AND
QUAKE/ The countries of one hundred worlds all
experience the six types of quakes. HIS ILLUMINA-
TION'S REACH IS ALSO THUS/ The pervasive illumination of his light also shines upon the living beings of a hundred worlds. HE TRANSFORMS AND SAVES
ONE HUNDRED BEINGS/ As he shines upon the living
beings of a hundred worlds, he transforms and saves
all those hundred worlds' beings. TO ENTER IN ONE
HUNDRED DHARMA-DOORS/ The living beings of the
hundred worlds all attain a hundred Dharma-doors.
HE CAN KNOW ONE HUNDRED KALPAS' MATTERS/ He is
able to know all of the events of a hundred previous kalpas, of a hundred kalpas afterwards, and
of a hundred present kalpas, knowing the entirety
of the past, the present, and the future. AND AP-
PEAR WITHIN ONE HUNDRED BODIES/ He is also able
to appear and transform, having as many as a hundred Bodhisattva bodies. THERE THEN APPEAR ONE
HUNDRED BODHISATTVAS/ Every single body further
manifests as many as a hundred Bodhisattvas, ACTING

AS A RETINUE FOR HIM/ They act as that Bodhisattva's retinue, helping him propagate the Buddhadharma and teach and transform living beings."

SUTRA:

"IF HE USES COMFORT FROM HIS POWER OF
        VOWS,
THEIR NUMBER, LIMITLESS, SURPASSES THESE.

"I, AMONG THE MEANINGS OF THIS GROUND,
HAVE IN GENERAL SPOKEN A SMALL PORTION.
IF ONE WANTS TO ANALYZE MOST BROADLY,
ONE CANNOT FINISH IN A MILLION KALPAS.

"THE BODHISATTVA'S PATH, THE MOST SUPREME,
OF BENEFITTING ALL THE FLOCKS OF BEINGS--
DHARMAS SUCH AS THOSE, OF THE FIRST
        GROUND,
I HAVE NOW ALREADY FINISHED SPEAKING."

COMMENTARY:

"IF HE USES COMFORT FROM HIS POWER OF VOWS/
THEIR NUMBER, LIMITLESS, SURPASSES THESE/ Should
it be that the Bodhisattva has made vows of sovereign, as-you-please comfort, the merit, virtue,
and wisdom far surpass that by an unknown amount,
surpassing it by a hundred kalpas, a thousand kalpas, a hundred thousand kalpas, kalpas so many
that words cannot express these principles. I,
AMONG THE MEANINGS OF THIS GROUND"/ Vajra Treasury Bodhisattva says, "I, within the meanings and
principles of this First Ground, "HAVE IN GENERAL
SPOKEN A SMALL PORTION/ I have not completely
discussed them. Were I to speak them completely
IF ONE WANTS TO ANALYZE MOST BROADLY/ If they
were discussed extensively and in full detail,
ONE CANNOT FINISH IN A MILLION KALPAS/ These
principles could not be discussed completely in
a quadrillion aeons.
    "THE BODHISATTVA'S PATH, THE MOST SUPREME/
which is cultivated by Bodhisattvas, OF BENEFIT-
TING ALL THE FLOCKS OF BEINGS/ What matters most
to them, their creed, is to benefit all living

beings, benefitting themselves by benefitting
others, crossing themselves over by crossing over
others, enlightening themselves by enlightening
others. DHARMAS SUCH AS THOSE OF THE FIRST GROUND/
The kinds of dharmas I previously discussed, those
Dharma-doors of the First Ground, I NOW HAVE AL-
READY FINISHED SPEAKING/ Now I have already finished my very general explanation of them. All
of you should thoroughly investigate them, and
then you will be able to understand them."

END OF THE FIRST GROUND

INDEX

Dharma, cont.
  doors, 26;29-30
  Eye, Selective 13;16
  Eye Treasury, Proper 70
  non-outflowing 15
  outflowing 15
  Realm xiii; 80
  Requesting of 8
  Wisdom 23
  Wheel 70
Dharmas
  World-transcending 14
  Worldly 14
  of Attraction, Four 97, 107
Discriminating Eloquence 36
Doubt 27, 31
doubts 65
Dying, fear of 59-63

Efficacy 69
Eight Marks of Accomplishing the Way 70;77
Eighteen Realms 47
Eloquence,
  Discriminating 36
  Unobstructed 16,18
Emitting Light, Bodhisattva Ground of 21-22
Emperor Tai Tsung (600-649) xii
Empress Wu, also Tse-tien xii
Empty Space 69
"Essay on the Gold Lion" xii
Evil Destinies, Fear of 59-63
Evil Destinies, Four 45
Fa-shang (495-580) xi
Ta-tsang (643-712) xii
Faith 27, 65, 84
False thinking 126
Fear 59-63
Fears, Five 116-117
Filial Piety iv
Five desires 57,108

Five Fearsome Matters 59-63; 116-117
Five Precepts 130
Five Skandhas 47
Flattery and Deceit 86
Four Evil Destinies 45
Four Dharmas of Attraction 97,107
Four Limitless Minds 111-112
Four Requisites 96
Four Virtues of Nirvana 5
Four Wisdoms 14

Ghosts
  Hungry 32
Giving 62,97,124
Gold Mountain Doctrine viii
Gold Mountain Monastery Establishment of viii
Good-knowing Advisors 66
Good Roots 13;19;65-66; 111;128
Good Wisdom, Bodhisattva Ground of 21
Great Medicine King Tree 77
Great Wisdom Light Samadhi 11-13;17,19
Greed 61-62;66;117
Greed, Hatred, Stupidity 87
Ground of Blazing Wisdom (Fourth of Ten Grounds) 21
Ground of the Dharma Cloud (Tenth of the Ten Grounds) 21
Ground of Emitting Light (Third of the Ten Grounds) 21-22
Ground of Good Wisdom (Ninth of the Ten Grounds) 21
Ground of Happiness (First of the Ten Grounds) 21,22;54

Dharma Protector Wei T'o Bodhisattva with his Jeweled Pestle

Verse of Transference

May the merit and virtue accrued from this work,
Adorn the Buddhas' Pure Lands;
Repaying four kinds of kindness above,
And aiding those suffering in the paths below.

May those who see and hear of this,
All bring forth resolve for Bodhi,
And when this retribution body is over
Be born together in Ultimate Bliss.

THE BUDDHIST TEXT TRANSLATION SOCIETY

Chairperson: The Venerable Master Hua, Abbot of
Gold Mountain Temple, Chairperson of
the Sino-American Buddhist Association, and Chancellor of Dharma Realm
Buddhist University

PRIMARY TRANSLATION COMMITTEE:

Chairpersons: Bhikshuni Heng Yin
Bhikshuni Heng Ch'ih

Members: Bhikshu Heng Kuan
Bhikshu Heng K'ung
Bhikshu Heng Sure
Bhikshu Heng Shun
Bhikshu Heng Tso
Bhikshu Heng Teng
Bhikshu Heng Kung
Bhikshu Heng Chi
Bhikshuni Heng Hsien
Bhikshuni Heng Ch'ing
Bhikshuni Heng Chen
Bhikshuni Heng Hua
Bhikshuni Heng Ming
Bhikshuni Heng Chai
Bhikshuni Heng Wen
Bhikshuni Heng Tao
Upasaka Kuo Jung (R.B.) Epstein
Upasaka Kuo.Chou (David) Rounds
Upasaka Chou Kuo Li
Upasika Kuo Ts'an (Terri) Nicholson
Professor Wu-yi
Professor Hsing Tsun Lee

REVISION COMMITTEE:

Chairpersons: Bhikshu Heng Tso
Upasaka Kuo Jung Epstein

Members: Bhikshu Heng Kuan
Bhikshu Heng Sure
Bhikshu Heng Teng
Bhikshu Heng Kung
Bhikshu Heng Chi
Bhikshuni Heng Yin
Bhikshuni Heng Ch'ih
Bhikshuni Heng Hsien
Bhikshuni Heng Ch'ing

Bhikshuni Heng Chen
Bhikshuni Heng Hua
Bhikshuni Heng Tao
Upasaka Kuo Chou Rounds
Upasaka Chou Kuo Li
Upasika Phuong Kuo Wu
Upasika Kuo Chin (Janet) Vickers
Upasika Kuo Han Epstein
Upasika Kuo Ts'an Nicholson
Upasika Hsieh Ping-ying
Professor Wu-yi
Professor Hsing Tsun Lee

EDITORIAL COMMITTEE:

Chairperson: Bhikshu Heng Kuan

Members: Bhikshu Heng K'ung
Bhikshu Heng 'Sure
Bhikshu Heng Shun
Bhikshu Heng Lai
Bhikshu Heng Ch'au
Bhikshu Heng Chi
Bhikshuni Heng Yin
Bhikhuni Heng Ch'ih
Bhikshuni Heng Hsien
Bhikshuni Heng Ch'ing
Bhikshuni Heng Chen
Bhikshuni Heng Chu
Bhikshuni Heng Hua
Bhikshuni Heng Jieh
Bhikshuni Heng Ming
Bhikshuni Heng Tao
Upasaka Kuo Jung Epstein
Upasaka Yu Kuo K'ung
Upasaka Kuo Chou Rounds
Upasaka Chou Kuo Li
Upasaka Kuo Tsun (Randy) Dinwiddie
Upasika Kuo Chin (Janet) Vickers
Upasika Kuo Ts'an Nicholson
Upasika Kuo Lin (Nancy) Lethcoe
Upasika Kuo Shun (Theresa) Nolan
Professor Wu-yi
Professor Hsing Tsun Lee

CERTIFICATION BOARD:

Chairperson: The Venerable Tripitaka Master Hua

Members: Bhikshu Heng Kuan
Bhikshu Heng Sure
Bhikshu Heng Tso
Bhiksuni Heng Yin
Bhikshuni Heng Ch'ih
Bhikshuni Heng Hsien
Bhikshuni Heng Ch'ing
Bhikshuni Heng Tao
Upasaka Wong Kuo-chun
Upasaka I Kuo-jung (R.B. Epstein)
Upasika T'an Kuo Shih
Upasika Kuo Chin Vickers

THE EIGHT REQUIREMENTS FOR TRANSLATORS WITH THE BUDDHIST TEXT TRANSLATION SOCIETY:

1. Translators must free themselves from all motives of personal fame and profit.
2. Translators must cultivate an attitude free from arrogance and conceit.
3. Translators must refrain from aggrandizing themselves and denigrating others.
4. Translators must not establish themselves as the standard of correctness and suppress the work of others with their fault-finding.
5. Translators must take the Buddha Mind as their own mind.
6. Translators must use the wisdom of the Selective Dharma Eye to determine true principles.
7. Translators must request Elder Virtuous Ones from the ten directions to certify their translations.
8. Translators must endeavor to propate the Teachings by printing Sutras, Vinaya texts, and Shastras when their translations have been certified as accurate.

THE GUIDING PRINCIPLES OF DHARMA REALM BUDDHIST UNIVERSITY:

1. Explaining and Propagating the Buddha's Teachings.
2. Developing Straightforward Minds.
3. Benefitting Society.
4. Enlightening All Living Beings.

PUBLICATIONS OF THE BUDDHIST TEXT TRANSLATION
SOCIETY: AVAILABLE AND FORTHCOMING

The Wonderful Dharma Lotus Flower Sutra, Volume III
The third of a series, this volume contains Chapter Two,
Expedients. Shakyamuni Buddha addresses Shariputra, the
wisest of the Sound Hearers, and starts to reveal his
use of expedients to describe the profundity of all
Buddhas' knowledge and vision, wisdom and suchness.
Then he stops himself, saying that the actual Dharma is
too difficult to hear and understand. Shariputra requests three times to be taught, and Shakyamuni Buddha
finally consents. As he begins to speak, five thousand
people, out of arrogance, leave the Assembly. To those
of true faith who remain, the Buddha explains the One
Great Matter for which all Buddhas appear in the world.
Paperbound, around 200 pages.

Shurangama Sutra, Volume II
This volume, accompanied by the outline of Dharma Master
Yüan Ying, and with thorough commentary by the Venerable
Master Hua, includes discussion of the ten manifestations
of seeing and individual and collective karma.
   *"When the Buddhadharma begins to disappear, the very first
   Sutra to disappear will be the Shurangama Sutra. The Shurangama Sutra lays bare the deviant knowledge and deviant
   views of those who misuse their powers. The Sutra text
   exposes their eccentricities and tactics so vividly that
   it is referred to as a 'monster-spotting mirror,' a demon-
   pounding pestle,' and a 'demon-cutting sword.' It breaks
   up the deviant and manifests the orthodox, destroys all the
   heavenly demons and those of external ways, and reveals the
   human capacity for proper knowledge and proper views. So,
   if we are to protect the Proper Dharma, we should investigate
   the Shurangama Sutra, understand the Shurangama Sutra, and
   protect the Shurangama Sutra. When people come to understand this Sutra, the heavenly demons and those of external
   ways will spontaneously disappear, world wars will cease,
   and all mankind will be at peace."*
                                        —*Tripitaka Master Hua*
Paperbound. 172 pages.

With One Heart Bowing to the City of Ten Thousand Buddhas, Vol. II
The second volume in the series presenting the daily records of two American Buddhist Monks, Bhikshu Heng Sure and Shramanera Heng Ch'au, as they make a pilgrimage bowing once every third step from Gold Wheel Temple in Los Angeles, California, to the City of Ten Thousand Buddhas near Ukiah in Northern California. By purifying their own bodies and minds they seek to influence humanity to cease all hatred and hostility and to prevent disasters, wars and suffering of all kinds.
Paperbound, 320 pages.

Songs for Awakening
A book of songs and music inspired by the teachings of Shakyamuni Buddha and the Venerable Master Hua.

Study Buddhism

I'm really lucky to study Buddhism.
Because last life, I planted good seeds,
Now in this life, I've met good friends,
And a good-knowing one to teach me deep wisdom.

I think that I will go to Buddhahood real soon.
I hope so.
My Dharma friends and I together will go
To Perfect Enlightenment.

Illustrated with photographs and pictures.

Open Your Eyes, Take A Look at the World
In the summer of 1978, a history-making event occurred in the course of world Buddhism: the delegation to Asia of the Sino-American Buddhist Association and Dharma Realm Buddhist University. Headed by the Venerable Master Hua, at the request of Southeast Asian Buddhists, ten delegates brought the Buddhadharma for the first time in this fashion from the West back to the East. Dynamic and outspoken, this book will open many eyes.
Bilingual.

Listen to Yourself; Think Everything Over
In this volume is plain and simple instruction on how to meditate using two traditional methods: Ch'an and Pure Land, from instructional talks by the Venerable Master Hua. Paperbound with photographs and illustrations, 153 pages.

The Heart of Prajna Paramita Sutra and Standless Gatha Commentary by the Venerable Master Hua. "Because nothing is attained, the Bodhisattva through reliance on Prajna-Paramita is unimpeded in his mind. Because there is no impediment, he is not afraid and he leaves distored dream-thinking far behind—ultimately Nirvana!" The *Heart Sutra* expresses the essence of Prajna Paramita, the great and perfect wisdom taught by the Buddha. Many practicing Buddhists recite the Sutra daily. The Venerable Master Hua's verses and commentary clearly explain each passage of the text. Available soon. Bilingual.

THE WONDERFUL DHARMA LOTUS FLOWER SUTRA, VOLUME I, paperbound, 88 pages.
THE WONDERFUL DHARMA LOTUS FLOWER SUTRA, VOLUME II, paperbound, 357 pages.
THE SHURANGAMA SUTRA, VOLUME I, paperbound, 250 pages.
WITH ONE HEART BOWING TO THE CITY OF TEN THOUSAND BUDDHAS, VOLUME I, paperbound, 173 pages.
THE AMITABHA SUTRA, paperbound, 204 pages. Also in Spanish.
THE VAJRA SUTRA, paperbound, 192 pages.
THE DHARANI SUTRA, paperbound, 352 pages.
THE SUTRA OF THE PAST VOWS OF EARTH STORE BODHISATTVA, hard cover and paperbound, 235 pages.
THE SIXTH PATRIARCH'S DHARMA JEWEL PLATFORM SUTRA, hard cover and paperbound, 380 pages.
THE SUTRA IN FORTY-TWO SECTIONS, paperbound, 94 pages.
THE SHRAMANERA VINAYA AND RULES OF DEPORTMENT, paperbound, 112 pgs.
PURE LAND AND CH'AN DHARMA TALKS, paperbound, 72 pages.
BUDDHA ROOT FARM, (Amitabha Buddha Recitation Instruction), paperbound, 72 pages.
RECORDS OF THE LIFE OF THE VENERABLE MASTER HSUAN HUA, VOLUME I, paperbound, 96 pages. Also in Spanish.
RECORDS OF THE LIFE OF THE VENERABLE MASTER HSUAN HUA, VOLUME II, paperbound, 229 pages.
WORLD PEACE GATHERING, paperbound, 128 pages.
THREE STEPS, ONE BOW, paperbound, 156 pages.
THE TEN DHARMA REALMS ARE NOT BEYOND A SINGLE THOUGHT, verses and explanation, paperbound, 72 pages.
CELEBRISI'S JOURNEY, paperbound, 178 pages.
VAJRA BODHI SEA/CITY OF TEN THOUSAND BUDDHAS, monthly magazine.

You may order books published by the Buddhist Text Translation Society by writing to:

The City of Ten Thousand Buddhas
2001 Talmage Road, Ukiah, California 95481 U.S.A.
telephone (707) 462-0939
        or
Gold Mountain Monastery
1731 15th Street, San Francisco, California 94103
U.S.A.   telephone (415) 621-5202 or 861-9672

California residents pay an additional six and one half percent sales tax. A full Buddhist Text Translation Society booklist will be sent upon request. Prices are subject to change without notice.

The Heart of Prajna Paramita Sutra and Standless on the Commentary by the Venerable Master Hua, A Vegetable cooking in a Tsienun, one pointed... through radiance of Buddha Paramitas is unimpeded in his mind. Because there is no indolence, he is not afraid and he leaves Sila is... permanent...nking The period—ultimately Nirvana. The seat Sutra expresses the essence of Prajna Paramita, the great and perfect Wisdom taught by the Buddha. Many...standing Buddhists recite the Seat Sutra. The Venerable Master Hua's verses and commentary clarify the plain each passage of the text. Available now. Bilingual.

THE WONDERFUL DHARMA LOTUS FLOWER SUTRA, VOLUME 7... paperbound,
80 pages. ... ...

THE WONDERFUL DHARMA LOTUS FLOWER SUTRA, VOLUME 13, paperbound,
82 pages. ...

THE SHURANGAMA SUTRA, VOLUME 1, paperbound, 290 pages.
WITH THE HEART SUTRA AND TO THE GATES OF TEN THOUSAND BUDDHAS,
VOLUME 2, paperbound, 193 pages.

THE AMITABHA SUTRA, cased hard, 204 pages, ...

THE VAJRA SUTRA, hardbound, 256 pages.

THE DHARANI SUTRA, paperbound, 261 pages.

THE SIXTH PATRIARCH'S GREAT STORE DOHS... hardbound boxed
and paperbound, 183 pages.

THE SIXTH PATRIARCH'S DHARMA JEWEL PLATFORM SUTRA, soft cover and
paperbound, 200 pages.

THE SUTRA IN FORTY-TWO SECTIONS, paperbound, 96 pages.

THE SHRAMANERA (VINAYA AND RULES OF DEPORTMENT, paperbound, ... 1890)

FILLY LAND AND AN IMPARTIAL TALKS, paperbound, ...

BUDDHA ROOT FARM, (Pureland Dharma Recitation Retreat Talks), paperbound, 72 pages.

RECORDS OF THE LIFE OF THE VENERABLE MASTER HSUAN HUA, VOLUME 1,
paperbound, 76 pages. ...

RECORDS OF THE LIFE OF THE VENERABLE MASTER HSUAN HUA, VOLUME 2,
paperbound, 200 pages.

WORLD PEACE GATHERING, paperbound, 128 pages.

THREE STEPS ONE BOW, paperbound, 184 pages.

THE TEN DHARMA REALMS ARE NOT BEYOND A SINGLE THOUGHT, paperbound,
OPEN ENLIGHTENMENT, paperbound, 95 pages.

CELEBRISE AGORAS, paperbound, 173 pages.

VAJRA BODHI SEA (MONTHLY OF THE TEN THOUSAND BUDDHAS, MONTHLY)

You may order books published by the Buddhist
Translation Society by writing to:

... or ...ten thousand Buddhas
... Talmage Road, Ukiah, California ... U.S.A.
... telephone (707) 462-0939 or ...

Gold Mountain Monastery
1731 15th Street, San Francisco, California 94103,
U.S.A. ... telephone (415) 863-0102 or (415) ...
California residents pay an additional ... and one half
percent sales tax. A full Buddhist Text Translation
Society booklist will be sent upon request. Prices are
subject to change without notice.

南無普賢菩薩

大方廣佛華嚴經淺釋

老兒山僧書

大方廣佛華嚴經華嚴海會佛菩薩

過新年

今逢一九八〇年

衲請各位上法船

同遊華嚴毘盧海

再登妙高極樂山

宣化上人寫於萬佛城

無言堂

大方廣佛華嚴經卷三十四

十地品第二十六之一

唐于闐國三藏法門實叉難陀譯

美國金山寺　宣化上人講述

弟子　恆華記錄

中美佛教總會一九八〇年出版

英文翻譯：恒賢

　　　李杏邨教授

修正：　恒持

　　　恒道

編修：　恒持

證明：　宣化上人

　　　恒道

中文記錄：恒華

編修：恒道

校對：周果立、蔡寶珠居士

寫在前面

三步一拜　比丘恒朝

「如渴思冷水，如饑念美食，

如病憶良藥，如蜂貪好蜜，

我等亦如是，願聞甘露法。」

——華嚴十地品，歡喜地——

金剛藏菩薩承諸佛威神力所加，證入菩薩大智慧光明三昧而宣演十地。法會中的大衆皆爭先恐後，「願聞甘露法」。可是金剛藏菩薩似乎有點猶豫，保持緘默。爲什麼呢？

因爲他感到十地的義理太深遠，太難捉摸，難說難受，雖然會中聽法者皆是大菩薩，他仍然覺得難以啓齒。

十地品是諸佛至高無上之源，所謂「非念離心道」，是言語道斷，心行處滅的境界。

必定要有大公無私，善根深厚的衆生，才能聽聞，才能信受這種廣博無涯的智慧。不然，聽了還會生出迷惑和懷疑心。所以又說：

「持心如金剛，深信佛勝智，

知心地無我，能聞此勝法，

如空中彩畫，如空中風相，

牟尼智如是，分別甚難見。」

——初地品——

一個下雨天，從南加州一個小鎮上，一位消防員和一位教師，前來探訪兩位三步一

拜的比丘。大家一起擠在老爺車裡。他們供養食物和熱茶，專誠來聽華嚴經。每天午飯

之後，我們都誦讀華嚴經。恒實朗誦中文，然後翻譯。恒朝在旁以英文記錄。

「這真有意思！」教員說。

「對了，真好！」消防員說：「請你再讀一次，我要把它抄下來！」

恒實重複唸了一次。

「我可以細嚼這義理，幾年也受用不盡！」教員若有所思地說。

在加州摩洛灣，有三四對青年夫婦，每個週末，携同他們的家眷，前來聆聽經典

之王—華嚴經。在公路的路肩或者在樹蔭底下，他們一同坐在氈子上，傾聽比丘每

天誦讀的經文。其中一個說：「我從未聽過這樣真實的言詞！」

全世界都在追求「真實的東西」，如飢如渴。在路上遇到很多人，都被華嚴經的力量

所吸引而來。他們大體有兩種感受：第一，華嚴經的文字，純真自然，填補了他們心靈

上的空虛。第二，他們看到那妙不可言的「中文」，翻譯成淺易簡明的英語，覺得

甚為驚喜。因此他們會自動自發的一再前來聽經。

科學愈昌明，物質愈富裕，卻使更多的人墮入沮喪頹唐和絕望之中。我們拜了八百

英哩，途中所遇到的眾生，他們心裡都渴望真理，都在尋求「真實的東西」。他們知

道，從外在的物質去尋求安樂，是緣木求魚，毫無希望。我們都要面對生死大事，都願意找到究竟的安樂。因此，初地（歡喜地）品似乎與時代更相爾、更實際、更貼切。

真正的快樂，是在心裡面，不在心外面。初地菩薩的甚深喜悅，來自勤修戒定慧，息滅貪瞋癡。並且，他們快樂的緣故，是因為放下了最大的累贅——自我。他們不再被憂慮所擾，因為他們沒有自我。

「此菩薩離我想故，當不愛自身，何況資財……；遠離我見，無有我想。」

—初地品—

對我個人而言，直到我拜了好多個月，「華嚴境界」方才生動起來，變成活的境界。為什麼？倒不是經典本身令人迷惑，而是我的思想太混濁，「我見」太深，所以不能聞睹「甚深微妙法」。拜了半年，恒常懺悔，在這期間沒有接近電視、書信、也不講話，淨持齋戒；然後，華嚴經才慢慢在我眼前開啓，揭露其玄妙幽微的旨趣。從前的自私和我慢，令我如聾如盲。

西方的科學及理智性的傳統，已面臨到存亡絕續的邊緣；這是必然的現象。我們生命及心靈的發展也同樣地阻滯不前。面對着諸法空相，「無我」的真諦，好像面臨中途截斷的橋樑，令我們無所適從，不知去向。「自我」的觀念，是西方人士的處世觀及其身分存在的基石。你要是告訴他，「自我」本來是幻覺，是虛妄的，必然會令他們不寒而

慄。有如在中世紀末年，西方人士發現地球原來是循太陽周行，而並非宇宙的中心；那

時候他們也曾一度大爲震驚。這是同樣的道理。

目前，在最契機的因緣下，佛教的出現，能夠把那已截斷的橋樑從此連接起來，使我們同

登彼岸。面對「無我」的眞諦，人們不但不應該把它視作可怕的盡頭；反而，應該歡迎

這個眞實智慧的開端，慶幸得見眞正快樂的泉源。

所以說：「捨不了死，換不了生。

捨不了假，成不了眞。」

包括小孩子在內，他們都被華嚴經所吸引。他們以直覺來認識這部經典—超過心思

言說—而是從心底裡產生直接的感應。

一九七七年的耶誕節，我們在加州海洋邨的沙灘上紮營。四個男孩子坐在木造的火

車構腳架上，靜靜地觀察我倆。然後，他們緩緩地走過來，不久，開始踴躍地討論人生

及佛教的問題。這些男孩子不怕路上的雨和淤泥，一心觀察著、諦聽著當天華嚴經文的

翻譯。在一盞搖曳不定的油燈下面，經文特別發人深省，孩子們無不「如蜂貪好蜜，如

渴思甘露」，盡量吸收經典的妙義。

之後，他們再度回來，把各人的零錢湊起來，作爲供養。還有半盒燕麥、一張卡片

，上面寫著：「積奇、新尼、波比、約翰祝好」。可是，他們回來的最大目的，是來聽

華嚴經。看著恒實「要那奇妙的法術」——把陌生的中國文字，翻譯成容易接受的英文。

他們都極爲欽佩，肅然起敬。

「這是我一生中前所未聞的！」其中一個孩子說。

「這是真實的！」另一個說：「而他能夠這樣暢順地讀出來，令我們也明白，太妙了！」

最後，約翰（他是四人當中最多疑的）說：「你們既不是向上帝祈禱，又不願上天堂……這不是很空虛，沒有意思嗎？」

當我們還未有機會回答他這個問題，新尼却直視他的朋友，冷靜地說：

「一切唯心造。約翰，一切在乎你怎樣看，你明白嗎？你若下了決心，幹什麼事都能成功的！」

在佛經裡有云：「心佛與衆生，是三無差別」。

華嚴經的妙理，在一切衆生心裡，每個衆生心裡都具有這種智慧，都能演說華嚴經。可是三毒煩惱，遮蓋了純真本然的自性光明。我們雖然忘失自性，但這個自性沒有暫離我們片刻；它在等待我們去把冰塊溶解。諸經典皆是從衆生心中自性流出，是一切衆生本有的財產。

初地菩薩的歡喜心，就在我們自性裡面，是我們自性本來具有的歡喜。只要去修道

，便能體會出這種無上的妙樂。人人都能夠辦得到。新尼說：「你若下定決心，幹什麼事都能夠成功！」這個小孩子，一語道破華嚴經的宗旨。他是無師自通；因爲華嚴經活在他底自性裡。所以說：

「若人欲了知，三世一切佛，
應觀法界性，一切唯心造。」

南無大方廣佛華嚴經！
南無華嚴海會佛菩薩！

西曆一九八〇年二月三日於萬佛城

按：恒實、恒朝兩位比丘，於一九七七年五月發宏大願，從洛杉磯金輪寺沿途三步一拜，直達北加州萬佛城，全程八百餘哩。其目的是爲祈求世界和平，消災解難，迴向功德與法界一切眾生。一九七九年十月，此兩位法師完成兩年半的艱巨旅程。自回城之後又發願，繼續三步一拜，直至萬佛功德圓滿。迄目前仍環繞萬佛殿外三步一拜，早晚精進，尚不休歇。

六

寫在前面

三步一拜　比丘恒實

—華嚴十地品—

「寂滅佛所行，言說莫能及，
地行亦如是，難說難可受，
如空中鳥跡，難說難可示，
如是十地義，心意不能了。」

很不容易執筆代序，寫及我對華嚴經的感想。要真正體驗這部經典，惟有把它的教理當衣
服穿，當飯吃，當覺睡。這樣，它就變得真實。這部經裡有深不可測的神通妙用，經文能在意
識心上，掀起不可思議之作用，令人切心立志去改惡向善。此外，還要身體力行，篤實履踐，
才有受用。就像吃飯，不管菜單把飯菜形容得如何，自己不去吃，還是不飽腹。

最主要的，此經闡釋圓滿人道的規範，教人如何淨化身、口、意三業。經裡開示諸佛菩薩
採用的法門，如何從凡夫地直至正覺的果位。而他們的光明如此灼亮，行門如此高妙，弟子根
本不能夠言說。

最實用的方法，**惟有請大家打開經典，諷誦經典、禮拜經典、讚歎供養經典、在經典前懺悔
，還要篤行實踐。這樣，智慧藏的玄門會自然開啓，燦爛的光芒能照徧寰宇，使黑闇隱退。**

七

「慈悲及願力，出生入地行，
次第圓滿心，智行非慮境。」

華嚴經像一面神奇的鏡子。鏡子裡現出華嚴法會諸大賢聖的圓滿德智。我們把自己暗淡無光的反影與這個景象相形之下，頓時生出大慚愧。於是，我們盡量改過自新。改過並不容易，有很多痛楚，但這是健康的痛楚。華嚴經以慈悲來指引我們向善，經典上說：「每一個眾生都能作菩薩，你可以獲得安穩和甚深的喜悅。只要依教奉行，勤策心念，淨化思慮，改邪歸正，謹慎言詞。只要守規矩，必定有效果！」

我們禮拜華嚴經，思惟華嚴經，知道佛法是本然自性裡「最深刻的輪廓」。它能超越一切種族、年齡、性別、國籍、言語、時空的界限，普徧成為攝受一切眾生的教義。它是永恒不變的真諦。能夠奉持五戒十善，修習六度萬行以及普賢十大願王，即是奠定正命正業的基礎。這是圓滿人道最根本的模範和準繩。所以說：「人道圓滿，佛道自成」。

這部經典並不艱深晦澀，並沒有和今日的局面脫節。反之，它更是暢發天機、窮理盡性的藍圖。我們愈認識真地履行經典的教義，我們的習氣毛病便愈清晰地展現眼前。就在我們自性裡本有充分的光芒去「明心見性」。只因為有妄想執著，所以暫時把智慧光明遮蔽了。能放下假的，真的便目然出然現出來。我向來只是為自己找麻煩而已；我的貪瞋癡大

到極點，皆因無明作怪，生出這三毒。依照經典的甚深智慧去修行，敦品勵德，日以繼夜，久而久之，終於會破除黑暗，重視光明。愈不自私自利，憂慮就愈少；並能回歸自然，契合大道，方能安穩自在。倘使能夠放棄意識的計度，萬事萬物愈顯得相得益彰圓融無礙。愈努力去修道，我們也愈加快樂。

在三步一拜途中，有一天在加州南灣燈塔下面拜。一輛大型房車在沙塵滾滾的轉角停下來，一個身裁高大、衣著華麗的中年男子從車裡出來，走到正在禮拜的出家人身旁。他的臉上呈現出悲喜交集的感情，顯得有點衝動。

「我的名字叫維里，你們是佛教徒嗎？佛！佛……你們知道嗎？我坐了五年牢，在監獄中，就靠一本佛教寓言的小册子，支持了我整整五年。那些故事深深地感動我，你明白嗎？你們是美國人？西方人？」

恒朝答道：「佛教是沒有國家或民族的界限……」

維里又搶著說：「也沒有顏色或種族之分，是在心裡、自性裡……對不對？」

「對了！」

他又說：「我正開車到洛杉磯，途中看到你們拜。告訴你，我見過基督徒、kris-hma教徒、回教徒、猶太教徒，還有些宗教，是前所未聞的，統統見過。（此時他已熱淚盈眶）。可是，從未這樣的把我感動！我在牢裡讀那些佛教故事是真的，你們在這兒

九

拜，就是躬行實踐。不得不告訴你，這對我有多大的影響（說著眼淚已由他的面頰簌簌

而下），佛教是屬於一切人，一切處的！

維里離開我們，他一邊哭，一邊顫抖，心裡洋溢一種不可言說的情懷。他的眼睛明

亮得如水晶盆子。

華嚴十地品的初地（歡喜地），目前以漢英對照的方式出版，就像朝陽衝破陰霾，

光明普照大地。

「是境界難見，可知不可說，

佛力故開演，汝等應敬受。」

恒道譯於萬佛城國際譯經院

西曆一九八〇年二月三日於萬佛城

前言 華嚴境界

李杏邨

(一)歷史背景

大方廣佛華嚴經為大乘教華嚴宗的立宗聖典，關於這部經典的出處，一般佛教信徒都接受這樣一個傳說：釋迦牟尼佛於菩提樹下觀明星悟道以後第廿七日，為文殊、普賢等深行菩薩講說圓滿修多羅，彙集成秩，名為大方廣佛華嚴經。該經闡揚圓頓義理，以一心貫穿萬法，即無障礙一真法界也。此法界本具三世間四法界，一切染淨諸法相融相即，全此全彼，互無障礙。色空無二，悲智一如，「觀色即空，成大智不住生死。觀空即色，成大悲而不住涅槃。」此經乃總會諸教，無法不收。佛陀暢演華嚴玄義，深入藏海，理趣淵沖，一般機淺聲聞，茫然不解，如聾如盲。職此之故，佛陀乃應機施教，為機淺徒眾宣講四阿含等小乘教理，因其義理較淺，易於悟解。

在華嚴宗成立以前，地論宗已在中國應運而生，其立宗經典為無著世親所傳的十地經。後來此宗信徒對十地經的講解，意見分歧，互不相下，乃分道揚鑣，各樹一幟，成立北道派與南道派。地論宗分裂的初期，北派一枝獨秀，壓倒南派，因其開山祖師道寵大師德高望重，聲名遠播，偏及洛陽及其它中國各大都市，門下徒眾不下萬人。道寵大師為陳隋兩代方外高人，名重朝野，恩遇殊隆。紀元後五五七至五八七年，陳朝皇室冊封為六

大賢良之一。紀元後五八九年至六一八年，又名列隋朝十大賢良之內。道寵大師遷化以後，北道派聲勢大減，江河日下，終至銷聲匿跡，不爲人知了。

南道派在慧光大師（紀元四六八─五三七）統馭之下，如日中天，盛極一時，凌駕北派之上。慧光大師精通梵文，善解十地經，爲佛門龍象，衆望所歸。十大入室弟子均享盛名，尤以法上大師（紀元四九五─五八〇）爲人所稱道。

華嚴宗的開創人爲杜順大師（紀元五五七─六四〇），爲唐代有數之佛學權威。在杜順時代，地論宗已漸式微，因而併入華嚴宗。杜順、法名法順，頗爲唐太宗所推重。曾一度詔宣入朝與太宗論道，上心甚悅，賜名「帝心尊者」。杜順總括華嚴玄義，作法界觀一卷及五教止觀一卷，爲該宗奠立始基。杜順弟子智儼大師（紀元六〇二─六八）傳其衣鉢，爲華嚴第二祖。智儼聰慧過人，深入華藏，作華嚴略疏五卷、華嚴還源觀，及華嚴義海百門等書。華嚴第三祖法藏（紀元六四三─七一二）承前啓後，總其大成，然後百尺竿頭再進一步。融滙印度哲學、老莊、周易、含英咀華，截長補短，發揚一眞無礙法界觀，使中國佛學自成蹊徑，大放異彩。法藏大師著有探玄記二十卷，章疏廿餘部。除著述外，法藏大師不辭辛勞各方奔走，隨緣應機，宣講華嚴義理。故華嚴一宗至法藏而登峰造極，大行於世。宋高僧傳記載：「藏爲則天（唐武后則天）講新華嚴經，至天帝網義十重玄門，海印三昧門，六相和合義門，普眼境界門，此諸義章皆是華

二

嚴總別義綱，帝於此茫然未決。藏乃指鎮殿金獅子為喻，因撰義門，徑捷易解，號金獅子章，列十門總別之相，帝遂開悟其旨。」由此可知，法藏大師名重朝野，故唐武則天亦詔宣入宮，暢演華嚴玄義。金獅子章係以金喻本體（本源眞性），以獅子喻現象（世出世間諸法）、闡明十重玄門，即㈠初明緣起、㈡辨色空、㈢約三性、㈣顯無相、㈤說無生、㈥論五教、㈦勒十玄、㈧括六相、㈨成菩提、㈩入涅槃。

㈡華嚴哲學

華嚴哲學可說是中國的宇宙有機論。它像一個大熔爐，把印度哲學、中國儒學、道學及周易等思想體系，經過揀選調配，溶為一體。像其他的大乘佛學一樣，華嚴哲學以一心貫穿萬法。故華嚴經云：「若人欲了知，三世一切佛，應觀法界性，一切唯心造。」世出世間一切諸法，無分染淨，不出一心，如大海水，全波即水、全水即波。真心法性為萬象之源，萬動之本。自法性觀之，性相無二，波水一如，但性因相顯、相因性起，波水不分。性相融通，隨心迴轉，互入無礙。見相知性，知波即水，事理交徹，圓融無礙，大中見小，小中見大，蔚藍一角，不異長天，寒碧半泓，何慚秋水。顯中見隱，隱中見顯，「於有為界示無為法而不滅有為之相。」「於無為界示有為法而不分別無為之性。」故觀空而不昧有、觀有而自證空。由此可知，華嚴自在無礙一眞法界觀，建

三

立在性相不分，空有無二的理論基礎上，故華嚴經說：「一切從此法界流，一切還歸此法界。」

總括而言，華嚴的眞如性海與老莊的道，儒家易經的乾元，頗有大同小異，融通交澈之處：

「大道氾兮其可左右、萬物持之而生不辭，功成不名有，衣養萬物而不爲主，常無欲可名爲小，萬物歸焉而不爲主，可名爲大，以其終不自爲大，故能成其大。」～老子道德經卅四章～

「東郭子問於莊子曰：「所謂道？惡乎在？」莊子曰：「無所不在」，東郭子曰：「期而後可（指定了才可以）」，莊子曰：「何其下邪？」曰：「在螻蟻。」曰：「何其愈下稗。」曰：「何其下邪？」曰：「在瓦甓。」曰：「何其愈甚邪？」曰：「在屎溺」，東郭子不應，莊子曰：「夫子之問也固不及質！正穫之問於監市履狶也，每況愈下，汝唯莫必，無乎逃物，至道若是……」

「周、徧、咸三者，異名同實其指一也。」莊子第廿二章。

「大哉乾元。萬物資始，乃統天。」周易卷一。

總上所述，「大道氾兮」，「道在屎溺，」「大哉乾元，萬物資始」，無非指明本體與現象不一不異，交融互澈，全此全彼也。作華嚴無礙法界觀者，見色明空，見空知

四

色，塵塵剎剎，皆是大法界心。正如清涼國師所說：「若知觸物皆心，方了心性。」

但是華嚴一眞無礙法界之意趣深遠，尚非一心萬法，所能蓋括。三世間四法界一切

染淨諸法，以一心爲經，以緣起爲緯、融通交澈、此隱彼顯，主伴相隨，無礙容持。如

萬鏡對照，光光相入，交相輝映，一中見多，多中見一，理事圓融。「華藏世界一一塵

，一一塵中見佛剎。」差別相即一合相，一合相即差別相。何有一心？何有萬法？何有

性相？何有色空？明乎此則平等性智何由不現？老子說：「昔之得一者，天得一以清，

地得一以寧，神得一以靈，谷得一以盈，萬物得一以生。」

從相對的觀點來說，天地間萬事萬物都是建立在時空的間架上。我們說這個城市像

古羅馬那樣大，那位老年人的年齡和我祖父相埒，都離不開時空的本位。如果從無量無

邊的太空來看，天地間的一切物體都無大小、粗細之分；如果用無始無終的永恒尺度來

衡量，人類無所謂老幼壽夭之別。用絕對的眞理來印證，相對的事物何有此壽彼夭，此

大彼小的區別呢？在眞理的熔爐裏，一切矛盾差別，和相對的事物都滙爲一體，無分軒

輕。所以莊子說：「天下莫大於秋毫之末而泰山爲小，莫壽乎殤子而彭祖爲夭。天地與

我並生，而萬物與我齊一，既已爲一矣，且得有言乎？既已謂之一矣，且得無言乎？」

～莊子齊物論。～

華嚴世界是一個結構精細、脈絡分明，而且具有機動性的有機體。它是一切事物活

動的場地。在那裏，此一事物與彼一事物，如波濤相接，此起彼伏、主伴互異，秩然有

序，完全合乎精密的宇宙律。這種相融相即，交互爲用的協和動作和連瑣關係，實屬「

法爾自然」，並非來自外力。華嚴經所講的一切事物，相即相入，一多互攝，體相不變

，隱顯互異，重重無盡，名爲因陀羅網境界。「天帝之宮、覆一寶網，綴有千萬明珠，

星羅棋佈，秩然有序，風起網動，珠光閃耀，交互射入，顯現重重，光影雜沓，美不勝

收。明珠雖重重亦映，鑑物照形，眞妄交錯，重重無盡，但影象不變，歷歷分明。」此

一寶網代表共相，每一明珠代表別相。共相爲體，別相爲用。體用不二，雜中見純、純

中定雜，無秩序中有秩序，有秩序中無秩序。

一眞法界，本攝三世間四法界爲一，貫穿時空的大法界緣起。性海圓融，緣起無性

，一念萬刼，三世本空，理事交澈，互奪雙亡；但性不礙相，月不棄影，心物一體，眞

妄無別。理法界、事法界，理事無礙法界，事事無礙法界，圓俱六相、十玄。「諸佛與

衆生交徹，淨土與穢土融通，法法皆彼此互收，塵塵悉包含世界。」由眞觀妄，萬法皆

空，以妄顯眞，萬相繁興。古語云：「三世古今始終不離乎當念，十方刹土自他何隔乎

毫。」一言道出華嚴一眞無礙法界的底蘊。

華嚴經卷三十四十地品第二十六之一

美國金山寺　宣化禪師　講述

弟子　恒華記錄

華嚴經有三十九品，八十一卷，我現在所講的是經內的第二十六品─叫十地品。為什麼叫十地品呢？因為地能生長萬物，一切萬物也是依地而生，依地而長，依地而成，依地而得到解脫。

地內又有種種的寶藏，種種貴重的物質，所以人們才能在地內發掘出金礦、鑽石礦、銀礦、銅礦、鐵礦等等的礦產。

十地品內也有一切的礦；如佛的礦、菩薩的礦、聲聞緣覺的礦、天上的天人礦、人間的礦、畜生的礦、還有餓鬼的礦、和地獄的礦。十法界，每界在地內都有這種礦，只是人們不知去發掘，如能知道去發掘，就能得到種種的成果。所以說一切萬物因地而生，因地而增長，因地而成熟，因地而得到解脫。

十地法門包括一切的法門，與一切的法門都有密切的關係。我們如要想修行菩薩道，就必須因地而生起菩薩道。我們如要增長菩薩道，就要藉十地法門來增長。我們如要成熟菩薩道，也要藉十地法門來成熟。我們如要想得到解脫菩薩道，更要依持十地的法門來修行，才能得到解脫的菩薩道。

一

這種十地法門在華嚴經品內是第二十六品，現在講的祇是第二十六品的第一部分，因之叫十地品第二十六之一。

爾時世尊，在他化自在天王宮，摩尼寶藏殿，與大菩薩衆俱。其諸菩薩，皆於阿耨多羅三藐三菩提不退轉。悉從他方世界來集，住一切菩薩智所住境，入一切如來智所入處。勤行不息，善能示現種種神通，諸所作事，教化調伏一切衆生而不失時。爲成菩薩一切大願，於一切世，一切劫，一切刹，勤修諸行，無暫懈息。具足菩薩福智助道，普益衆生而恒不匱。到一切菩薩智慧方便究竟彼岸。

金剛幢菩薩說完了十迴向品之後，還未說十地品之前。這時釋迦牟尼佛正在天上的他化自在天王宮裡。他化自在天王宮的意思；是能以他人的快樂視同自己的快樂。很任運自在的天王的宮殿裡。這座宮殿是用摩尼寶藏所造成的。同時還有許多大菩薩中的大菩薩。大菩薩就是老菩薩，言其有相當的道德，有相當的智慧，有相當的修行。衆俱是形容很多很多的、不是少數、是無量無邊那麼多的菩薩在一起。這些大菩薩們，他們都已能對這無上正等正覺不退轉了。念也不退於無上正等正覺，行也不退於無上正等正覺，位也不退於無上正等正覺。三不退；即念不退、行不退、位不退。

無上正等正覺：正覺—菩薩和二乘人都修得了正覺。但二乘人未得到正等，所以不

能覺他，只是正覺而已。菩薩不但能自覺，還能覺他。菩薩得到了正覺，又能修正等與佛的法門，所以叫正等。可是還沒有到無上，就是還有上師，菩薩又稱為有上師，因為上面還有佛。你們各位想一想：做人並不是自己以為了不起，自認為到了如何如何的程度，就真的是那麼一回事的。一切的成就，是要別人來公認才算是真的成就。二乘人修得正覺，能自覺、不能覺他，也沒得到正等，所以只能說正覺。菩薩修得了正覺、能自覺、能覺他、又能等覺。等於佛的覺悟，與佛差不多一樣，這叫正等，可是還未能無上。阿耨多羅三藐三菩提的意思，就是無上正等正覺。這些大菩薩雖然還沒有完全得到無上，但決不會退轉了，退轉於二乘。將來一定會成佛的。悉從他方來集：這些大菩薩並不是這個婆婆世界的，他們都是從十方無量微塵數那麼多的世界而來此集會的。住一切菩薩智：他們都已修得了菩薩的智慧，達到了菩薩所住的境界。他們不但已住於菩薩的境界，就連佛的智慧也有了。佛所知道的一切，他們也都知道，不過所知沒有佛那樣深切。佛的智慧所證得的境界，他們也將近證得。勤行不息：因為他們都能勇猛精進，勤修菩薩道而從不休息的。善能示現種種神通：他們能以種種的智慧，顯現種種的神通。諸所作事：他們的所行所作，都本着菩薩的職責—教化眾生、調伏眾生、令一切的眾生都能早成佛道。而不失時：就是教化眾生、調伏眾生，要知道把握時機，就是剛好對着機緣，如

三

果不對機；不是應該對他說法的時候你去對他說，不應該教化他的時候，你去教化他。

時機未成熟時，不特不能令他接受，反而使他害怕，令他狐疑不信，令他永遠不想再聽

佛法了，這就是**失時**，失去了機宜。菩薩教化眾生，就能恰到好處，把握着最恰當的時

機。譬如農夫種地，他就知道該下種的時候才播下種子，如果在不該下種的時候下種，

那就不會生長，豈不是白費工夫，浪費時間？菩薩教化眾生，就如農夫下種，知道何時

可為眾生下種，他就乘時為眾生播下菩提種子，就來開發他的心地，教他發菩提心。給

他種下菩提種子，令它一點點的生長，一點點的成熟，一點點的得到解脫，這便是**不失**

時。所以我們要教化人時，最要緊的，就是應該知道**而不失時**。失去時機，就不對機了

。**為成菩薩一切大願**：大菩薩們為了成就修菩薩道時所發的大願心。**於一切世**：在所有

的世界裡。**一切劫**：在無量無邊劫長的時間裡。**一切刹**：在所有諸佛的刹土裡。**勤修諸**

行：他們都是自己非常勤謹而勇猛精進的修行菩薩所有的行門。**無暫懈息**：從不稱為懶

惰，也不休息的。**具足菩薩福智助道**：具足了菩薩的福德和智慧來幫助自己修道。**普益眾**

生：不只自己修行，還要時時刻刻不忘記普益眾生。**而恒不匱**：就是不疲倦、不懶惰

、不論何時也不說不行菩薩道，不利益眾生的。**到達一切菩薩智慧方便**：能到達一切

菩薩的智慧，和知道運用一切的方便。**究竟彼岸**：而得到最高的果位，進入清淨的涅槃

彼岸，證得常樂我淨的快樂。

四

示入生死及以涅槃，而不廢捨修菩薩行。善入一切菩薩禪定解脫三昧，三摩鉢底，神通明智。諸所施爲皆得自在，獲一切菩薩自在神力。於一念頃無所動作，悉能往詣一切如來道場衆會爲衆上首，請佛說法。護持諸佛正法之輪，以廣大心，供養承事一切諸佛。常勤修習一切菩薩所行事業。其身普現一切世間，其音普及十方法界，普見三世一切菩薩所有功德，悉已修行而得圓滿，於不可說劫，說不能盡。

示入生死：修行菩薩道的菩薩，他是生死自由，他是生死即涅槃，煩惱卽菩提的。他的一切都爲了示現；示現種種的生，示現種種的死，示現各種的衆生，示現有情的身體，上自天、人，阿修羅，下至地獄、餓鬼、畜生，每一道內菩薩都去示現明白生死的痛苦，所以菩薩才示現入生死的境界。及以涅槃：菩薩示現了如何的生，如何的死的各種生死痛苦，是用以教化衆生的。然後又示現修苦行，令衆生知道如何變化生死入於涅槃。而不廢捨修菩薩行：菩薩他如此在每類衆生中行菩薩道，而並未廢捨他修菩薩行。不管在那類衆生中，他都行菩薩道來利益一切的衆生。令一切的衆生發大菩提心。善入一切菩薩禪定解脫三昧：他善於證得菩薩所修行的禪定、菩薩所修行的解脫、菩薩所修行的正定正受。三摩鉢底等至的意思。神通明智：明白一切的智慧及三明六通的妙用。三明是──天眼明、天耳明、宿命明或者說是：

五

漏盡明。六通是──天眼通、天耳通、他心通、宿命通、神足通、漏盡通。諸所施為皆得自在：菩薩的一切作為，都能任運自在。獲一切菩薩自在神力：他示現生死、涅槃，及示現修菩薩道，時時都可得到一切菩薩所有的任運自在的神通妙用的力量。

於一念頃：就在一念之間。無所動作：不須要有何動作。你如見他在走路，其實他正週遍十方。你如見他在吃飯，他的神通已入了一切如來的道場。你如見他正在睡覺，他却已化身到了其他諸佛的國土。你如見他坐在那兒，一事未幹，可是他已化身到無量無邊的諸佛國土內教化衆生去了。所以菩薩的一切表現，決不是我們可隨便定論的。諸位；千萬不要用凡夫的眼光錯認菩薩，菩薩也不可能隨便冒充。悉能往詣一切如來道場衆會：他隨時隨地可以去朝觀十方諸佛、禮拜十方諸佛、供養十方諸佛。他隨時都在觀察十方的衆生，如有任何災難，需人救濟幫助時，他就會化身去拯救、度化。所以菩薩能到達一切如來的道場衆會，而為上首，為一切法會中的大衆之領袖。請佛說法：菩薩他到處護持諸法的人，右繞三匝，佛才說法，就是轉大法輪。護持諸佛：菩薩他到處護持諸佛的衆會道場。正法之輪：轉正法輪，這不是件平常的事，任何地方轉正法輪時，都是驚天動地的，護法諸天，及諸大菩薩都會蒞臨護持和聽法的。我們金山寺在美國是經常轉正法輪的，可惜無人認識，譬如三藩市久旱不雨，我們一求，就下雨了

，這就是我們經常說正法、轉正法輪的感應。不特人需要諸佛的護持，諸佛也需要

諸菩薩護持的。以廣大心、供養承事一切諸佛：菩薩以廣大的真心，來供養諸佛，

仰承諸佛的教言，而去度化衆生。常勤修習一切菩薩所行事業：恒常不斷的修習菩

薩應作的事業。其身普現一切世間：他的身體普遍現到十方一切的世界。其音普及

十方法界：這些位菩薩，不特他們的身體普現十方世界，他們的音聲也同時普及到十方

法界。心智無礙：他們的心和智慧也已達到了圓融無礙。普見三世一切菩薩所有功

德：他們都能普徧見到三世—過去、現在、未來世的一切菩薩所有的功德。悉已修

行而得圓滿：所有一切菩薩具有的功德，他們也都修行圓滿了。於不可說刼、說不

能盡：這些菩薩們的修行功德、神通妙用，在漫長的時刼裡，說都說不完。

其名曰：金剛藏菩薩、寶藏菩薩、蓮華藏菩薩、德藏菩薩、蓮華德藏菩薩、日藏菩薩、

蘇利耶藏菩薩、無垢月藏菩薩、於一切國土普現莊嚴藏菩薩、毗盧遮那智藏菩薩、妙德

藏菩薩、栴檀德藏菩薩、華德藏菩薩、俱蘇摩德藏菩薩、優鉢羅德藏薩、天德藏菩薩、

福德藏菩薩、無礙清淨智德藏菩薩、功德藏菩薩、那羅延德藏菩薩、無垢藏菩薩、離垢

藏菩薩、種種辯才莊嚴藏菩薩、大光明網藏菩薩、淨威德光明王藏菩薩、金莊嚴大功德

光明王藏菩薩、一切相莊嚴淨德藏菩薩、金剛燄德相莊嚴藏菩薩、光明燄藏菩薩、星宿

王光照藏菩薩、虛空無礙智藏菩薩、妙音無礙藏菩薩、陀羅尼功持一切衆生願藏菩薩

、海莊嚴藏菩薩、須彌德藏菩薩、淨一切功德藏菩薩、如來藏菩薩、佛德藏菩薩。解脫

月菩薩、如是等無數、無量、無邊無等，不可數、不可稱、不可思、不可量、不可說諸

菩薩摩訶薩眾。金剛藏菩薩而爲上首。

在這個法會中的諸位菩薩，他們的名號，都是以修行證得的功德而爲名號的。所以

我們口誦菩薩的名號，心內思惟，就明白了這位菩薩的聖號，就是他德行的代表。

在會的菩薩，是無數、不可數。無量、不可稱。無邊、不可思想。無等、不可衡量

。說也說不清楚的這樣多的大菩薩衆在一起。金剛藏菩薩是這些大菩薩中的上首，

——就是衆菩薩中的領袖。

爾時金剛藏菩薩承佛神力，入菩薩大智慧光明三昧。入是三昧巳，即時十方各過十億佛

刹微塵數世界外，各有十億佛刹微塵數諸佛，同名金剛藏而現其前，作如是言；善哉！

善哉！金剛藏！乃能入是菩薩大智慧光明三昧。善男子！此是十方各十億佛刹微塵數諸

佛，共加於汝，以毗盧遮那如來應正等覺本願力故、威神力故、亦是汝勝智力故。欲令

汝爲一切菩薩說不思議諸佛法光明故。所謂令入智地故，攝一切善根故，善簡擇一切佛

法故。

這時；金剛藏菩薩仰承釋迦牟尼佛及十方諸佛的威神之力的緣故，入了大菩薩的大

智慧、大光明的正定正受中。入是三昧巳∴入了這三昧（正定）後，一切的境界都

現前了。即時十方各過十億佛刹微塵數世界外：立刻在十方各過去十億佛刹微塵數

那樣多的世界以外的佛刹。各有十億佛刹微塵數諸佛：各有十億佛刹微塵數

的諸佛。同名金剛藏而現其前：同樣都名金剛藏菩薩一齊出現在這位金剛藏菩薩的

定裡。作如是言：對金剛藏菩薩這樣說：善哉！善哉！金剛藏！：好呵！金剛藏菩

薩呀！你眞好呵！乃能入是菩薩大智慧光明三昧：你能入於這樣的大菩薩的大智慧

、大光明的正定正受。善男子！此是十方各十億佛刹微塵數諸佛，共加於汝：這是

十方佛刹微塵數的諸佛、共同加被於你，使你能入此三昧的。

以毘盧遮那如來應正等覺本願力故：以這位遍滿一切處的無上正等正覺的佛，以他

本來的願力的緣故，來加被於你。威神力故：更以他的威德神通的力量來加被你，

令你能入此正定。亦是汝勝智力故：也是你自己修菩薩行得到的殊勝智慧的力量，

故能入這種正定。欲令汝爲一切菩薩說不思議諸佛法光明故：希望你爲法會中的諸

位菩薩宣說諸佛所說的，最勝智慧、光明微妙的佛法。所謂令入智地故：就是宣說

能令一切的衆生入智慧之地的佛法。攝一切善根故：攝一切衆生所修集的善根的緣

故。善簡擇一切佛法故：使衆生能有選擇的擇法之眼，能明白諸佛所說的法的意趣。

知諸法故，善能說法故，無分別智清淨故，一切世法不染故，出世善根清淨故，得不

議智境界故，得一切智入智境界故，又令得菩薩十地始終故，如實說十地差別相故，

緣念一切佛法故，修習分別無漏法故，善選擇觀察大智光明巧莊嚴故，善入決定智門故，隨所住處次第顯說無所畏故，得無礙辯才光明故，住大辯才地善決定一切諸法故，憶念菩薩心不忘失故，成熟一切眾生界故，能徧至一切處決定開悟故。

廣知諸法故：佛法不是世間的知識，以俗慧可以瞭解的，必須深入經藏，才能求得智慧如海。佛法如大海，沒有廣大的大智大慧，怎能廣知諸法。單自己知道一切諸法，不能算真知，還要**善能說法故**：說法也不是件簡單的事，要善於運用一切方便、權巧的方法，宣說諸法。**無分別智清淨故**：還要在沒有分別的智慧中，才能明瞭一切清淨的妙法。清淨就可生智慧。智可分：成所作智。妙觀察智。平等性智。大圓鏡智。**一切世法不染故**：一切的世間法，只要能轉過來，就是不染的清淨法。能轉過來的意思就是能改惡向善。世間法是染污的，出世間法就是不染污的，清淨的。**出世善根清淨故**：能夠理解出世法，修出世間的善根，就可得到清淨法。**得不思議智境界故**：得到了不可思議的智慧及它的境界的緣故。**得一切智人智境界故**：一切智人，就是指所有的佛。得到了諸佛的智慧，才能入智慧的境界。**又令得菩薩十地始終故**：又令得到菩薩十地—從初地到十地的修行過程。初地是開始，第十地是十地的終了。由初地到十地，其中種種不同的修持經歷，都要明白，都要證得。修道者是初地不知二地的境界，十地不知等覺的境界。各人的境界，各自不同。修道者

的工夫、法門也是各自不同的。**如實說菩薩十地差別相故**：實實在在的來解說菩薩在十地中各自修證的不同相狀。因為修行的法門不同，得到的境界各異，修證的相狀自然有差別了。金剛藏菩薩知道、瞭解，所以希望他如實解說此中的差別。**緣念一切佛法故**：緣念；就是順着諸佛所說的佛法去思念。又可作專一講；專一至念諸佛所說的法。**修習分別無漏法故**：修；就是修行。習；就是學習。修行也要學習，才能明白甚麼是有漏法？甚麼是無漏法？有漏法裡有多少種有漏法，無漏法內又有多少種無漏法。一邊修行、一邊學習，一邊研究。認真研究，詳細分辨，才明白甚麼是有漏法。一邊修行，一邊學習，一邊研究。**善選擇觀察大智光明巧莊嚴故**：善選擇就是善於用擇法眼，以大智慧來觀察諸法。有大智慧就如大光明。有智慧之光，才能善巧莊嚴諸佛國土。**善入決定智門故**：善能入於決定一切的智慧之門。很純淨的分辨一切，無所懷疑。**隨所住處次第顯說無所畏故**：菩薩隨他的所在地，有次第的，有條不紊的，很明顯的，宣說正法，而毫無畏懼。**得無礙辯才光明故**：得到辯才無礙的大智慧。**住大辯才地善決定故**：住於有大辯才的果位，就能決定諸法的善巧妙用。**憶念菩薩心不忘失故**：就是令一切的衆生常常憶念諸佛菩薩的功德，而心總不忘失。**成熟一切衆生界故**：就是令一切的衆生，未種善根者，令種。已種善根的，令增長。已增長的、令成熟。已成熟的，令他得到解脫。這就是成熟一切衆生界。能徧至一切處決定開悟故：能到十方三世一切

十一

諸佛的剎土，一切的道場衆會裡去。決定開悟是說可得大智慧、大辯才、得大壽命、得大安樂。開悟一切諸法，證得一切諸法的實相。

善男子，汝當辯說此法門差別善巧法，所謂承佛神力，如來智明所加故：淨自善根故，普淨法界故，普攝衆生故深入法身智身故，受一切佛灌頂故，得一切世間最高大身故，超一切世間道故，清淨出世善根故，滿足一切智智故。

十方諸佛也來勸請稱讚金剛藏菩薩說：善男子！你應當用你的無礙辯才、善巧的方法，宣說十地這種大智光明的法門和他的差別。承佛神力，如來智明所加故：你仰承十方諸佛威神之力、毘盧遮那佛的大威神之力、本師釋迦牟尼佛的大威神之力，和如來的智慧光明加被於你之故。淨自善根故：清淨自己的菩提善根。普淨法界故：普遍令法界得到清淨。普攝衆生故：普遍攝受一切衆生。深入法身智身故：深入一切的法身和智慧之身中。受一切佛灌頂故：受十方三世諸佛來給你授記、灌頂、加被的緣故。得一切世間最高大身故：得到一切世間裡最大的智慧，最高的法身。超一切世間道故：能超過一切世間所有的法門道路。清淨出世善根故：得清淨出世的菩提善根。滿足一切智智故：滿足一切的智慧，也令一切的衆生能得到智慧中的智慧。

爾時十方諸佛與金剛藏菩薩無能暎奪身，與無礙樂說辯，與善分別清淨智，與善憶念不

忘力，與善決定明了慧，與一切處開悟智，與成道自在力，與如來無所畏，與一切智

人觀察分別諸法門辯才智。，與一切如來口妙身語意具足莊嚴。

這時十方諸佛給與金剛藏菩薩無能暎奪身：就是加被金剛藏菩薩無上勝威德之身，

如像國王處在大衆之中，任何人的光輝都不能蓋過他的光輝。又加被給予金剛菩

薩無礙樂說辯：一種圓融自在樂於為衆生說法的清淨無為的智慧。與善分別清淨智：又加

被給予金剛藏菩薩善於分辯正法的清淨無為的智慧。與善憶念不忘力：又加被給予

金剛藏菩薩善於憶念正法之名義，不異說，不忘本宗。與善決定明了慧：又加被給予

金剛藏菩薩種種善巧方便，能見機、能隨所應，舉比喻說明的斷疑智慧。與至一切

處開悟智：又加被給予金剛藏菩薩隨處都能明瞭真諦、俗諦、中道第一義之真理的

智慧。與成道自在力：又加被給予金剛藏菩薩佛的十力，使令敎化衆生能斷惑、出

離煩惱、得到果位，所以說成道自在。與如來無所畏：又加被給予金剛藏菩薩佛的

大無畏的威神力。與一切智人觀察分別諸法門辯才智：又加被給予金剛藏菩薩一切

智人就是諸佛的觀察，分別各種法門的無碍辯才。與一切如來口妙身語意具足莊嚴

：諸佛更加被給予金剛藏菩薩殊勝的三業，具足了菩薩的莊嚴。

何以故？得此三昧法如是故。本願所起故。善淨深心故。善淨智輪故。善積集助道故。

善修治所作故。念其無量法器故。知其清淨信解故。得無錯謬總持故。法界智印善印故。

是甚麼緣故金剛藏菩薩能得到諸佛的加被呢？能得此殊勝的三昧法門？本願所起故

這是他在因地所發的宿願深重，定要證得此十地的智光三昧。善淨深心故：也是

在因地修菩薩行時，有信樂至極的善根和清淨心的原故。善淨智輪故：智慧清淨，

好像日輪能圓滿普照法界，是金剛藏菩薩的智德清淨。善積集助道故：他生生都是

善根深厚，清淨無為，所以能積集助道，這是金剛藏菩薩的福德。善修治所作故：

金剛藏菩薩善能調伏心、清淨善根、斷除煩惱習氣，這是他的修治工夫。念其無量

法器故：金剛藏菩薩能聞持無量的佛法，憶念不忘失，真是難得的法器。知其清淨

信解故：金剛藏菩薩以他的清淨智慧，令眾生對佛法有深入的信心，有明確的理解

。得無錯謬總持故：使佛法流通，眾生信奉誦持，對正法的真理前後都沒有疑惑，

也不違背，總一切法，持一切正法之義理。法界智印善印故：法界眾生，得奉持正

法，知出離生死的因果，以如實智印可，善法印證。

爾時十方諸佛，各伸右手摩金剛藏菩薩頂。摩頂已。金剛藏菩薩從三昧起；普告一切菩

薩眾言：諸佛子！諸菩薩願善決定無雜不可見，廣大如法界，究竟如虛空。盡未來際，

徧一切佛剎，救護一切眾生，為一切諸佛所護。入過去未來現在諸佛智地。

這時十方的諸佛。（十方是：上、下、東、南、西、北、及四維。）都伸出右手來

摩金剛藏大菩薩的頭頂。佛摩頂以後，金剛藏菩薩就從定中起定了。普告一切菩薩

衆言：並且普徧的對法會內諸位菩薩說：各位佛的弟子！諸菩薩願：諸位菩薩所發的大願，善決定無雜：是用他所得到的眞智慧，揀擇善法而沒有一點夾雜的。這個願，是菩薩所發的大願。視之不見，雖說看也看不見，可是他卻廣大到徧滿法界，

究竟如虛空：他的究竟處，就像虛空樣找不着邊際。盡未來際，徧一切佛利，救護一切衆生：菩薩救護所有的衆生從不計較時間，不怕是盡未來際。也不考慮到任何地方，徧一切諸佛的利土都去到。為一切諸佛所護：因此受到十方三世諸佛的護持和懷念。入過去未來現在諸佛智地：他已證到過去佛、未來佛、現在佛，諸佛的智慧之地了。

佛子！何等為菩薩摩訶薩智地：諸位佛的弟子！甚麼叫做菩薩中的大菩薩，修集種種善根的大菩薩們的智慧之地、和諸佛的智慧之地呢？

佛子！菩薩摩訶薩智地有十種。過去、未來、現在諸佛已說、當說、今說，我亦如是說。各位佛的弟子！菩薩修行菩薩行時集具的種種善根的智慧之地，略說有十種，如要詳細的說；有無量無邊那麼多種。是過去諸佛已說的，未來諸佛將要說的，現在諸佛正在說的。我也要如三世諸佛一樣要說這種菩薩十種的利益和智慧之地的地相和地體。

何等為十？一者歡喜地。二者離垢地。三者發光地。四者燄慧地。五者難勝地。六者現

十五

前地。七者遠行地。八者不動地。九者善慧地。十者法雲地。

甚麼叫十地呢？十地的名稱是：第一叫歡喜地；菩薩修到了這地的時候，非常歡喜

。第二叫離垢地；菩薩修到了第二地時，把一切的塵垢、妄想、見惑、思惑、塵沙

惑都斷淨了。第三叫發光地，因為把一切的塵勞妄想都沒有了，就現出了本有的智

慧光呢，所以叫發光地。第四叫燄慧地，到此地時，不特發光；而且放出了智慧的

火燄。第五叫難勝地，修行不易修到這種地位，因為不容易達到，所以叫難勝地。

第六叫現前地，一切的智慧都現前了。第七叫遠行地，菩薩修到此地時，能飛行變

化，行動自如了。第八叫不動地，就是不動道場，而有可徧遊十方的神通。第九叫

善慧地，菩薩修得了變化自如，徧遊十方的神通，更得到了殊勝的般若智慧。第十

叫法雲地，菩薩修行的功德，像雲樣普徧蔭護着一切的衆生。

佛子！此菩薩十地，三世諸佛已說當說今說：金剛藏菩薩又稱一聲各位佛的弟子！這種

菩薩修行的十地法門，是三世諸佛；過去佛已經說了，未來佛應該說的，現在佛正

在說的。

佛子！我不見有諸佛國土，其中如來不說此十地者。何以故？此是菩薩摩訶薩向菩提最

上道，亦是清淨法光明門。所謂分別演說菩薩諸地。佛子！此處不可思議，所謂諸菩薩

隨證智。

金剛藏菩薩又稱一聲各位佛的弟子！我不曾看見任何一個佛的國土內的如來不說這

十地法的道理的。甚麼緣故？就因爲**此是菩薩摩訶薩向菩提最上道**：這個法，是菩

薩中的大菩薩修行菩提的最上道路。**亦是清淨法光明門**：也是因爲十地法是修行的

清淨而光明的智慧之法。**所謂分別演說菩薩諸地**：十地法是非常正確的，詳細的演

說了菩薩修行十地的過程，顯示一切菩薩的智慧及所知的法。各位佛的弟子！**此處

不可思議**：這十地的道理，是沒法想像得到的。**所謂諸菩薩隨證智**：這種道理就是

諸位菩薩，隨着他們所修行的功德，而證得的智慧。

爾時金剛藏菩薩說此菩薩十地名已。默然而住，不復分別。是時一切菩薩衆，聞菩薩十

地名，不聞解釋，咸生渴仰。作如是念，何因何緣，金剛藏菩薩唯說菩薩十地名而不解

釋。

這時金剛藏菩薩說完了這菩薩修行的十地法門的名字以後，就默默的不開口了，也

不繼續分別解釋十地法門的義理。這時一切菩薩衆，這些十方來的諸大菩薩們，聽

了金剛藏菩薩說了十地法門**的名字**，而聽不到他解說其中的道理，大家都像**如渴思

飲**的仰望着他，等着他來解釋。同時也在心中生起了疑念！是甚麼因？甚麼緣

？令得金剛藏菩薩單單只說十地法門的名字而不加解釋呢？

解脫月菩薩、知諸大衆心之所念，以頌問金剛藏菩薩曰：何故淨覺人　念智功德具　說

諸上妙地　有力不解釋？

在法會中的解脫月菩薩，祂知道諸菩薩這時心中所生起的疑念，於是用偈頌向金剛藏菩薩請問。說：為什麼？您這位清淨覺悟的菩薩！念清淨、智慧光明、一切功德都具足的菩薩！說了最好的十地法的名字之後，您有能力而不為大家解說呢。

一切咸決定　勇猛無怯弱　何故說地名　而不為開演。

金剛藏菩薩！你對於一切的事理，都能明辨是非，也有決定一切的智慧。你又是一位勇猛精進修菩薩道，而無所恐懼的大菩薩，為什麼只說十地的名字，而不為大家明白的解說呢？

諸地妙義趣　此眾皆欲聞　其心無怯弱　願為分別說。

這十地法的每一地，一定都有很不可思議的、微妙的義趣。現今在此法會的大眾，都想聽你解說。這些大菩薩們，他們的心裡也是無所恐懼的，所以都很高興的希望你分別解說這十地法給他們聽。

眾會悉清淨　離懈怠嚴潔　能堅固不動　具功德智慧。

如今在這道場眾會中的諸位大菩薩們，他們都是身心清淨無濁的，遠離了一切的塵垢，勇猛精進而不懈怠，威儀嚴謹，不貪名圖利而廉潔，不為境界所轉移，無雜染異想，菩提心永不退轉或動搖。因為這些大菩薩們已具足了大功德、大智慧了。

相視咸恭敬　一切悉專仰　如蜂念好蜜　如渴思甘露。

大家都非常恭敬、誠懇、而專心一意的、仰望您金剛藏菩薩來為他們解說這最微妙而殊勝的十地法。這種情況好比蜜蜂一心想做好牠的蜜糖，又像人渴極了，想得一滴甘露來活命那樣的急切專一地等待着。

爾時大智無所畏金剛藏菩薩聞說是已。欲令眾會心歡喜故，為諸佛子而說頌言。

這時，這位有大智慧而又無所懼怕的金剛藏菩薩，聽了解脫月菩薩所說的偈頌後，想令大眾法會中的諸位菩薩都生起歡喜心，也用偈頌來對諸大菩薩說。

菩薩行地事　最上諸佛本　顯示分別說　第一希有難

菩薩在因地修菩薩行時的事，就是十地中應做的事。這些事是再沒有比它更高尚的了。十地中所修行的，就是成佛的根本法門。如果要很明顯的來分別演說，真是最上第一的、最稀有的、難逢難遇的。

微細難可見　離念超心地　出生佛境界　聞者悉迷惑。

菩薩行微細微妙、深義妙理，不容易明白，很難看見的。要達到離念超心地這種境界的法門，是言語道斷心行處滅，超出一切的思慮，這時所生出的一切，都是佛的境界，不是沒有相當修行功德的人可以了解的，如果忽然聽聞說此法的境界時，很容易引起人的懷疑和迷惑。

十九

持心如金剛　深信佛勝智　知心地無我　能聞此勝法。

生了疑惑是因衆生沒有智慧，所以對這種殊勝的法門，不會明白，如果能修持到信心如金剛般堅固，深信佛的殊勝智慧，對佛所說的教言－－十地法門，理解了無我相就能聽聞這種殊勝的法門了。

如空中彩畫　如空中風相　牟尼智如是　分別甚難見。

要能聽到這種殊勝的法，而明白受用，而能不執着，就要像在空中畫有彩色的畫，又要像想看到風在空中的形相樣，知道這都是不可能有的而不執着，才可以明白受用。釋迦牟尼佛的智慧就是這樣不執着的。所以很難分別解說，也不容易使人明白，令人看見。

我念佛智慧　最勝難思議　世間無能受　默然而不說。

因此我想念到佛的智慧，眞是最殊勝，最不可想像到的。世間上恐怕沒有人能明白這種法，也沒有人能領受這種道理，所以我只有默默的不向諸位解釋。

爾時；解脫月菩薩聞是說已。白金剛藏菩薩言：佛子！今此衆會皆悉已集，善淨深心、善潔思念、善修諸行、善集助道、善能親近百千億佛，成就無量功德善根，捨離痴惑，無有垢染。深心信解，於佛法中不隨他教。善哉佛子！當承佛神力而爲演說。此諸菩薩於如是等甚深之處、皆能證知。爾時；解脫月菩薩欲重宣其義，而說頌曰：

這時解脫月菩薩聽了金剛藏菩薩所說的偈頌後，接着再對金剛藏菩薩說：：你是佛的大弟子！現在已聚集在這大衆法會中的諸位菩薩，他們都已**善淨深心**，因已修得了一切善行，連心的深處都已清淨了。**善深思念**，他們的思想和念慮也都清淨了。**善集助道**也明白怎樣用悲智、勝念來助他修諸行，在修持上也知道怎樣精進用功。**善修諸行**，在修持上也知道怎樣精進用功。行正道。也知道增長智慧，必須親近多佛，發願生生見佛，受持妙法，才能**成就無量善根**。因爲曾經親近過百千億佛，才成就了無量的善根，也才能把愚痴和迷惑都捨離了，更沒有了染汚的塵垢。**深心信解**：用他們最清淨的心，虔誠的、深深的信奉理解佛法。一心學習佛法，從不輕信旁門外道的邪說。最崇高的金剛藏大菩薩！你是佛的好弟子！請你仰仗着佛的大威神力，來爲大衆演說這佛法吧。在這法會中的諸位菩薩，對於這種甚深微妙之極的十地法，他們都能證得，而明白的。這時解脫月菩薩爲了要想重說一遍他的意思，就用偈頌的方法來表達：：

願說最安隱　菩薩無上行　分別於諸地　智淨成正覺。

這時解脫月菩薩說：：我願意金剛藏大菩薩呀！現在就請你來說這最好而最安隱的佛法，菩薩修行的最上法門。分別解釋十地的道理，令一切衆生可以得到清淨的智慧，將來都能成佛。

此衆無諸垢　志解悉明潔　承事無量佛　能知此地義。

二二

在這大法會中的諸位菩薩，都已遠離了所有的染汚和塵垢，他們的志願和理解，都已非常清淨和明白了。他們也曾經承事供養過無量諸佛，他們亦 能瞭解十地的義理。

爾時金剛藏菩薩言：佛子！雖此衆集，善淨思念，捨離愚癡及以疑惑，於甚深法不隨他教，然有其餘劣解衆生，聞此甚深難思議事，多生疑惑，於長夜中受諸哀惱。我愍此等，是故默然。爾時金剛藏菩薩欲重宣其義，而說頌曰：

說：佛子！雖然在這大法會中的諸位菩薩，都已善淨了身心的思念，捨離了愚癡和疑惑，對於甚深微妙之法已深信無疑了，也不會隨旁門外道而轉變了。可是還有其他一些根器拙劣的、不甚明白的衆生，聽了這種甚深微妙的不可思議的大法以後，很容易生出疑惑。在愚癡無明的長夜裡—這是形容無知衆生，不明白大法，生死昏昧，輪轉無際之意—看不破，放不下、得不到自在，自己苦惱自己。我因爲可憐這類衆生，所以默然不說。這時金剛藏菩薩唯恐大家不明白，又用偈頌說一遍：

雖此衆淨廣智慧　甚深明利能決擇　其心不動如山王　不可傾覆猶大海。

金剛藏菩薩說：雖然在這道場中的諸位菩薩，都是清淨的，沒有染汚了，也有了廣大的智慧，更有甚深的般若，深心信解，決擇正邪的功能，他們的信心就如須彌山王樣，不會被外境所動搖，也像大海樣沒有人能把它到過來。

有行未久解未得　隨識而行不隨智　聞此生疑墮惡道　我愍是等故不說。

可是在這大衆中，也有修行不久的初發菩提心的菩薩，他們對於**解**的智慧還不夠，只是跟著識來分別一切境界，沒有真正的智慧去認識一切的境界。識只能分別，智才能認識決擇。當他們一聽到這十地的法門，恐怕會生起懷疑而不信。不信此大法，就會墮入三惡道裡去——餓鬼、畜生、地獄。我憐愍這些眾生，所以不說。

爾時解脫月菩薩，重白金剛藏菩薩言：佛子！願承佛神力、分別說此不思議法，此人當得如來護念而生信受。何以故？說十地時，一切菩薩法應如是、得佛護念。得護念故，於此智地能生勇猛。何以故？此是菩薩最初所行、成就一切諸佛法故。譬如書字數說、一切皆以字母為本，字母究竟，無有少分離字母者。佛子！一切佛法皆以十地為本。十地究竟，修行成就，得一切智。是故，佛子！願為演說，此人必為如來所護，令其信受。爾時解脫月菩薩、**欲重宣其義而說頌曰**。

在這個時候，解脫月菩薩又再對金剛藏菩薩說：佛的弟子！希望大菩薩您秉承著十方諸佛和本師釋迦牟尼佛的威德神力。**分別說此不思議法**：很詳細地分別解說一下這種不可思議的法門，令能聽到這種法門的人，破除他的疑惑，而生信心，就會得到諸佛的護持，而生起信心的力量。甚麼緣故呢？因為說十地法門的時候，**一切菩**薩聽到了這法，一定都會是這樣的，一定會得到諸佛的護念的。**得護念故**：因為得

了諸佛的護念，聽得了這大智慧的十地法以後，能生勇猛：就能生出很大的勇猛心

。何以故呢？此是菩薩最初所行：因為這個法門，是一切菩薩最初所修行法門。成

就一切諸佛法故：修持這法門，就能成就所有諸佛所說的法。譬如書字數說：舉個

譬喻，好像學寫字，開始就要知道每個字有一定的構造，有一定的字母（中國字有

部首、英文有母音子音），有一定的寫法順序。數說：就是聯合許多單字成為一個

有意思的句子。字母究竟：如果你能正確地寫出每個字的字母，決不會有絲毫錯誤

的。所有的字也沒有離開字母而可以成為一個字的。佛的弟子！一切佛法皆以十地

為本：所有諸佛所說的法，都是以十地法為基本的。十地究竟：如果把十地法修行

圓滿，就可以得到一切的智慧了。所以要請佛子您，為此

法會中的諸位菩薩們演說這個法門，令聽到這法的人，必定會為諸如來所護念，也

令他生起信心，依教奉行的。這時解脫月菩薩想再把他的意思說一遍，就說了下面的

偈頌：

善哉佛子願演說　趣入菩提諸地行　十方一切自在尊　莫不護念智根

本。

解脫月菩薩又讚一聲金剛藏菩薩說：您是佛的大弟子，希望您憐憫一切眾生，為眾

生演說這十地法門，彼能使這些菩薩走入菩提的覺道中，學習修持十地中各地的行

門。十方的諸佛世尊，祂們都是常常要加持、護念這些聽聞十地法門的人，和修行

十地法門的人。因爲十地法是智慧的根本。

此安住智亦究竟　一切佛法所從生　譬如書數字母攝　如是佛法依於地。

「此安住智」是指十地法的智，意思是說十地法的智慧，是最徹底的、最正確的、最圓滿的、最殊勝的智慧。爲什麼叫地呢？因爲諸佛所說的法，都是從十地所生出的。譬如學寫字，一定要根據字母，學作文一定要先從聯字做起。一切佛法依十地爲基礎而生起，修學佛法也應以十地法爲依據。

爾時諸大菩薩衆，一時同聲，向金剛藏菩薩而說頌言：

解脫月菩薩說完了上面的偈頌以後。這時在法會中的十方無量微塵數一般多的大菩薩們，同時同聲，一齊用偈頌向金剛藏菩薩請法。說：

上妙無垢智　無邊分別辯　宣暢深美言　第一義相應。

佛的大弟子、金剛藏菩薩！您是已證得了最上微妙、離垢的清淨大智慧了。你的辯才也是無量無邊的，說得很詳細、很有道理。現在希望你對我們宣說無上甚深的微妙道理、與第一義相應的十地法門。

念持清淨行　十力集功德　辯才分別義　說此最勝地。

這些菩薩都是念和修行，一切都清淨了的人，他們修持佛的十力，也集具了種種的功德。他們也已有分別一切義理的智慧和無礙的大辯才。就請大菩薩你，說這最殊

二五

勝的十地法門。

定戒集正心　離我慢邪見　此衆無疑念　惟願聞善說。

在這法會中聽你解說的人，都是修定而持戒、有正知正見的老修行，他們早已遠離了貢高我慢，也沒有邪見的思想了，他們對十地法門也不會有懷疑的念頭。大家都誠心專一的想聽你宣說這十地法門。

如渴思冷水　如饑念美食　如病憶良藥　如蜂貪好蜜。

好像人又熱又渴的時候，想喝一杯冰水一樣。冷：是清涼的意思。又像人餓了，想有點好吃的東西來充饑。又好像人有病了，就想能找到好藥，一吃病就好了。又好像蜜蜂天天探蜜，為的是希望做一窩好蜜多天享受。

我等亦如是　願聞甘露法　善哉廣大智　願說入諸地　成十力無礙　善逝一切行。

在這法會中的大衆，也是如同上面所說的思想一樣，希望聽到能解渴、能充饑、能去病、能解除一切貪的妙法。您這位崇高有廣大智慧的金剛藏菩薩！願你說說如何進入十地的法門。因為您已成就了如佛的十力，而達到了無障礙的果位，也已修證到如同佛一樣的一切行門。

爾時世尊，從眉間出清淨光明，名菩薩力燄明。百千阿僧祇光明以為眷屬，普照十方一切世界，靡不周徧，三惡道苦皆得休息。又照一切如來衆會，顯現諸佛不思議力。又照

十方一切世界，一切諸佛所加說法菩薩之身。作是事已，於上虛空中，成大光明雲臺而住。時十方諸佛，悉亦如是，從眉間出清淨光明，其光名號眷屬作業，悉同於此。又亦照此娑婆世界佛及大眾，并金剛藏菩薩身師子座已，於上虛空中，成大光明雲網台。

時光臺中，以諸佛威神力故，而說頌言：

大眾菩薩們說完了上面的頌言以後，這時釋迦牟尼佛從兩眉的中間，放出一股很清淨的光，這光的名字叫菩薩力燄明。是菩薩法力之火焰的光明。百千阿僧祇光明以為眷屬，另外還有種種無量的光明，作這光明的眷屬。普徧照到十方所有諸佛的世界，沒有一處不照到的。徧三惡道苦皆得休息。就連地獄、餓鬼、畜生三惡道中正在受苦刑的也都停止了。又照到所有諸佛的道場法會中。顯現諸佛不思議力：用這種光燄來顯示諸佛不能想像的法力。又照到十方所有的世界中，並一切備受諸佛佛力加持而又正在說法的菩薩身上。作是事已，這樣照了之後，就在上面的虛空中，結成大光明雲網台而停住了。這時其他十方的諸佛也悉亦如是，同樣從兩眉中間放出這種光明雲網台，也叫菩薩力燄明。其光名號眷屬作業，他的作用是作釋迦牟尼佛的光明的眷屬，如同他的親屬，來陪同、擁護的作用。悉同於此，也同世尊的光樣普徧照十方世界。又照到娑婆世界、和佛、和法會大眾、和金剛藏菩薩、和他師子之座。之後；同樣在上面的虛空中，結成一個大光明雲的網臺而停住。在光明臺中，以釋迦牟

二七

尼佛和諸佛的大威德神通的法力，而說出下面的頌言：

佛無等等如虛空　十力無量勝功德　人間最勝世中上　釋師子法加於彼。

佛是沒有任何事物可與祂比較的，就像虛空那樣微妙。佛有十種力量，又有無量的殊勝功德。在人間來說，佛最殊勝，在世間上來說，他是最高尚的。凡是能**釋師子法**；解釋法王之法的人，佛力必加被於他。

佛子當承諸佛力　開此法王最勝藏　諸地廣智勝妙行　以佛威神分別說。

佛子！金剛藏菩薩：您應當仰承釋迦牟尼佛及十方諸佛的威神力，為大眾開演法王具有的最殊勝的菩薩行門。因為十地法中，各地有各地的廣大智慧，各有不同的微妙修行法門，必須佛力加持，才可以詳細的分別解說。

若為善逝力所加　當得法寶入其心　諸地無垢次第滿　亦具如來十種力。

假若你得到了佛力的加持，（善逝是佛的十號之一）就等於無量法寶的法門進入了你的腦海中一樣，演說佛法時，格外說得圓融無礙，義理分明。十地每一地都是清淨無垢的，如能依着次第修持，一定可以證得圓滿的果位，也會具有如同佛樣的十力。

雖住海水劫火中　堪受此法必得聞　其有生疑不信者　永不得聞如是義。

雖然你就是住在像海水這樣多，這樣深成、住、壞、空後的劫火中，也應該忍受這種

刼難之苦，週有講十地法時，必定要聽的。（這意思是說，寧忍受三惡道之苦，也

不被「八難」所障礙聞法）。如有對十地法生疑惑而不相信的人，他是永遠沒有機

會聽到這種勝義之法了。

應說諸地勝智道　入住展轉次修習　從行境界法智生　利益一切衆生故。

金剛藏菩薩！您應該向大衆解說菩薩在十地各地中得到殊勝智慧的道理。使大衆能

入於十地法內，展轉流通，令衆生循次第漸漸修習，從修行的境界中，生出法智，

超俗的智慧。希望這樣可以利益法會中一切的衆生。

爾時金剛藏菩薩觀察十方，欲令大衆增淨信故。而說頌曰：這時金剛藏菩薩觀察法會中

大衆的因緣，希望能令大衆增加清淨的信解心的緣故：又用偈頌說：

如來大僊道　微妙難可知　非念離諸念　求見不可得。佛就像大僊道一樣。大僊道就

是聖人之道。他的微妙之處，是不可想像的。當你已能離念的時候，還要更進一步

的連這個離念　的念頭也要捨離。如果你想以聲、色求見佛，以聲色求見法，色見

聲求，那是不可能明白這十地法門的。案：僊與仙通。

無生亦無滅　性淨恒寂然　離垢聰慧人　彼智所行處。這十地法門，就是我們本有

的佛性，本有的智慧，本有的本性光明藏。它們的本性是不生不滅的，不垢不淨的

，不增不減的。它也是常常清淨的，因爲常清淨，所以是常常寂然不動的。去一分

二九

染污，增一分清淨。染污與清淨是對待法。增加清淨就是增加智慧；增加染污，就是增加愚痴。有智慧就日漸上升，愚痴就日漸墮落。中國的古聖人說：君子上達，小人下達，就是這意思。我們修行的目的，就為的啟智慧，滅愚痴。世間法中最不清淨的，最染污的，就是男貪歡、女貪愛。都為此數所縛而不能超出，其原因就是不能學聖人轉染污為清淨。凡是能離開染污而恢復清淨的，就得到了真正的聰明智慧，才是真正的聰明有智慧的聖人。諸位都是佛的弟子，都已離了一切的染污而恢復了本有的清淨，成為真有智慧的聖人。聰明有智慧的人的智慧，以及菩薩所修行的，就是這十地法門。

自性本空寂　無二亦無盡　解脫於諸趣　涅槃平等住。

我們每個人的自性，本來是清淨的，本來甚麼也沒有的。就因為自己背覺合塵，染苦為樂，因之增加了許多煩惱。自性雖然一個也沒有，無形無相，無人無我，無眾生，無壽者，但也不能說沒有，就如虛空，不能說沒有虛空。這十地的智慧，能得清淨自在的解脫，是得之於四惡趣裡面。四惡趣—地獄、餓鬼、畜生、修羅。你如能明白十地法門，就能明白生死、涅槃是平等的。所謂生死即涅槃，煩惱即菩提。如不明白這十地法門，則生死、涅槃自是涅槃，兩者毫無關係可言。

非初非中後　非言辯所說　出過於三世　其相如虛空。

十地法門的智慧，不能分為

初中後的階段來說。菩薩發心，得菩提，永不退轉，亦無先後。只可智會，不能言詮。所以我（金剛藏菩薩）不願解說。因為這種法門，超過了三世一切法，它真實的相狀，就如同虛空。

寂滅佛所行　言說莫能及　地行亦如是　難說難可受。　這種法門是寂滅相的。視之不見，聽之不聞，齅之無味的。乃是佛所行的，最微妙的。如要我用言語來解釋，真沒法說明白。十地中所說的修行法門，就像我在前面所說的比喻一樣，是不容易說明白的。所謂言語道斷、心行滅，眾生也不容易信奉，也不容易接受的。

智起佛境界　非念離心道　非蘊界處門　智知意不及。　這由智慧中生出來的境界，是佛所證得的境界。就如前面說的言語道斷、心行處滅的意思。應即念離念，念而無念，即為非念。離開心裡所想像的一切。這種法門也不是從修五蘊—（色、受、想、行、識），十八界—（六根—眼、耳、鼻、舌、身、意。六塵—色、聲、香、味、觸、法。六識—眼識、耳識、鼻識、舌識、身識、意識）。十二處—（六根六塵）裡可以得到的。是要用智慧才能了解，用意念和思想是沒有法子明白的。

如空中鳥跡　難說離可示　如是十地義　心意不能了。　好像鳥在空中飛行，有什麼蹤跡可說？有什麼痕跡可表示？十地法所包含的義理，也是不能用眾生的心和意念可以了解的。

慈悲及願力　出生入地行　次第圓滿心　智行非處境。

菩薩能演說十地法門，都是
仰承諸佛的慈悲和願力，出在世間來修行這十地法門，依着各地的次第，令智慧心
圓滿了，令覺悟的菩提道也就了。這是由智慧修行的法門，不是用人心思慮可明白
的境界。

是境界難見　可知不可說　佛力故開演　汝等應敬受。

這種境界是很難見到的，知
道這法門還比較容易，如果要解釋演說，就不容易了。必須仰承十方諸佛加持的力
量，才能演說。你們各位菩薩能聽到這法門，都應該恭敬聽受這法。

如是智入行　億劫說不盡　我今但略說　真實義無餘。

這種用智慧來修行的法門，
就是用無量劫的時間也說不完。現在我（金剛藏菩薩）祗好略略說一下，真實的義
理是無窮無盡的。

一心恭敬待　我承佛力說　勝法微妙音　譬喻字相應。

諸位菩薩，一心一意，恭恭
敬敬的等待着，我仰承十方諸佛的大威神之力，來演說這微妙殊勝的法音——十地法
。沒有什麼相當的，能與十地法門相應的字句用作譬喻。

無量佛神力　咸來入我身　此處難宣說　我今說少分。

無量無邊的諸佛，以他們的
神通之力，一齊加持到我的身上。因為十地法門難於宣說，也不可能說得完，所以
我現在就說個大概。

佛子，若有衆生深種善根，善修諸行，善集助道，善供養諸佛，善積白淨法，爲善知識善攝，善淸淨深心，立廣大志，生廣大解，慈悲現前。爲求佛智故，爲得十力故，爲得大無畏故，爲得佛平等法故，爲救一切世間故，爲淨大慈悲故，爲得十力無餘智故，爲淨一切佛刹無障礙故，爲一念知一切三世故，爲轉大法輪無所畏故。

金剛藏菩薩又稱一聲諸位佛的弟子們：假設有這樣的衆生；已深深的種植了善根，又能修行六度萬行的法門。又能修聚幫助他成道的法門。又最會供養十方三世一切諸佛。又最懂、最明白怎樣修集所有的最上法門。又能攝受衆生，敎化衆生，爲衆生的大善知識。又能知道調伏身心，遠離塵垢得淸淨心。並且能**立廣大無邊**的志氣，拔度衆生無分別心。發大願，不怕艱辛。**慈悲現前**。**生廣大解**，對於佛的正法生起無量無邊廣大的信心，和堅固的理解力。**慈悲現前**；修道的人應該對任何人，都要有慈悲心，他們是沒有時間性和地域觀念的。爲了求得如佛的智慧，爲了修得佛的十力，爲了想有最大的，無所怖畏的智勇，爲了得到佛的平等法門，爲了拔救所有世界的衆生。**爲淨大慈悲故**的意思就是要得到最大的，淸淨的，慈悲心，即出世間的正智。**爲得十力無餘智故**，爲了想盡得佛的大智慧，爲了莊嚴淸淨所有諸佛的刹土，沒有一點障礙，爲了想達到一動念，就能知一切三世的因果，爲了能常常轉無上的大法輪，而沒有一點恐懼之心，爲了這種種緣故，必須聽受這種十地法門。

三三三

佛子，菩薩起如是心，以大悲爲首，智慧增上，善巧方便所攝，最上深心所持，如來力無量，善觀察分別，勇猛力、智力、無礙智現前。隨順自然智，能受一切佛法，以智慧教化。廣大如法界，究竟如虛空，盡未來際。佛子，菩薩始發如是心，即得超凡夫地，入菩薩位，生如來家，無能說其種族過失，離世間趣，入出世道，得菩薩法，住菩薩處，入三世平等，於如來種中，決定當得無上菩提。菩薩住如是法，名住菩薩歡喜地，以不動相應故。

金剛藏菩薩又稱一聲諸位佛的弟子！菩薩生起以上種種心念的時候，以大悲爲首；因大悲心能拔衆生的苦，令衆生離苦得樂，故說以大悲爲首。智慧增上；修菩薩法，就能得到菩薩的智慧，多修一點菩薩行；智慧就會增上。說法時，就會有善巧方便的智慧，辯才無礙的能力。又有無量善於觀察一切的智慧和分別一切境界的能力。很勇猛佛的無量威神之力。所攝持的是最上微妙的深心，所恃的是的向前精進修行。不論任何境界現前，他都有不受其障礙的智慧應付。常有一種很自然的智力，使他能領受一切諸佛所說的法門。用智慧來教化一切衆生。這種境界廣大得像法界，徧一切處。究竟徹底的程度，就如虛空樣無障無礙。可以窮盡未來所有的時間。諸位佛的弟子！行菩薩道的大菩薩，一開始發這樣的大悲心時，即刻就得到超出了凡夫的地位，進入到菩薩的地位了。生到了如來的家族中，沒有能找出菩薩和佛的眷屬（種族）是有何過錯可說的。離世間趣；離開世間四種惡趣——

地獄、餓鬼、畜生、阿修羅。證得超出三界的聖道，得菩薩修持的一切法門，住在菩薩所住的清淨處，不捨世間，也能方便不染。更得到三世平等的智慧。**於如來種中：**在深種了佛的種性中，決定會得到再沒有比這更高尚的菩提覺果的。**菩薩住如是法，名住菩薩歡喜地。**菩薩修到了這種法門，這就是十地中的初地，名叫歡喜地，因為他證到了初地，生起大歡喜心來了。這種歡喜，是因定力而生出的，所以說以不動相故與定相應了。

佛子，菩薩住歡喜地，成就多歡喜，多淨信、多愛樂、多適悅、多欣慶、多踴躍、多勇猛、多無鬥諍、多無惱害、多無瞋恨。金剛藏菩薩又稱一聲諸位佛的弟子！在歡喜地的菩薩們，證入了歡喜地後，成就了很多種的歡喜。如**多淨信**對佛法的清淨信心，也增深厚了。對於佛法，更生起了無量的愛樂心。無論何時都覺得很快樂，很安祥。到什麼地方也沒有一點障礙。極令遇着了障礙，也不生煩惱，總是感到滿足的。**多欣慶**常常欣喜而慶幸自己能聞到佛法彼能修行菩薩道。**多踴躍、多勇猛：**他們時刻都勇猛精進，從不懶惰。與人交接，也從不發生鬥爭和諍論。不去惱害他人，不障礙別人修行。證入了**歡喜地**的初地菩薩們，對於任何人，任何事，也不會生起瞋恨心了。

佛子，菩薩住此歡喜地，念諸佛，故生歡喜。念諸佛法，故生歡喜。念諸菩薩，故生歡

三五

喜。念諸菩薩行，故生歡喜。念清淨諸波羅蜜，故生歡喜。念諸菩薩地殊勝，故生歡喜

。念菩薩不可壞，故生歡喜。念如來敎化衆生，故生歡喜。能令衆生得利益，故生歡喜

。念入一切如來智、方便、故生歡喜。

金剛藏菩薩又稱一聲諸位佛的弟子！菩薩證得了歡喜地的果位之後，爲什麼這樣歡

喜呢？因爲他們都常常憶念一切的諸佛，所以生歡喜心。不像凡夫俗子，每天都生

活在嫉妒障礙中，沒有道心。菩薩能專一憶念諸佛，就不會生嫉妒障礙之心。又念

諸法，常常記得諸佛所說的一切佛法，依法修行，所以也生大歡喜。念諸菩薩，他

不但憶念諸佛諸法，還常念十方三世一切的賢聖僧，和大菩薩們所以心生

歡喜。凡是修道的人，都應常常憶念三寶的心，不使心生外務而專意挑剔別人。若

常常迴光返照，就不會生異心而障道了。又常念諸菩薩所修行的一切成佛的法門，因

爲所有的大菩薩都是未來的諸佛，他們勤修六度萬行，不捨度衆生。菩薩們就是不明白

證入了這十地法門後，自己仍不懈怠，仍修一切法門。所以生大歡喜，又念清淨諸波羅蜜將來

都能成就圓滿清淨的智慧和成佛的功德，這也是歡喜的根源。又念諸菩薩的地位，

特別殊勝，也生大歡喜。又念菩薩證得了三不退，一念不退，位不退，行不退。再

沒有天魔外道能破壞他，也生大歡喜。又常常想到如來敎化衆生，慈悲爲懷，令衆

生離苦得樂。而生大歡喜。又念諸佛常使衆生聞法得度，了生脫死，這是令諸衆生

得大利益的最好法門。諸菩薩有這些殊勝的因緣，可以作很多的大事，所以就生出了大歡喜心。念入一切如來智方便；證到歡喜地的菩薩，他也有念，不過他們的念是清淨的。而眾生有念，他們的念是染污的—財、色、名、食、睡—五欲的境界。菩薩所想的是佛、法、僧及六度萬行，種種清淨的境界。因為他們知道自己已經證入一切如來的智慧，得到了種種的方便，所以生大歡喜。

復作是念，我轉離一切世間境界，故生歡喜。親近一切佛，故生歡喜。遠離凡夫地，故生歡喜。近智慧地，故生歡喜。永斷一切惡趣，故生歡喜。與一切眾生作依止處，故生歡喜。見一切如來，故生歡喜。生佛境界中，故生歡喜。入一切菩薩平等性中，故生歡喜。遠離一切怖畏毛豎等事，故生歡喜。何以故？此菩薩得歡喜地已，所有怖畏悉得遠離。所謂不活畏、惡名畏、死畏惡道畏、大眾威德畏、如是怖畏，皆得永離。

得到歡喜地果位的菩薩們，又作這樣的想法，我轉離一切世間境界，我把世間法，一切的都放下了。（轉離就是放下）把它轉變過來了。轉凡成聖，轉迷為悟，轉染污為清淨把整個世界的境界都轉變過來，所以生大歡喜。譬如在金山寺內聞法的人，就比在外面社會中的人清淨多了。這就是轉離的好例子。證得初地果位的菩薩，就常能見佛，因親近佛所以生歡喜。凡夫所想的，所求的，他都不想、不求。他之想求均為凡夫所不要的，而他便去學習，所以他能遠離凡夫的地位，轉

凡成聖，故生歡喜。遠離了凡夫的地位，就是遠離了無明愚痴。親近善知識，就是**近智慧地**，所以生歡喜。證入初地的菩薩，就已**永斷一切惡趣**，不會再墮落到四惡趣內了，除非他發願到四惡趣內去教化眾生，那是爲度生，行菩薩道，不是行惡而墮落。菩薩教化一切眾生，使離苦得樂，給予眾生一種安穩的感受，因此眾生均樂於把他作爲**依止**的地方，所以生歡喜。常常見到佛，又常生在佛的境界中，與一切菩薩同處在**平等性中行菩薩道**。又能遠離一切使人恐怖得毛髮都豎起的種種事。有這些難求難遇的好處，所以生起大歡喜心。何以故呢？菩薩證到歡喜地的果位後，對於一切都看破了，放下了，沒有甚麼使他懼怕的了，一切的怖畏，自然遠離。（怖畏即煩惱業苦之意）凡夫所怖畏的，如**不活畏**，生怕不能活下去。**惡名畏**怕人毀謗，名聲受污。**死畏**，人人怕死，都想求長生。**惡道畏**怕墮到四惡趣中。**大衆威德畏**，在大群廣衆中，不敢說話，爲了怕受衆人的奚落，被大衆的氣勢所威脅。這些怖畏，都是發於心裡，如果能修行，有定力，就甚麼都不怕了。

何以故。此菩薩離我想故。尚不愛自身，何況資財。是故無有不活畏。不於他所希求供養，唯專給施一切衆生，是故無有惡名畏。遠離我見，無有我想，是故無有死畏。自知死已，決不離諸佛菩薩，是故無有惡道畏。我所志樂，一切世間無與等者，何況有勝，是故無有大衆威德畏。菩薩如是遠離驚怖毛豎等事。佛子！此菩薩以大悲爲首，廣大志

樂無能沮壞，轉更勤修一切善根而得成就。

菩薩為什麼沒有了這些怖畏的呢？因為他遠離了一切恐怖毛豎等的事。是甚麼力量使他能遠離的呢？這就是能修行、肯發菩提心、願行菩薩道，因而證得歡喜地的這位菩薩，達到了離我想的工夫的緣故。他沒有了自己，不但沒有自己，連想都不想有這個自己。因為他早已把這個自身布施給了眾生，為眾生作事，不自私，不自利。**自身都不愛**，何況資財？資財──金銀珠寶，城廓妻子，這都是身外之物，他完全看得破，放得下，得到了真正的自在。是故無有**死畏**。因為這樣，所以菩薩不怕自己不能生活，也就沒有不活畏了。既不想自益，他就根本沒有希求，所謂到無**求處便無憂**，無求自然沒有憂愁了。為什麼會有貪求？就因為有貪求，有貪求，便有憂愁。菩薩不貪求名聞利養，也不貪求五欲──財、色、名、食、睡。菩薩對這些都不在乎了，更不會貪圖好供養。**唯專給施一切眾生**，就因他專一修行布施，不論甚麼供養，他都拿來給所有的眾生。至於外人對他的好壞議論，他也不去理會，不貪求虛名，也不生歡喜與煩惱。因為菩薩已有超出好壞境界之外的智慧，所以他沒有**惡名畏**的恐懼心了。菩薩沒有自己就是**無我**，沒有我，自然也不會有**我見**、我想了。沒有了我，那會有誰死、誰不死的想法呢？故沒有**死畏**。菩薩他知道自己死後，不會墮到四惡趣裡，因為他常行菩薩道。也決定不會離開諸佛，一定還是與

三九

諸菩薩在一起，所以沒有**惡道畏**。我的志願，和我所樂做的事，世間上沒有能與我相比的，沒有比我再好的，或能勝過我的，所以沒有**大眾威德畏**。這種想法，並不是菩薩有貢高我慢的思想，只是金剛藏菩薩說明證得歡喜地果位後的菩薩，他的境界就是這樣的。菩薩遠離了以上五種怖畏，就不會有驚怖毛豎的事發生了。諸位佛的弟子！這些菩薩做事都是以**大悲心為第一**作出發點的。因為悲能拔苦。**廣大志樂**菩薩有廣大的志願—救度眾生。無量的快樂。沒有任何天魔外道能破壞他及擾亂他的修行，或阻擋他行菩薩道。所以他**轉更勤修**，一天比一天精進，一天比一天用功。所有一切善根、菩提根因之都圓滿成就。

所謂信增上故，多淨信故，解清淨故，信決定故，發生悲愍故，成就大慈故，心無疲懈故，慚愧莊嚴故，成就柔和故，敬順尊重諸佛教法故，日夜修習善根無厭足故，親近善知識故，常愛樂法故，求多聞無厭足故，如所聞法正觀察故，心無依著故，不耽著利養名聞恭敬故，不求一切資生之物故，生如寶心無厭足故，求一切智地故，求如來力無畏共佛法故。

菩薩證到歡喜地後，無時不在大歡喜中。因為他勤修一切的善根，很快就成就了，信心日漸增多不會減退，這就是信增上的緣故。因信心上增，清淨的信念也跟着增多，不像過去雖有信心，還不免有點染污。現在信心既增強又無一點染污，只有清淨，返本還原了。為什麼會令信心增強有這種清淨的境界的呢？因為菩薩他知道如今已沒有一點懷疑了，信心堅固決定了。信；十方佛，信；十方諸佛所說的法，信；十方一切的賢聖僧，都是自己的法友。因為自己也是三寶之一，就生出了悲愍眾生的心，度一切眾生。悲心；令眾生離苦。慈愛眾生的心，令眾生得一切的快樂。求佛法日日精進修行。勇猛行道，也日勝一日，從不感到疲倦和有懈怠的情緒。慚愧莊嚴；常生慚愧，慚其前愆，愧其後過。用自己所有的功德來莊嚴十方國土。成就柔和，修忍波羅蜜，成就忍辱的力量，對任何事故，都有逆來順受的忍耐工夫，決定不會再有與人爭勝負的心，和剛強的態度。恭敬諸佛，順受諸佛的

四一

教言，尊重奉行諸佛所說的教法。日夜修習善根無厭足畫夜六時，精進修習種種善根，不會有厭倦和滿足的心。菩薩知道親近善知識，能多聞廣學，獲大利益，法喜充滿，常在法樂中。勤修戒定慧，息滅貪瞋痴，從不自滿。自己在諸佛處聽來的正法，不時正心思惟，觀察諸法實相。心中無一點執著，執著我執、法執，無一點依賴。不耽著利養、名聞、恭敬故：菩薩他決不會去耽心供養，貪圖名聞，和希望虛偽的奉承。更不會希求物質的享受，和一切豐富的身外之物。生如寶心：（如寶心；就是好像稀世之寶一樣的心。）菩薩他只一心求菩提心，金剛心而沒有厭足的意思。求得如來的力量

求一切智地只希望求得一切智慧的果位和達到無上智慧的地步。求得如來的力量得到四無所畏，和求得十八不共於二乘的佛法，這種種的利益。

求諸波羅蜜助道法故，離諸諂誑故，如說能行故，常護實語故，不汙如來家故，不捨菩薩戒故，生一切智心如山王不動故。不捨一切世間事，成就出世間道故。集助菩提分法無厭足故，常求上上殊勝道故。

前面說的修 菩薩行的菩薩，證得到歡喜地後，能得到佛的力量，四無所畏，及十八不共於二乘等等佛法，又繼續追求諸波羅蜜的修持，以幫助自己的道業。捨離一切不應有的言行，如諂媚富人，和打妄語，不欺世盜名。如說能行尊奉佛所說的法，切不應有的言行，如詔媚富人，和打妄語，不欺世盜名。如說能行尊奉佛所說的法，老老實實的去修行。做到言行一致，常護實語。—（就是常常保護自己所說的都是真

（實話）不汙如來家：身為佛的弟子，知道菩薩是最清淨高尚的，決不能做出有汙穢佛家風的行為，也就是不能有汙道場的事。更不能有稍捨去菩薩戒律的表現。要能守持身、語意的清淨戒律，就能生出一切的智慧心，好像須彌山王一樣，永不會為外事外物所動搖。不需要放下一切的世間事，也能成就出世間的道法。修行積聚能幫助自己成就菩提分法的法門和功德，決不會生出厭倦的心，和已功德圓滿的傲慢之心。因為菩薩是經常都在追求一切最高尚的、最殊勝的、最圓滿的、上上的佛道心。

佛子！菩薩成就如是淨治地法、名為安住菩薩歡喜地。佛子！菩薩住此歡喜地，能成就如是大誓願、如是大勇猛、如是大作用。所謂廣大清淨決定解，以一切供養之具，恭敬供養一切諸佛，會無有餘。廣大如法界，究竟如虛空，盡未來際，一切劫數無有休息。又發大願、願攝一切佛法輪，願攝一切菩提，願護一切諸佛教，願持一切諸佛法。廣大如法界，究竟如虛空，盡未來際，一切劫數無有休息。又發大願，願一切世界佛興于世，從兜率天宮沒，入胎，初生、出家、成道、說法、示現涅槃，皆悉往詣親近供養，為眾上首、受行正法，於一切處一時而轉。廣大如法界，究竟如虛空，盡未來際，一切劫數無有休息。

諸位佛的弟子！菩薩修菩薩行，成就了如前面所說的，這種清淨修治所證得的法門，這就是菩薩修證的初地——歡喜地的果位。因為成就了淨治地法，永不會退轉於

二乘了，所以說從此安住在歡喜地，再繼續修證以下各地法門。諸位佛的弟子！菩

薩證得歡喜地，成就大誓願大勇猛，把他在因地所發的大誓願；別人不能做的，一

般人做不到的，他都能用他的智慧勇猛而技巧地達到目的，使其有利益於眾生生大

作用。對微妙的佛法，能生出一種廣大、清淨、而又、毫無疑惑的決定性的理解和明

瞭的智慧。用他所有的，最好的、一切能供養的東西，恭敬供養所有的諸佛，無一

佛不供養。這種廣大供養具的誠心和法門，大到週徧法界。無一處不到。究竟得像

虛空一樣的清澈。菩薩並不是偶然如是的，他盡未來所有無盡的時間，永遠都不停止休

息的。菩薩又發大願，願意接受一切佛所轉的大法輪，繼續說法。又願攝受佛的一

一切覺道，常常修習。又願對諸佛所說的教法，一一護持。又願受持諸佛所說的

法門。菩薩發這大願，廣大得充滿法界，究竟得好像虛空。在時間上是盡未來際無

窮無盡的劫數，他都從不休息的。菩薩又發大願；希望所有的世界，都有佛出興於

世，處處佛法興隆。佛從兜率天宮下降到人間—從入母胎，住母胎，初生，出家修

行，成道後，說法，到入涅槃，示現這八相成道的過程。他都能去親近、承事供養

為法會中眾生的上首，受行正法，在所有的地方同一個時間，而轉大法輪。廣大到

徧滿法界究竟得猶如虛空。窮盡無量的時劫，都不休息。

又發大願；願一切菩薩行，廣大無量不壞不雜，攝諸波羅蜜，淨治諸地，總相、別相、

同相、異相、成相、壞相，所有菩薩行，皆如實說，教化一切，令其受行，心得增長，廣大如法界，究竟如虛空，盡未來際，一切劫數，無有休息。又發大願；願一切衆生界，有色、無色、有想、無想、非有想、非無想、卵生、胎生、濕生、化生、三界所繫，入於六趣、一切生處，名色所攝，如是等類，我皆所化，令入佛法，令永斷一切世間趣，令安住一切智智道，廣大如法界，究竟如虛空，盡未來際，一切劫數，無有休息。

菩薩又發大願；願一切菩薩所修的行門，都是廣大得、不能計量、包括一切，不被天魔外道所破壞，也沒有善惡的因素夾雜在內，都是與一切波羅蜜互相攝卽相應的。以這些功德，幫助修行清淨的十地法。一切事事物物的成因；如總相、別相、同相、異相、成相、壞相等的一切行門，我都實實在在的對衆生解說，教化所有衆生，令他們接受並領悟、接受，老實去修行，使清淨的菩提心因而增長。這種願心，也是廣大到徧滿法界，究竟得猶如虛空。盡未來無窮的刼數，我亦不停止或休息的。菩薩又發大願；願一切的衆生界，如有色、無色的衆生，有想的衆生、無想的衆生，非有想的衆生、非無想的衆生，卵生的、胎生的、濕生的、化生的等各品類的衆生，凡爲三界所繫縛，在六道中，輪迴、各類的衆生，以及凡受名色所攝的這些種類的衆生，我都要去教化他們，令他們能深入佛法，依教奉行，能永遠脫出這六道輪迴的世界，令他們安住在最具智慧的聖道。這

種願心，也是廣大到徧滿法界，究竟得猶如虛空，盡未來一切的時刻，我亦不停止或休息。

又發大願；願一切世界廣大無量、麤細、亂住、倒住、正住、若入、若行、若去、如帝網差別，十方無量種種不同，智皆明了，現前知見。廣大如法界，究竟如虛空，盡未來際，一切刼數無有休息。

菩薩又發大願：願每個世界，不論仰的、覆的、長的、方的、都是那樣的廣大，不論有多少。其中有粗的、有細的、有亂住的，沒有次第的。又有倒住，顛倒的。有正住，有條不紊，很規矩的。有人的，有常常行動的。有的很多變化的，各各皆不同。就如大梵天王殿上的網羅幢一樣各各不同。十方的形狀種種各異。但菩薩的智慧都可明瞭。凡可現在眼前的，一概明白。這種智慧的願望，也是廣大得徧滿法界究竟得猶如虛空。盡未來一切刼數，永不休息的。

又發大願，願一切國土入一國土。一國土入一切國土。無量佛土普皆清淨，光明衆具以爲莊嚴。離一切煩惱，成就清淨道。無量智慧衆生充滿其中，普入廣大諸佛境界，隨衆生心而爲示現皆令歡喜。廣大如法界，究竟如虛空。盡未來際，一切刼數無有休息。又發大願，願與一切菩薩同一志行，無有怨嫉。集諸善根，一切菩薩平等一緣，常共集會。能知一切如來境界威力智慧，得不退如意，不相捨離。隨意能現種種佛身，任其自心。能知一切如來境界威力智慧，得不退如意

神通，遊行一切世界，現形一切眾會，普入一切生處，成就不思議大乘，修菩薩行。廣

大如法界，究竟如虛空。盡未來際，一切劫數無有休息。

菩薩又發大願；希望所有的國土，變爲一個國土，這個國土又變入一切的國土，這是互相圓融無礙，相卽相入的法性作用。所有的佛土，都成爲清淨的佛土。**光明眾**

具，以清淨光明，作爲佛土的莊嚴。**離一切煩惱**，沒有貪瞋痴三毒，成就**戒定慧**清淨的聖道。有無量無數具大智慧的菩薩和有智慧的眾生充滿在這國土中，大家都證得了諸佛的境界，常隨應眾生的心念，而爲示現一切的境界，令所有的眾生得到歡喜。這種心願，也是廣大到徧滿法界，究竟得猶如虛空，窮盡未來一切的劫數，也不休息的。菩薩又發大願；願意常與一切志同道合的菩薩一起修行，互相愛護，彼此也沒有仇視和妬嫉的思想。積聚所有善的善根，與眾菩薩處在平等平等的法緣中。經常在一處修行而不分離。隨各人的意念，呈現各種佛身，在自己的心裡，便知道所有諸佛如來的境界，與威神之力和智慧。得到隨心如意的變化和不退轉的神通，遊行到一切世界，參加各處所有的法會，普徧去到一切眾生的地方。成就不可想像的大乘法門，菩薩所修行的一切萬行。這個願心，也是廣大得像法界一樣，究竟得猶如虛空。窮盡到未來一切的劫數，我亦不休息。

又發大願；願乘不退輪，行菩薩行。**身語意業悉不唐捐，若暫見者，則必定佛法。**暫聞

四七

智影則得實智慧。才生淨信，則永斷煩惱。得如大藥王樹身，得如意寶身，修行一切菩薩行。廣大如法界，究竟如虛空。盡未來際，一切劫數無有休息。又發大願；願於一切世界，成阿耨多羅三藐三菩提。不離一毛端處，於一切毛端處，皆悉示現初生、出家、詣道場、成正覺、轉法輪入涅槃，得佛境界大智慧力，於念念中，隨一切眾生心示現成佛，令得寂滅，而不斷菩薩行。示大智慧地安立一切法。以一音說法，令一切眾生心皆歡喜。示入大涅槃，以一三菩提，知一切法界即涅槃相。廣大如法界，究竟如虛空。盡未來際，一切劫數無有休息。以法智通、神足通、幻通、自在變化、充滿一切法界。

菩薩又發大願；希望乘不退轉的法輪，修菩薩所修行的法門。身語意三業都清淨，不造惡業，沒有罪過，決不會是空過的。假設有人能暫時見到菩薩的，必定能種善根，明白佛法。能暫時聽到菩薩的聲音的，就能得到像寶貝一樣的真實智慧。如果他清淨的信心剛剛才生起來，就能永遠斷除煩惱，得到像大藥王樹一樣的身體，能治眾生的病，又可得到像如意寶一樣的身體，修一切菩薩所修行的行門。這種願心也是廣大如法界，究竟如虛空，盡未來的時刻，也不休息。菩薩又發大願；希望全世界的眾生，同時都能證得無上正等正覺。不離開一毛端，和一切的毛端處，都能示現從兜率天宮降生人間、出家、學道、到各道場、菩提樹下成正覺、轉大法輪、說法度眾生，最後入涅槃。徧法界中，一一毛端極小量處，都在其中示現這八相成道

。得到如佛的境界，如佛的大智慧之力。在一念之中，隨眾生的心念，示現成佛，

令一切眾生，也得到寂滅之樂。以一種的正覺，就知一切法界，就好像一個大涅槃

相。用一種聲音說法，使所有的眾生聽到都生歡喜心。雖示現入了大涅槃，但還是

在這世界上不斷的行菩薩道。示大智慧地，大智慧地就是佛智，因智能生萬物，能

領萬行，所以能安立一切。令眾生知道一切依大智慧而安立。以法智通的意思，是

能了知法無性相而生的智慧神通。神足通是能於自身顯現生、住、滅，長短時劫，

能隨心自在。幻通是轉變外事，無不隨心所欲。運用自在，變化無窮充滿所有的法

界。這種願心也是廣大如法界，究竟如虛空，窮盡未來一切劫數，也不休息。

佛子！菩薩住歡喜地，發如是大願，如是大誓願，如是大勇猛，如是大作用。以此十願門為首，滿

足百萬阿僧祇大願。佛子！此大願以十盡句而得成就，何等為十？所謂眾生界盡，世界

盡。虛空界盡、法界盡、涅槃界盡。佛出現界盡、如來智界盡、心所緣界盡、佛智所入

境界界盡。世間轉、法轉、智轉界盡。若眾生界盡、我願乃盡。若世界乃至世間轉、法

轉、智轉界盡、我願乃盡。而眾生界不盡，乃至世間轉、法轉智轉界不可盡故，我此

大願善根，無有窮盡。

金剛藏菩薩恐怕諸位菩薩有時放逸，或不注意聽他說這華嚴經中的法門，又稱一

弊諸位佛的大弟子！你們知道菩薩修證到了歡喜地，他已修得種種的善根，成就了

種種波羅蜜的功德，達到登彼岸的地位，所以他時時都生出大歡喜心，發出前面所發的那些大願。他能以發大勇猛心，衆生不敢修行的法門，他敢來修行。衆生不敢作的事，他敢去作。好像前面所說的種種大作大用，他都以這十種的大願爲第一，來滿足，他在百萬阿僧祇刼中所發的一切大願，一切的大願亦依此十大願而完成。金剛藏菩薩又稱一聲諸位佛的大弟子！這個大願，是修行菩薩道的菩薩**以十盡句而得成就**的。（盡字在這兒要當不能**斷盡**講。這十句是用十項不能盡者爲譬喻，不能盡的十大願作比量。）那十種呢？如所說的衆生界盡了，世界也窮盡了，虛空界也盡了。（這三者是說的世間。）法界也盡了，涅槃界也沒有了，佛出現界盡。（這三者是指法說的）。如來的智慧也沒有了，心裡所想像的，所依據的也沒有了，佛的智慧所證得的，所瞭解的，明白的，這種境界也亦沒有了，（這三者是說的佛智）**世間轉**（轉字在這兒也是不可盡的意思）**法轉，智轉界盡**。這些都轉盡盡沒有了。以上衆生等界都盡了，我的願心才算完了。假若世界乃至於世間轉、法轉、智轉界盡，我的願才能盡。然而衆生以及世間轉、法轉、智轉界等是不能盡的，所以我這種大願，是不可能盡的，永遠存在的。所修的善根，也不會有窮盡的。

佛子！菩薩發如是大願已，則得利益心、柔軟心、隨順心、寂靜心、調伏心、寂滅心、

謙下心、潤澤心、不動心、不濁心。成淨信者；有信功用，能信如來本行所入。信成就諸波羅蜜，信入諸勝地，信成就力，信具足無所畏，信生長不可壞不共佛法，信不議佛法，信出生無中邊佛境界，信隨入如來無量境界，信成就果。舉要言之：信一切菩薩行，乃至如來智地說力故。

金剛藏菩薩又稱一聲諸位佛的大弟子！菩薩發了以上的大願以後；就得到了十種信心：利益心：菩薩在沒有發大願以前，想利益眾生，總是發不出心來，想做也做不到，因爲沒有力量。發了這些大願以後，無形中就增加了他幫助眾生的力量。柔軟心：因爲有願心的力量，把過去剛強的脾氣也變柔軟了，對眾生也能忍耐了，也和氣了，教化眾生時自然能身心調伏而不生煩惱了。隨順心：沒有發菩提心的人，不行菩薩道的人，都喜歡命令人，要別人聽我指揮。等到發了大願以後，就知道必須隨順眾生，然後才能使眾生隨順。沒有我的成見，就沒有了我執。寂靜心：常常心平氣和，沒有煩惱，不管在鬧的靜的地方，都能修行用功，不受外境的影響。調伏心：在這娑婆世界，一切人、事、物都是難調心難伏的，處在這環境中，不要說調伏眾生，就連自己也很難調伏的。菩薩發了大願心後，自然就調伏了身心，也能善巧的調伏了眾生。寂滅心：諸法從本以來，常是寂滅的。如果自心不知寂滅，何能對外物寂滅。菩薩發了大願後，了知諸法寂滅之道。謙下心：沒有發大願以前，常

五一

易犯貢高我慢的毛病，生出許多無謂的煩惱。發此大願以後，這些不好的習氣，自

然消除，由貢高我慢而轉變爲謙和了。潤澤心因爲有了大願心的力量，內心常感到

如甘露潤澤的舒適，沒有枯燥的煩悶之感了。不動心念動百事有，念止萬事無。不

生雜念就沒有妄想的煩惱，心念清淨，智慧油然而生可幫助萬行。不濁心因爲有如

是的大願，心念清淨，那還會有濁心、染污心呢。有了上面這些願力的信心，就成

了一位有清淨信心的德人了。這種信心的功用，能使進入佛本來所修行的行門，能

由信成就十種的波羅蜜，能信就能進入這殊勝的十地的地位，能信也就能成就神通

的力量，由信心也具足一切大無畏的力量，經上說信爲道源功德母，長養一切諸善

法。信能生長不可爲外道所破壞的佛法。信不可以言語形容的，不能想像的，佛所

說的眞理。信佛所說的，不落於兩邊的境界。因爲佛的境界是時時刻刻，在在處處

都不着於空、不落於空。不着於有，不落於有的。佛所提倡的是中道。信能隨入佛

的不可限量的境界。信能成就一切的果位。總結舉其重要的說一點：信一切菩薩所

修行的法門，乃至於達到如來的智慧之地，這都是由信生起的力量的

緣故。

佛子！此菩薩復作是念；諸佛正法、如是甚深、如是寂靜、如是寂滅、如是空、如是無

相、如是無願、如是無染、如是無量、如是廣大。而諸凡夫，心墮邪見，無明覆翳，立

憍慢高幢，入渴愛網中，行謟誑稠林，不能自出。心與慳嫉相應不捨，恒造諸趣受生因緣。貪恚愚痴，積集諸業，日夜增長。以念恨風，吹心識火，熾然不息。凡所作業，皆顛倒相應欲流、無明流、見流、相續起心意識種子，於三界田中，復生苦芽。所謂名色，共生不離。此名色增長生六處聚落，於中相對生觸，觸故生受。因受生愛，愛增長故生取。取增長故生有，有生故有老死憂悲苦惱。如是衆生，生長苦聚。是中皆空，離我我所，無知無覺，無作無受，如草木石壁，亦如影像。然諸衆生，不覺不知。菩薩見衆生於如是苦聚，不得出離，是故即生大悲智慧。復作是念；此諸衆生，我應救拔，置於究竟安樂之處，是故即生大慈光明智。

金剛藏菩薩又稱一聲諸位佛的大弟子！證得歡喜地的菩薩，又作這樣的想法；諸佛正法眼藏，是這樣的深，深得好像大海不能見到底。如是寂靜；法的本體，是寂靜的，不會被任何外來的境界所動搖。而且寂滅的，無有形相可見。也像虛空，空得無量無邊，沒有一定的相狀。也沒有什麼願，一切都空。也無任何染汚和着處。法體就是這樣的不可限量而廣大無際。然而一般凡夫，却墮入邪知邪見的思想，顛倒行事，不知修行。無明就像天空的烏雲，把日光遮蓋。自己豎起憍慢的高幢，深入渴愛的網羅中，蹈進謟媚欺誑的密林裡，輾轉不能出來。心性與慳貪嫉妒糾纏不清，不捨，永遠在四惡趣中自造受生的因緣。因無明的緣故，就生出貪妄、瞋恚愚痴的

思想，做出種種業果，日積月累，增長不息。生起念恨的邪風，吹動心識的邪火，燃燒不息。凡所作所為，都是顛倒而不合理法的，隨順貪欲。在三界內順應有流，跟着無明、見惑去跑。這種種子在心意識裡相續不斷的生起，保留。在三界的田中又生出苦痛的苗芽。這是佛講的十二因緣。十二因緣第一是無明。由無明顛倒就生出行，就是愛欲的行為。有了行為，就生出了意識的種子。因意識的種子種到三界的田裡，就生出了苦芽。這苦芽就是名色。（名色；如說男的、女的。）因名色就生出六處聚落。（六處聚落乃指眼、耳、鼻、舌、身、意六根。又叫六入，六根為內六入。六根、六境互涉入而生六識，故又名六處。）聚落就是六入同在母胎內生長。因之就生出觸塵。因觸塵又生出領受。因領受生出愛欲。因愛欲的增長，又生取。因取生有。由有生出生。由生就有生、老、病、死、憂悲、苦惱，隨着而來。像這樣的眾生，生長成為苦的聚落。雖然這樣說法，如果能明白這道理，一切就是空的，終歸幻滅，而離開我和我所，就無知無覺了。十二因緣的本身，就是無知無覺的。無作者，也無受者，就像無情的草木石壁。明白了這道理一切就如像影像。可是眾生在這種中間，他不覺不悟，不知本來是空。菩薩看見眾生在十二因緣中生殁，為愛欲所繫縛，受其苦聚，不能出離。因之菩薩生起大悲心的智慧，又這樣想；像這些眾生，我應該拯救他們，把他們救出到最安適快樂的地方。所以就生出了

大慈的心而發出了光明的智慧。

佛子！菩薩摩訶薩隨順如是大悲大慈，以深重心住初地時，於一切物無所恪惜，求佛大智，修行大捨。凡是所有，一切能施，所謂財、穀、倉庫、金銀、摩尼、眞珠、瑠璃、珂貝、璧玉、珊瑚等物，珍寶、瓔珞嚴身之具，象、馬、車乘、奴婢、人民、城邑、聚落、園林、臺觀、妻妾、男女內外眷屬，及餘所有珍玩之具，頭目、手足、血肉、骨髓、一切身分，皆無所惜，爲求諸佛廣大智慧。是名菩薩住於初地大捨成就。

金剛藏菩薩因恐有些菩薩常在定中，沒有注意，於是又稱一聲諸位佛的大弟子！修行菩薩道，積聚種種善根的大菩薩，他是常常隨着大悲大慈行道的。因爲大悲心住在初地——歡喜地的時候，對於任何貴重的物質，都沒有貪戀和吝惜心，都能毫無不捨的意思捨於別人。唯一的他只想求得和佛一樣的大智慧，所以他修行布施法門，大大的布施。凡是他所有的，一概能捨得布施。如像外財：錢財、穀米、倉庫能拔救衆生出於苦海，大慈能給予衆生眞心的快樂。以深不可測的心，愼重嚴謹的心住在初地——歡喜地的時候，對於任何貴重的物質，都沒有貪戀和吝惜心，都能毫無不捨的意思捨於別人。唯一的他只想求得和佛一樣的大智慧，所以他修行布施法門，大大的布施。凡是他所有的，一概能捨得布施。如像外財：錢財、穀米、倉庫內的金銀，摩尼寶、眞珠寶，瑠璃寶，珂貝寶，最好的玉石，珊瑚等寶物。又如日常使用的象、馬、名貴的車。又如莊嚴身體，使人顯得高貴的珍寶瓔珞的飾物。居住的園林、樓臺、亭閣聰明靈慧的侍者，和屬於自己的人民、廓城、鄉村聚落，甚至自己的妻、妾、兒子、女兒、內外親眷家屬以及所有珍貴玩物等等的東西都

五五

能布施。如果有人來乞求他的內財如頭、目、手、腳、血、肉、骨髓，凡是身上所
有的，他也絕不吝惜，一切能捨。這樣的大布施，他是為了求得諸佛廣大的智慧。這
就是菩薩住在初地時成就的大捨善根功德。

佛子！菩薩以此慈悲大施心，為欲救護一切眾生，轉更推求出世間諸利益事，無疲厭
故，即得成就無疲厭心。得無疲厭心已，於一切經論，心無怯弱，無怯弱故，即得成就一切經論
智。獲是智已，善能籌量應作不應作。於上中下一切眾生，隨應隨力，隨其所習，如是
而行，是故菩薩得成世智。成世智已，知時知量，以慚愧莊嚴，勤修自利利他之道，是
故成就慚愧莊嚴。於此行中，勤修出離，不退不轉，成堅固力。得堅固力已，勤供諸佛
，於佛教法，能如說行。

金剛藏菩薩又稱一聲各位佛的大弟子！歡喜地的菩薩發這種大慈大悲大布施的大願
一段發心，是為了救拔一切眾生，使得離苦，愛護一切的眾生使他們獲真樂。於是他又更進
一步的推求，在世間如何利益眾生，出世間又如何利益眾生。常常修此菩薩行，從
不生厭倦疲乏的心，這樣很自然而沒有疲厭的心了。得到了無疲厭
智，圓滿了一種精進不懈的力量，對於一切的大乘經典論說，再不會有畏難畏多的怯弱
心。此後，一種疑難也不能作障了，也不怕佛法如大海，不敢去攝受了。凡佛所說的經典，一見就能一目了
然，照了諸法實相。深入經藏，智慧如海。成就了研究一切經論的智慧。

菩薩獲得了深入經藏，智慧如海的智慧以後、對於一切事理、都能很仔細的計劃，對的甚麼事應該做，甚麼事不應該做，都能分別認識清楚。遇着上根上智的眾生、中根中智的眾生，下根愚拙的眾生，他都能隨應自己的力量，了解眾生的愛惡習性，應該用甚麼方法和身份才能度他，都能得心應手，順事而行的去教化眾生。因之菩薩就成了世間法的智慧。菩薩成就了世間的智慧以後，有了「知時知量」的決斷力，清楚知道一切眾生的機緣是否成熟，何者眾生應先度，應用何法，何者眾生機緣未熟，還不應度，他均能酌量而行。隨時都警策自己，發慚愧心，以「慚愧」來「莊嚴」自己，修福修慧，聚積福德。精進勤修一切能自利又能利他的聖教道理。因之成就了慚愧行，而自莊嚴的功德。在這種修行的行門中，精勤修習出三界的法門是，就不會退轉於阿耨多羅三藐三菩提，成就了修行的堅固不退的勝進。得到了這種「堅固力」以後，殷勤供養一切諸佛，對於佛所說的一切教法他都能如是說如是奉行。

佛子！菩薩如是成就十種淨諸地法，所謂信悲慈捨無有疲厭。知諸經論，善解世法。慚愧堅固力，供養諸佛，依教修行。佛子！菩薩住此歡喜地已，以大願力得見多佛。所謂見多百佛，多千佛、多百千佛、多億佛、多百億佛、多千億佛、多百千億佛、多億那由他佛、多百億那由他佛、多千億那由他佛、多百千億那由他佛。悉以大心深心，恭敬尊

重，承事供養。衣服、飲食、臥具、醫藥、一切資生悉以奉施。亦以供養一切衆僧，以

此善根，皆悉迴向無上菩提。」

金剛藏菩薩又稱一聲諸位佛的大弟子！菩薩像上面所說的一切，刻意修行，就成了

十種的「淨治諸地」的去障淨修法門。就是要「信」佛所說的一切道理，救拔衆生

於苦難中，給予眞正的快樂而行大布施，如此修行，而不生「疲厭」。深入經藏，

瞭解三藏十二部。對於世間法，也很通達而善於方便運用。有「慚愧堅固」的力量

，供養一切佛，依佛所說，切實修行。諸位佛的大弟子！菩薩修證到初地——歡喜地

了，因爲他有種種大願力的緣故，所以他可以見到很多佛，多到無法計數，所謂「

見多百佛、多千佛、多百千佛、多億佛、多百億佛、多千億佛、多億

那由他佛、多百億那由他佛、多千億那由他佛、多百千億那由他佛」。總之；算數

校計，所不能知。初地的菩薩已經有這種隨心自在，隨時可以見佛的境界了。他們

隨時都以最大的願心，最深切的信心，恭恭敬敬，謹愼仔細的承事於諸佛之前，供

養衣服、飲食、臥具、醫藥等一切資生的東西，也以之行大布施，並供養諸位賢聖

僧。將這種善根功德，都迴向無上的妙覺佛道。

佛子！此菩薩因供養諸佛故，得成就衆生法。以前二攝，攝取衆生，謂布施愛語。後二

攝法，但以信解力故，行，未善通達。是菩薩十波羅蜜中，檀波羅蜜增上，餘波羅蜜，

非不修行，但隨力隨分。是菩薩隨所勤修，供養諸佛，教化衆生，皆以修行清淨地法。

所有善根，悉以迴向一切智地，轉轉明淨，調柔成就，隨意堪用。

金剛藏菩薩又稱一聲諸位佛的大弟子！這位證得歡喜地的菩薩，因爲廣修供養諸佛的緣故，得到的功德，成就了廣度衆生的四攝法。以前面的兩種方法，攝取衆生就是「布施、愛語」。菩薩是廣修布施，布施一切的內外財寶。愛語呢；就是以慈悲心愛護衆生，對他們說他們愛聽的話。沒有愛惡心用善巧的方法，發菩提心平等廣度衆生。另外二種方法，就是「利行、同事」：「利行」是用有利於衆生的善行；如在身、口、意、方面表現有利於衆生的行爲，使衆生由此而生親近的心，而受教化。「同事」則是菩薩以法眼觀衆生根性，隨衆生之所需，而示現身形，令衆生受到同化而度脫之。菩薩但以他的信解力而行，還有修行沒有完善通達的地方。初地菩薩在修十種波羅蜜的法門中，初地是以布施波羅蜜爲最增上的。（十種波羅蜜：布施、持戒、忍辱、精進、禪定、智慧、方便、願、力、智。）其餘九種，並不是不修，祇是隨自己的力量和因緣而行。「是菩薩」是指這位初地菩薩他一方面修行，同時亦殷勤供養諸佛，和教化衆生，他都是依據所修的清淨十地法門。如此「轉轉明淨」就日漸「一步一步」的修行進步，明淨除障。身心自在，內外調柔，隨自己的心意，運用佛法，教化衆

五九

生。

佛子！譬如金師，善巧鍊金，數數入火，轉轉明淨。調柔成就，隨意堪用。菩薩亦復如是。供養諸佛，敎化衆生，皆為修行清淨法地。所有善根悉以迴向一切智地。轉轉明淨，調柔成就，隨意堪用。佛子！菩薩摩訶薩住於初地，應從諸佛菩薩善知識所，推求請問於此區地點中，相及得果，無有厭足。為欲成就此地法故，亦應從諸佛菩薩善知識所，推求請問於此區地點中，相及得果，無有厭足。為欲成就彼地法故，亦應如是推求請問第三第四第五第六第七第八第九第十地中相及得果，無有厭足。為欲成就彼地法故。是菩薩善知諸地障對治、善知地成壞、善知地相果、善知地得修、善知地轉行、善知地地處非處、善知地地殊勝智、善知地地不退轉、善知地法清淨、善知地地轉治一切菩薩地，乃至轉入如來地。

金剛藏菩薩又稱一聲諸位佛的大弟子！現在我舉一個比喻：好像鍛鍊金子的匠人，他用種種的方法，一次又一次的把金子放在火裡燒，每燒一次，金子便亮一點，愈燒便愈亮。把所含的雜物去淨了，就柔軟了，不會折斷了。這時就能「隨意堪用」，隨人的意思，願意做什麼都可以，莊嚴佛事和裝飾一切。菩薩也是這樣的，他修治一切諸地法門，首先修廣行供養諸佛，和用慈悲、喜捨、忍辱、精進等波羅蜜來敎化衆生，令一切衆生都能修行這清淨的十地法門。所修行的一切善根，完全用以迴向一切智慧的果地。修行這十地法門的工夫，一天比一天進步，一

天比一天明淨。菩薩這時一點煩惱也沒有了，時時都能慈悲喜捨也能忍辱，成就了調柔忍辱的法門，隨自己的意思，願用什麼法門都可以。各位佛的大弟子！修菩薩行，積聚種種善根的大菩薩，在證得歡喜地的期間，應該依從諸佛、菩薩、和善知識的途徑，不斷的研究、思惟他現在修習的初地中，有些什麼相狀，和將來可得到何種的果位。對於有關修行此地法門，如有疑難，隨時請問諸佛、大菩薩、和善知識。日日如是，精勤不懈怠，也沒厭倦和自滿的心。為了想成就這第二地法門，也應該依從諸佛、大菩薩、和善知識的途徑，研究推求修行第二地法門中所經歷的相狀，和將來應得到如何的果位，為求得這些疑難得解答，從不曾生厭倦滿足的心。為了要成就這種十地法門，更應該深入研究，向諸佛、大菩薩和善知識請問第三地、第四地、第五地、第六地、第七地、第八地、第九地以及第十地，各地中所修行的經過和相狀，和各地修得如何的果位。這位菩薩，他善於瞭解修行初地法門時，有些甚的障礙，用甚麼方法來對治。這樣恆常精勤推求，從不曾厭倦自滿。這都是為了想成就這種十地法門的緣故。也知道怎樣修行可成就十地法，為什麼不能修證成功的原因。也明白修行十地法門經歷的一切相狀，和將來可能證得的果位。也知道要怎樣修行，才能進入二地。也知道十地法門是無上清淨的。也能體會得依次一地一地的，循序漸進的修行，從初地進入十地法門。也能認清修行每地的方法，怎

様才是正確 和 用甚麼方法方可避免有錯誤。也知道各地有各地的特別智慧和行門

。也注意到各地都有防止修行者不生退轉心的秘訣。也知善用智慧來對治菩薩地中

可能發生的諸障，而得到清淨，乃至轉入如來地的經過 層六次， 而 成 就 佛 果

的果位。

佛子！菩薩如是善知地相，始於初地，起行不斷，如是乃至入第十地，無有斷絕。由此

諸地智光明故，成於如來智慧光明。佛子！譬如商主，善知方便，欲將諸商人，往詣大

城，未發之時，先問道中功德過失，乃住止之處，安危可不，然後具道資糧，作所應作

。佛子！彼大商主，雖未發足，能知道中，所有一切安危之事。善以智慧籌量觀察，備

其所需，令無乏少，將諸商眾，乃至安隱到彼大城，身及眾人，悉免憂患。佛子！菩薩

商主，亦復如是。住於初地，善知諸地障對治，乃至善知一切菩薩地清淨，轉入如來地

。然後乃具福智資糧，將一切眾生，經生死曠野險難之處，安穩得至薩婆若城，身及眾

生，不經患難。是故菩薩常應匪懈，勤修諸地殊勝淨業，乃至趣入如來智地」。

金剛藏菩薩又稱一聲諸位佛的大弟子！菩薩像這樣修行，他就能知道每一地有每一

地不同的相狀和境界。從初地起，發心勤修十地法門，從未間斷。好像這樣繼續不斷

地修行，直到進入第十地，不曾停止。由於各地都能修證到智慧之光的緣故，因之

成就了如同佛一樣的智慧光明了。諸位佛的大弟子！我現在舉一個例來說：有一位

大商主，他很有頭腦，也很會運用善巧方便的方法，他將要帶領許多商人，到一座大城去做生意。當他還未出發之前，他就先打聽清楚所經旅途，何處路好走又平安，何處路不好走又危險，甚麼地方應該休息，甚麼地方可以住宿。他瞭解了這些安危的情形後，才着大家準備錢財貨物和預備一切應該準備的事情。各位佛的大弟子！像這位大商主他雖然還沒有啟程動步，他就能事先知道途中一切安危的事，這就是他能運用他的智慧事前計劃，各方觀察，準備週全，便不會臨時發生缺這少如那的阻礙，他才能很順利地帶着這些商人，到達那座大城。這樣自己和衆人，都能免去那些無謂的憂心與禍患。諸位佛的大弟子！菩薩也同這位商主一樣，住在初地的時候，就知道各地有些什麼障礙，應該用甚麼方法去對治，進而知道一切菩薩地的菩薩，是如何修清淨行門，才能進入佛的果位。然後他就廣修諸波羅蜜，積聚福德智慧的資糧，教化衆生，度衆生脫離生死輪迴的曠野，離開危險痛苦的地方，到達安穩智慧的城垣。自己本身，和衆生，大家都沒有了苦難。所以菩薩是應該常常不懈怠，精進勤修各地殊勝的清淨法門，和勤習各種道業，直到進入佛的智慧果位。

佛子！是名略說菩薩摩訶薩，入菩薩初地門，廣說則有無量無邊百千阿僧祇差別事。

諸位佛的大弟子！這是大略說說菩薩中的大菩薩，證入菩薩初地的法門中的一切實在情境，假如要詳細說，那就無法說得完，些無量無邊的不同事相。

六三

佛子！菩薩摩訶薩住此初地，多作閻浮提王，豪貴自在，常護正法。能以大施、攝取眾生，善除眾生慳貪之垢。常行大施，無有窮盡。布施、愛語、利行、同事。如是一切諸所作業，皆不離念佛不離念法，不離念僧，不離念同行菩薩，不離念菩薩行，不離念諸波羅蜜，不離念諸地，不離念力，不離念無畏，不離念不共佛法，乃至不離念具足一切種一切智智。

諸位佛的大弟子！證得初地果位的大菩薩，住在初地時，多數能做閻浮提王（即鐵輪王）。或者是大富大貴的人，生活得很如意自在。還常常護持正法。「能以大施」：常行大布施的法門，攝取眾生，也知道用方法教化眾生，除去眾生的慳吝和貪妄的毛病。他經常廣行大布施，沒有窮盡。「布施、愛語、利行、同事」布施財物，愛語教化眾生。幫助眾生，親切接近眾生，（以四攝法使他們受同化。）像這樣做出一切利他的善業，都不曾忘離念佛、法、僧三寶的心。也不曾離念十地中各地的法門及相狀。也不曾離念修菩薩行所應修的行門。也不曾離念十波羅蜜，也不曾離念同修行的菩薩，也不曾離念一切的願力。也不曾離念佛的四無畏法。也不曾離念佛的十八不共法。乃至於不曾離念一切，和一切智慧中的佛的大智慧。

復作是念：我當於一切眾生中，為首、為勝、為殊勝、為妙、為微妙、為上、為無上、

在這兒包含很多意思：如種子、種性、種智、種識、智慧等多意。（種字

為導、為將、為帥、乃至為一切智智依止者。是菩薩若欲捨家,於佛法中,勤行精進。

便能捨家妻子五欲,依如來教,出家學道。

住在十地—歡喜地的諸位菩薩,又作這樣的觀想:「為首」我應該在一切眾生中,作他們的領導者。「為勝」我應該有超人的智慧。「為殊勝」有超人的特別才能。

「為妙」有無礙的辯才。「為微妙」應善於運用微妙的言辭,令眾生離一切的痛苦而自在。「為上」應該修集完美的福德。「為無上」沒有人比我更完美的。「為導」

我應能為眾生分別法義。「為將」令眾生能得到證義,滅除一切煩惱。「為帥」令眾生能進入正知正見的正道中。令所有的眾生以我為他們的智慧之所依止的人。這

位菩薩當他想想出家的時候,在學習佛法的期間,要特別勇猛精進,就能捨掉世俗的家業、妻、兒、和財、色、名、食、睡)五欲。依着佛的教言,出家學道是出煩惱的家

、三界的家(色界、欲界、無色界)要能出這三界的家,才能算真正出家,才能修道。

既出家已,勤修精進。於一念頃,得百三昧,得見百佛,知百佛神力。能動百佛世界,

能入百法門,能示現百身。於一一身,能示百菩薩以為眷屬。若以菩薩殊勝願力,自在

能過百佛世界,能照百佛世界。能教化百世界眾生,能住壽百劫,能知前後際各百劫事

示現,過於是數。百劫千劫百千劫,乃至百千億那由他劫,不能知數。爾時金剛藏菩薩

,欲重宣其義,而說頌曰:

六六

六五

菩薩發菩提心，捨世俗家而出家，是為了求無上正道，這時他是勤奮不懈，勇猛精進的修行。就在一念之間，就可以得到百多種正定正受的智慧。既得到如許三昧，也見到了十方世界的百佛。見到佛後，也能知道這些佛的智慧，能用神通令十方佛世界六種震動。他的神通力量，能超過十方百佛的世界。他的壽命明也能照耀百佛的世界。也能在一念之間，教化百佛世界那樣多的眾生。他的光能夠住世一百劫。能知百劫前後的一切事故。能示現很多化身，而每一個化身，又能示現化出百菩薩，來作他的眷屬。假如這位菩薩有特別的功德和願力他更能非常自在的示現變化，還要超過百劫，甚至千劫、百千劫、百千億那由他劫，不能用算數校計。這時；金剛藏菩薩想重說一遍，就用偈頌的方式再說一遍：

若人集眾善　具足白淨法　供養天人尊　隨順慈悲道。

菩薩修所應修的行門，和積聚種種的善根。因善根功德具足了，就把一切的染汙除去了，就是無染汙的清淨法了。他能供養諸佛，又常用慈悲喜捨四無量心教化眾生。

信解極廣大　志樂亦清淨　為求佛智慧　發此無上心。

他的信心和理解能力，都是非常廣大的，他的志願和樂於所作的，也都是清淨的。為了想求得同佛一樣的智慧，發這種無上的菩提道心。

淨一切智力　及以無所畏　成就諸佛法　救攝群生衆。

清淨所有的智慧之力，和用大無畏的精神，成就諸佛所說的種種法門，救拔攝受那些苦難的衆生。

爲得大慈悲　及轉勝法輪　嚴淨佛國土　發此最勝心。

爲了得到大慈悲心，和轉一切殊勝的法輪，（就是廣對衆生演說大乘正法）用這種救攝衆生的大慈悲心，和演說大乘佛法的功德，來莊嚴清淨佛的國土。爲了這個目的，菩薩發這種最殊勝的菩提心。

一念知三世　而無有分別　種種時不同　以示於世間。

一念能知過去、未來、現在三世，而沒有分別，這是用智慧來知道的，不是以識來分別的。因爲三世的時間不同，所以示現於世間。

略說求諸佛　一切勝功德　發生廣大心　量等虛空界。

略略的說點諸佛的無上聖道，和諸佛的殊勝功德，菩薩發這麼廣大的願心，大得與虛空同等。

悲先慧爲主　方便共相應　信解清淨心　如來無量力。

以大慈悲心爲第一，以智慧爲主體。行一切方便善巧的方法，而能與佛法相應。以清淨的信解心，得到如來的無量神通力。

六七

無礙智現前　自悟不由他　具足同如來　發此最勝心。

得到了無礙的智慧，又得到了百千萬的三昧，這並不是別人賜給的。而是由自己修持證悟的。這些種種殊勝的智慧與神力，都可與佛同一樣了。菩薩發這種殊勝的菩提心。

佛子始發生　如是妙寶心　則超凡夫位　入佛所行處。

佛弟子剛剛發菩提心，如像金剛堅固的寶心，就與凡夫不同了。超出了凡夫的地位，進入了佛所行的道路。

生在如來家　種族無瑕玼　與佛共平等　決成無上覺。

證得歡喜地的菩薩，就是生在佛的家族中了。種族是高貴的，不是貧窮下賤。這樣的種族可說是一點汙垢也沒有了。一切與佛一樣，將來一定成佛的。

纔生如是心　即得入初地　志樂不可動　譬如大山王。

菩薩剛發起這菩提心和慈悲心，馬上便證入了歡喜地。他的志願和所樂於作的，都是菩薩道行的，菩薩道行的，誰也不能阻擋及破壞他，就好像大須彌山王一樣巍峨聳立而不被動搖。

多喜多愛樂　亦復多淨信　極大勇猛心　及以慶躍心。

證得了歡喜地的菩薩，時刻都是歡喜的，他愛護眾生，樂於接近眾生。同時也不懈於修

習清淨的法門，而堅固對佛法的信解心。發非常勇猛的精進心，更生起慶幸活躍的歡喜心。

遠離於鬪諍　惱害及瞋恚　慚敬而質直　善守護諸根。

菩薩證入了歡喜地的果位後，自然沒有了好勇鬪狠的傲慢心，也不事事與人爭論，也不惱害，和嗔恨別人了。只有慚愧而恭敬的誠懇、質樸、正直的菩薩心了。他善於守護自己的六根，不令放逸。

救世無等者　所有衆智慧　此處我當得　憶念生歡喜。

行普救衆生的菩薩道，除佛以外，沒有誰能與他相比。所有佛的智慧，我都應當證得。菩薩時常憶念三寶，及一切衆生，就生起大歡喜心。

始得入初地　即超五怖畏　不活死惡名　惡趣衆威德。

菩薩證入歡喜地時，就能遠離了五種的怖畏：一不能生活的怖畏。二不能活，就是怕死的怖畏。三怕受人的誹謗的怖畏。四怕受生到三惡道中的怖畏。五、在大衆中畏首畏尾的大衆威德畏。以不貪著我，及以於我所，是故諸佛子等，遠離諸怖畏。這些怖畏的生起，都是由於貪在我的執著偏見上，如果能破除了我見，還有甚麼可怕的呢。還有我所，就是受貪心的驅使，甚麼都是我所有的。把我見和我所都放下了，明白了一切都是空的。學佛法的佛弟子，就要能捨掉我及我所，自然遠離這些

怖畏了。

常行大慈愍　恒有信恭敬　慚愧功德備　日夜增善法。

常常行大慈大悲，愍念衆生。常常有誠懇的清淨信心，恭敬三寶。時刻懷着慚愧的心意一切的功德就具足了。這樣就可以日夜增長善法。

樂法眞實利　不愛受諸欲　思惟所聞法　遠離取著行。

歡喜佛法的眞實利益，不喜歡那些五欲的事情。能常常思惟觀想所聽聞的佛法眞實義意，遠遠的離開一切愛、取的執著行爲。

不貪於利養　唯樂佛菩提　一心求佛智　專精無異念。

不去貪圖名聞利養，唯一就喜歡學佛法，證得無上的菩提大道。一心只想求得如佛的智慧，精誠專一，不生二心，不起異念。

修行波羅蜜　遠離詔虛誑　如說而修行　安住實語中。

想求得如佛的智慧，必須修習十種波羅蜜。更應遠離詔媚心、虛榮心、和狂妄心。一定要切實依照佛所說的方法來修行。安然住在不打妄語的實語中。

不汙諸佛家　不捨菩薩戒　不樂於世事　常利益世間。

學佛法的人，要常能如理修行，護持三寶，不做有汙佛門的事，不敗壞如來的家風，令衆生一見就生起恭敬三寶的心，皈依佛門。時時刻刻要守着曾受過菩薩所

制定的四十八種輕重戒律。不要去染指世俗中的五欲惡事，要常做有益世間、利樂衆生的善事。

修善無厭足　轉求增勝道　如是好樂法　功德義相應。

修行善法是無止境的，是沒有厭倦滿足的。這樣日復一日勇猛精進，勤修無上殊勝的善道。如此愛好佛法，功德一定與佛法相應的。

恒起大願心　願見於諸佛　護持諸佛法　攝取大仙道。

時常生起大志願的心。希望常常見到十方三世諸佛。又應該發願護持諸佛所說的法，攝取諸佛的佛道。（大仙道就是佛道）。

常生如是願　修行最勝行　成熟諸群生　嚴淨佛國土。

時常發這樣的願心，修行最殊勝的法門，令一切衆生都能成熟善根？修行得到成就。將來一定都能成佛。莊嚴十方三世所有諸佛國土。

一切諸佛刹　佛子悉充滿　平等共一心　所作皆不空。

佛刹，佛的弟子都充滿其中。（佛子是指菩薩）這些菩薩們都是一心一意為救度衆生的，他們所作所為所修行的，都不會是白費工夫，一定有如願的成就和功德的。所有的世界，和無量無邊的

一切毛端處　一時成正覺　如是等大願　無量無邊際。

修行，同樣大家可在一時成佛果。像這樣不可思議的大願，是無量無邊不可度量的。菩薩發願在一切毛端的地方

七一

虛空與衆生　法界及涅槃　世間佛出興　佛智心境界。　虛空和衆生都是不可窮盡的，

法界和涅槃同樣是不可窮盡，世界上有佛出興，也是不可以預知的，佛的智慧和心

意的境界，是不可思議的。

如來智所入　及以三轉盡　彼諸若有盡　我願方始盡。佛的智慧所能到的，和虛空

一切界盡，衆生界盡，煩惱界盡，如果這些都能窮盡，我的願也就窮盡了。

如彼無盡期　我願亦復然　如是發大願　心柔軟調順。　如像前面所說的虛空界、衆

生界、煩惱界、法界這些都是沒有窮盡的，所以我的願心也同樣不會有盡期的。發

了這種大願，這種不可思議，廣大無邊，不可限量的大願，心就自然柔和、自在、

安詳了。　（大山道場彌陀殿）。

能信佛功德　觀察於衆生　知從因緣起　則興慈念心。　我們學佛的人，首先要認識

清楚學佛的宗旨，反省一下是否真正信佛，是否信佛有無量的功德。佛何以會有無量的

功德？正因為佛在過去生中，廣行大布施；內財：頭、目、骨、血，外財：廓城妻子

，一切難捨能施。我們既信佛有無量功德，就應常隨佛學，也要作種種的大布施，

所以要觀察一切的衆生。衆生是因緣和合而生，在過去無量劫中，與我們曾有過親

屬關係，或曾為父子、母子、兄弟、姊妹、夫妻、朋友等等，彼此有如業網交織，

輪迴輾轉。明白這種關係後，就應生起慈悲心，救護顧念他們，使衆生都能離苦得

七二

樂。

如是苦衆生　我今應救脫　爲是衆生故　而行種種施。

迴六道中，生生死死不能脫出。菩薩現在既已明白這種道理，就應該救度衆生出離苦海。爲了救這些受苦的衆生，就廣修種種布施。

王位及珍寶　乃至象馬車　頭目與手足　乃至身血肉。

我的王位和七寶、種種的名貴珠寶，以及華貴的大白象、千里馬、寶車等的外財。或尊貴的頭、眼、手、足、身體內的血，外面的肉，種種難捨的內財，沒有一樣保留而不能布施。

一切皆能捨　心得無憂悔　求種種經書　其心無厭倦。

聞欲一切內財外財，我亦能布施。布施之後，心中毫無一點捨不得的憂悔心。諸位學佛的信士！我們學佛；就應該學佛一切的行儀。信佛；就應該信佛所說的法──理，依教奉行。學佛難捨能捨的精神，廣修布施。菩薩誦念種種經典、持咒、修行，心無見異思遷，或厭煩疲倦。而誦經、持咒的用意，是去妄存真，使六根歸於清淨專一，善心生起。

善解其義趣　能隨世所行　慚愧自莊嚴　修行轉堅固。

誦經持咒是爲了明白一切道理，在誦經的時候，可以收攝心意，培養定力。繼而用到世間法上利益衆生。常常要反省過去的錯誤行爲，生慚愧心。以覺悟的清淨和誠直心來警策未來，衆善奉行，積聚功德，莊嚴自己。能心生大慚愧、發大菩提心，修行無上的菩提道，信

心就日益增長，更堅固了。

供養無量佛　恭敬而尊重　如是常修習　日夜無懈倦。

廣修供養十方諸佛。不獨供養，還懂得恭敬，和尊重諸佛。這樣生生世世，恆常不斷的修習，晝夜六時，亦無懈怠厭倦。

菩薩的信心日漸堅固了，就

善根轉明淨　如火鍊眞金　菩薩住於此　淨修於十地。

日勝一日的光明清淨了。好像冶金師傅用火鍛鍊金子一樣，一回又一回的燒鍊，直至無一點雜質留存，最後變成純金。菩薩住在初地時，修行的工夫，也是無有息歇，清淨無爲的修習十地法門。，了知十地的境界，最後才會得到十地的果位。

菩薩如此修行不懈，善根就

所作無障碍　具足不斷絕　譬如大商主　爲利諸商眾　問知道險易　安隱至大城　菩薩

住初地　應知亦如是。

菩薩行菩薩道，修一切善，滅一切惡，所以處事接物沒有任何障碍。具足了智慧之光，佛種不會斷絕。譬如一位大商主，爲利益許多的商人，聯合大眾到遠處經商，他必須知道路途各處安危的實在情形，準備週全，大家方能安穩地到達目的地。

菩薩住初地。應知亦如是　勇猛無障礙　到於初地中　作大功德王。

菩薩住在初地修行的時候，也同樣要了解各地的境界，和所證得的果位，方能達至佛的果位。這其間一切的過程。勇猛精進，沒有一點障礙，一直到第十地法雲

七四

地，都不會有障礙發生。住在歡喜地──初地的菩薩，作最大的功德之王，領導所有的菩薩向前修行。

以法化眾生　慈心無損害　統領閻浮地　化行靡不及　皆令住大捨　成就佛智慧　欲求最勝道　捨己國王位。

菩薩作功德王，在南閻浮提常作輪王，以佛法教化一切的眾生。化度眾生首先要有慈心，決不能有損害眾生的心。又常行布施，救濟眾生。菩薩做南閻浮地的國王，領導眾生，把這世界上一切壞的風俗，都一一把它轉變成良好的風氣。教化眾生修持五戒、八關齋戒，不殺生，不偷盜，不邪淫，不妄語，不飲酒，修學十善正法。又教導眾生修習布施法門，化除慳吝的障礙，常住在大喜捨中，使所有眾生亦得到如佛的智慧。菩薩自己求最的是最殊勝的佛道，他也教眾生求取無上聖道。

為求清淨殊勝的佛道，他就捨掉國王的地位，出家學道。

能於佛教中　勇猛勤修習　則得百三昧　及見百諸佛　震動百世界　光照行亦爾　化百土眾生　入於百法門　能知百刼事　示現於百身　及現百菩薩　以為其眷屬。

修菩薩行、求菩薩道的菩薩，捨掉了王位，出家修梵行，在佛的佛化中，他特別顯得勇猛精進，勤謹修習佛所說的各種法門，能在一念中得到百多的正定心得，也能在一念之間見到百世界的諸佛。這種修證的境界，震動了百世界，並有六種的

七五

震動。光明也能照耀到百世界，並遍及其間一切樂生。教化百世界的衆生，令彼等

都進入百種法門。菩薩這時能知道三世——過去、未來現、現在——百劫中一切事

情。又能示現變化百樣身形，每位身形又能變化出數以百計的菩薩形相，作爲他的

眷屬，來幫助他弘法利生。

若自在願力　過是數無量　我於地義中　略述其少分　若欲廣分別　億劫不能盡　菩薩

最勝道　利益諸群生　如是初地法　我今已說竟。

像那些願力已達到圓融無礙的大菩薩們，他們的功德和境界，當然超過了前面所說

的初地菩薩們的功德和境界無量倍劫，是無法說盡的劫數。我在講初地的義理時，

只能略略的說一點，如果要詳細的說明其中義理、相狀、境界等的差別，恐怕歷百千

億劫也沒有方法說盡。菩薩所修行的是最殊勝的菩薩道，他最主要的宗旨是利益衆

生，自利利他，自度度他，自覺覺他。前面所講的初地法門，我——金剛藏菩薩——現

在算大略的說完了。

第一地　初地　竟

廻向偈

願以此功德　　莊嚴佛淨土

上報四重恩　　下濟三途苦

若有見聞者　　悉發菩提心

盡此一報身　　同生極樂國